Alternative Approaches in Music Education

Case Studies from the Field

Edited by
Ann C. Clements

Published in partnership with
MENC: The National Association for Music Education

ROWMAN & LITTLEFIELD EDUCATION
A division of
ROWMAN & LITTLEFIELD PUBLISHERS, INC.
Lanham • New York • Toronto • Plymouth, UK

Published in partnership with MENC: The National Association for Music Education

Published by Rowman & Littlefield Education
A division of Rowman & Littlefield Publishers, Inc.
A wholly owned subsidiary of The Rowman & Littlefield Publishing Group, Inc.
4501 Forbes Boulevard, Suite 200, Lanham, Maryland 20706
http://www.rowmaneducation.com

Estover Road, Plymouth PL6 7PY, United Kingdom

British Library Cataloguing in Publication Information Available

Library of Congress Cataloging-in-Publication Data

Alternative approaches in music education : case studies from the field / edited by Ann C. Clements.
      p. cm.
   "Published in partnership with MENC: The National Association for Music Education."
   ISBN 978-1-60709-855-3 (cloth : alk. paper)—ISBN 978-1-60709-856-0 (pbk. : alk. paper)—ISBN 978-1-60709-857-7 (electronic)
   1. Music—Instruction and study—United States. 2. School music—Instruction and study—United States. I. Clements, Ann C., 1971– II. MENC, the National Association for Music Education (U.S.)
   MT3.U5A47 2010
   780.71—dc22

                                                            2010012383

∞™ The paper used in this publication meets the minimum requirements of American National Standard for Information Sciences—Permanence of Paper for Printed Library Materials, ANSI/NISO Z39.48-1992.

Printed in the United States of America.

Contents

List of Illustrations   vii

Preface   ix
Ann C. Clements

PART I: PREK–12 CASE STUDIES

1   Opening Spaces in the Instrumental Music Classroom   3
    Carlos Abril

2   Guitar Class and the Popular Music Ensemble   15
    Joseph Abramo

3   Toward a New Conception of World Music Education:
    The Virtual Field Experience   29
    Sarah J. Bartolome

4   Discovering World Music and Children's Worlds: Pedagogy
    Responding to Children's Learning Needs   41
    Lily Chen-Hafteck

5   The Lakewood Project: Rockin' Out with
    Informal Music Learning   57
    Megan Clay Constantine

6   Music Tech, Adaptive Music, and Rock Band 101:
    Engaging Middle School–Age Students in
    General Music Class   67
    Mary L. Cohen and Cecilia Roudabush

7   Rock 'n' Roll High School: A Genre Comes of Age in
    the Curriculum   83
    Robert Gardner

8   Lead Lines, Licks, and Everything in Between: Popular
    Music in a Preschool Music Classroom   95
    Beth Gibbs and Mark Ross

9   Starting Young: Developing a Successful
    Instrumental Music Program in Kindergarten   105
    Elizabeth M. Guerriero and Matthew Hoy

10 Music in Cyberspace: Exploring New Models in Education   111
    Sheri E. Jaffurs and Betty Anne Younker

11 Exploring the Creation of Music through Film Scoring   119
    Douglas C. Orzolek

12 Alternatives to Music Education: East Meets West
    in Music Education   131
    *Lisa M. Meyer, Catherine Odom Prowse, and
      Terese Volk Tuohey*

13 Steel Drums in a Middle School Setting   139
    Barbara J. Resch

14 Talkin' Turkey: Incorporating Music from Turkey in
    the Elementary General Music Class   151
    Christopher Roberts

15 Enhancing the Instrumental Music Program
    with Creativity   161
    Nancy Beitler and Linda Thornton

PART 2: SCHOOL TO COMMUNITY AND HIGHER EDUCATION CASE STUDIES

16 *O Passo* (The Step): A Critical Pedagogy for Music
    Education from Brazil   177
    Frank Abrahams

17 Cultural Bearers in the Children's Choral Ensemble   189
    Ruth O. Boshkoff and Brent M. Gault

18 A Unique Collaboration: The Fairview Elementary
    School String Project   201
    Brenda Brenner

19 New Wine in Old Skins: Making Music with Older Adults   213
    Don D. Coffman

20 Compose Yourself: Older People and GarageBand   227
    Jonathan D. Harnum

21 Democratic Jazz: Two Perspectives on a Collaborative
    Improvisation Jazz Workshop   243
    Victor Lin and Joshua S. Renick

22 If the Shoe Fits: Tapping into the Potential of an
    Undergraduate Peer-Teaching Experience to Promote
    Music Teacher and Music Teacher Educator
    Socialization and Identity   257
    Alison M. Reynolds

23 Crossing Borders: Building Bridges for an International
    Exchange in Music Teacher Education   271
    Janet Robbins

24 The Rock Project: Informal Learning in Secondary
    General Methods   283
    Katherine Strand and Daniel Sumner

25 Rekindling the Playful Spirit: Learning to Teach
    through Play   297
    Sarah H. Watts

About the Contributors   307

Illustrations

FIGURES

15.1   Phrase of "Shepherd's Hey" without articulation
and expression symbols   166
15.2   Patterns for modeling   167
15.3   Improvisational accompaniment   168

PHOTOGRAPHS

6.1   North Central Junior High School
general music classroom   68
6.2   Northwest Junior High School music lab   69
6.3   Northwest Junior High School music-lab guitars
and drums   69

TABLES

15.1   Assessment Rubric for Theme and Variation   171
24.1   Assessment Rubric for Rock Performance   289

24.2   Assessment Rubric for Musical Creation   290
24.3   Assessment Rubric for Journal   291

BOXES

3.1   Students' Comments Following a VFE in Ghana   34
8.1   "Good Morning"   99
8.2   "Take Your Hands"   100
8.3   "Flick a Fly"   101
8.4   "Mixed-Up Morning Blues"   101

Preface

Ann C. Clements

The purpose of the text is to provide music educators, preservice music education students, and music education faculty an opportunity to explore the creative ways in which music educators across the country are approaching emerging practices in music teaching and learning.

The following chapters offer personalized case studies of music programs that are engaging in alternative approaches. Each case is unique and offers a new and different perspective on music teaching and learning. Often the programs described fall outside of the standard music education curriculum offered in most teacher-preparation programs. These models of successful alternative approaches can be replicated in a variety of school, university, or community settings.

This project was supported by the Society for Music Teacher Education's (SMTE) Areas of Strategic Planning and Action on Critical Examination of the Curriculum, and a portion of the proceeds will be donated to this organization.

TO THE MUSIC EDUCATOR

Teaching music is a challenging art, growing only more complex as children and youth are increasingly influenced by popular culture, mass media, technology, and the rest of the world at the "click of a button."

One of the greatest difficulties for music educators can be staying current with new practices and approaches in music education. While some school districts provide opportunities for sharing ideas and state and national music organizations provide workshops and conferences, it remains difficult to know what new ideas are out there on a national level and which of these are working successfully.

Whether you are a new or experienced teacher, you are most likely looking for innovative ideas and methods of successful practice that you can incorporate into your own teaching. This text provides twenty-five models of alternative approaches to music education, presented as narrative case studies. Each was written by practicing music educators with a vast variety of experiences to share. Some were written by educators directly involved in the project or program being described, others by those who have had an opportunity to explore the projects and programs firsthand. Specifically, this text is intended to assist you, the music educator, in the following ways:

1. by offering a means for exploring alternative approaches and materials,
2. by presenting multiple examples of alternative approaches that you can consider for implementation into your own music classroom or program,
3. by providing opportunities for reflect on your previous experiences in traditional music education and for pondering new possibilities for music education as a whole, and
4. by serving as a means to garner administrative support for experimentation with and implementation of alternative approaches in your music program.

TO THE PRESERVICE MUSIC EDUCATION STUDENT

Congratulations on selecting the lofty career of being a music educator. As you may already know, teaching music is an art that requires an in-depth knowledge of educational practice, music and musicianship, and children, youth, and community. While you have been gaining experience through your music education coursework, ensembles, and the private studio and have been receiving general preparation through music theory and music history courses, you must also be prepared to understand the changing face of music education in this country.

You may have attended schools prior to your university that had strong bands, choirs, and orchestras. You may have even taken music classes that were alternative or less typical or that included new or unusual projects and assignments. However, it's unlikely that as a student participating in these atypical classes or projects you viewed them through the eyes of a teacher. Music education is in constant flux: As society changes, so should the profession. As our next generation of music educators you must understand who your students are, what they want to know, and how to creatively teach it. And so in the following chapters we've presented you with twenty-five case studies of alternative approaches to music education. Specifically, this text is intended to assist the preservice music education students in the following ways:

1. by offering examples of alternative approaches to music education,
2. by creating an opportunity for discussion of alternative approaches,
3. by showing how to apply alternative approaches and materials to contextual classroom situations,
4. by providing opportunities for discussion of uncommon issues and themes in music education with peers and faculty,
5. by giving you a chance to reflect on previous experiences in traditional music education and on the new possibilities for music education as you begin your teaching career, and
6. by specifying models that can be implemented in current and future teachings.

TO THE HIGHER-EDUCATION FACULTY MEMBER

It has been estimated that school music education, particularly at the secondary level, is reaching only a limited number of students through the traditional performance offerings of band, choir, and orchestra. In essence, music education is failing to reach the majority of students. A key remedy for this is to expand course offerings while exploring alternative approaches. However, many music education programs at the university level continue to focus the majority, if not all, of their methods and technique courses on traditional offerings. This, coupled with the amount of time most universities require students to spend in traditional ensembles and coursework, can set a poor example for incorporating alternative approaches. In order to equip future music educators with the skills, materials, and models they will need to be successful in an ever-changing music education profession, they must be introduced to alternative approaches, alongside traditional approaches, in the course of their music education.

Just as preservice music education students must prepare for changes in preK–12 music instruction, those in higher education must be aware that regulations and expectations for the profession at all levels are changing. The National Association of Schools of Music (NASM 2007) has recently altered the requirements for teacher-certification programs and has extended musical competencies to include alternative approaches and musicianship (93–97). NASM has recognized that music teaching now encompasses a wide range of traditional, emerging, and experimental purposes, approaches, contents, and methods (93). Of particular interest, NASM recognizes that, in addition to methods courses in general, vocal, and instrumental music, students must also have competencies in and experiences with specific fields and combinations of fields, including composition, electronic or computer music, guitar, music technology, and popular musics (95). Universities undergoing a NASM review must be able to demonstrate where these materials are being discussed and taught in the teacher-certification coursework.

The twenty-five case studies included in this book are examples of successful alternative approaches to music teaching and learning that can assist you, the higher-education faculty member, in the following ways:

1. by narrating multiple real-life cases of alternative approaches for discussion with students,
2. by creating flexibility for faculty in selecting appropriate readings that relate the specific materials and methods being taught, and
3. by suggesting alternative approaches being used in other higher-education institutions for possible experimentation or implementation in your classrooms.

BOOK STRUCTURE

This book is organized into discussion of case studies pertinent to K–12 and those pertinent to school to community and higher-education. As you can imagine, it was difficult to categorize the case studies, as some could have comfortably appeared in either section of the text. Additionally, case studies that focused on higher education could easily be transformed into models for preK–12, and vice versa. You are encouraged to explore the entire text to find the material of most interest and relevance to you.

The case studies discuss the aims of individual alternative approaches and programs, the construction of these courses and ensembles, the benefits and difficulties encountered during their construction, and the program outcomes from the teacher's perspective.

THE CASE STUDY

The case studies emphasize detailed contextual analysis of a limited number of events or conditions and their relationships. Researchers have used the case-study research method for many years, across a variety of disciplines. Social scientists, in particular, have made wide use of this qualitative research method to examine contemporary real-life situations and provide the basis for the application of ideas and extension of methods. Researcher Robert K. Yin (1984) defines the case-study research method as an empirical inquiry that investigates a contemporary phenomenon within its real-life context and when the boundaries between phenomenon and context are not clearly evident (23).

Each of our case studies is not merely a description of the specific program, although a brief description of the program has been included. Rather, its intention is to provide thorough yet succinct information relating to *what* the programs consists of, *why* and *when* the program was started or created, *who* participates in the program, *how* the program was started or created, and any difficulties or successes during its creation and the current successes of the program. In many ways the case study can serve as a how-to guide, helping the reader consider the different approaches and tools they can use to experiment with these approaches in their own teaching and learning situations.

Contributors were asked to follow a predetermined template to insure that all case studies consist of the same elements, the text as a whole maintains flow, and the suggestions are easy to use. The template was based on models of case-study research from both the fields of education and business (Yin 1984), melding an educational perspective with a straightforward business approach. While educational research tends to be in-depth and lengthy, employing a business model, which is more to the point, allowed us to include a greater number of case studies within the text. That said, while a template was provided, contributors were given latitude in utilizing the provided model and in selecting the style and format of writing that best fit the case they were describing.

PRIMARY PURPOSE

The primary purpose of this text is to provide music educators, pre-service music education students, and university faculty with real-life examples of the many creative approaches to teaching already established by practicing music educators so that the reader can implement them in their own emerging practices. This might lead the reader to develop nonperformance courses (such as music appreciation or general music courses) or alternative ensembles, or perhaps to augment preexisting performance and nonperformance courses with nontraditional units or curricular constructs, or perhaps even to extend music education beyond the walls of the school building out into the communities that surround them. Of particular interest are new practices that focus on popular and world musics; but we have also made sure to examine case studies that implement new approaches to music education within traditional settings.

The intent of this book is to provide an opportunity to explore some of the many alternative approaches to music education currently practiced in the field. Recent research has highlighted a disjunction between the musics explored within school buildings and those more commonly found outside the music classroom. While music educators and music teacher–certification programs often explore alternative approaches, it is impossible to understand what is being taught across the country without examining the personal experiences narrated by participants of the programs themselves.

Our intention is not to limit or prohibitively shape a future direction in music education. Rather, we wish to simply explore all the ways music is currently being taught that differ from the traditional approaches. We hope our studies will provide you many ideas for continuing to break down the barriers between music in school and outside of school and that as a result you may even spark the interest of young musicians not currently enrolled in traditional formal music offerings.

I thank each of the chapter authors for their ingenuity in finding new approaches to music education and for their willingness to share their case studies with us. I also offer sincere thanks to Beth Guerriero, my research assistant throughout this process, for dedicating much time, effort, and energy to seeing this project to fruition.

It is our hope that the diversity of real-world case studies provided, the thoughtfulness with which they were written, and the questioning and curiosity that they inspire will stimulate lively discussion, new innovations and approaches, and much food for thought.

REFERENCES

NASM. 2007. *Handbook 2007–2008*. Reston, Va.: National Association of Schools of Music.

Seperich, G. J., M. J. Woolverton, J. G. Beierlein, and D. E. Hahn, eds. 1996. *Introduction to the case-study method.* (Adapted from *Cases in agribusiness management*.) Scottsdale, Ariz.: Gorsuch Scarisbrick Publishers. www.uidaho.edu/ag/agecon/391/casestudmeth.html.

Soy, S. K. 1997. The case study as a research method. Unpublished paper. University of Texas at Austin. www.gslis.utexas.edu/~ssoy/usesusers/l391d1b.htm.

Yin, R. K. 1984. *Case study research: Design and methods*. Newbury Park, Calif.: Sage.

Part I

PreK–12 CASE STUDIES

1

Opening Spaces in the Instrumental Music Classroom

Carlos Abril

ABSTRACT

In an effort to respond to the cultural backgrounds of a growing body of Hispanic students in a suburban middle school, an instrumental music teacher decided to start a mariachi ensemble. While not a particularly innovative idea in certain regions of the United States, this program was a first of its kind in the school district where this teacher worked. This chapter does not advocate for or explain how to start a mariachi or any less-traditional school music ensemble. Rather, this chapter is about giving voice to students whose diverse backgrounds offer teachers a perspective from which to examine their practices. It is the hope that teachers may be inspired to take a path less traveled in the instrumental music classroom, a path where members of a learning community delve beyond the surface of notes, rhythms, and fingerings to consider the sociocultural and political constructs that shape and are shaped by the musical experience. This case seeks to provoke readers to rethink traditional pedagogical practices in instrumental music education.

INTRODUCTION

Over the last three decades increased attention has been paid to cultural diversity in music education. One of the more common ways music educators have responded to the call for more cultural diversity and to multicultural mandates is through the selection of repertoire. This seems like an important and logical step, as music usually lies at the center of music curricula. In school instrumental ensembles, nods to multiculturalism have taken the form of arrangements based on traditional folk tunes and musical fantasies of varying degrees of quality and cultural validity (Campbell 2002). Yet in recent years greater emphasis has been placed on selecting music that serves as a valid and respectful representation of specific cultural groups (Abril 2006a). Yet while repertoire selection is important, it only comprises one part of the planning process. Teachers must also consider how to situate the music in individual lessons as well as the curriculum as a whole. In so doing, the focus begins to shift from thinking of music as object to thinking of it as practice or experience.

Contextualizing music in the classroom, both historically and culturally, heightens awareness and deepens understanding of the music being studied. In fact, context is thought to be so vital to understanding music that it may very well determine exactly how music is conceptualized (Merriam 1964). National and international music education organizations—such as MENC: The National Association for Music Education and the International Society for Music Education (ISME)—have considered these examinations and discussions to be an important part of music teaching and the learning processes (McCarthy 2004; Consortium of National Arts Education Associations 1994). Music must be experienced in its context, "historical, cultural, and political, in order to be grasped appropriately; that is, 'knowing about' becomes an essential ingredient of artistry and of listening" (Reimer 2003, 98). Unfortunately, these practices are less common in traditional instrumental music classes, where skill development and final products (i.e., polished musical performance) are paramount. How can these seemingly disparate yet closely connected facets of music learning be reconciled?

Educational practices that include learning about music and culture may meet multicultural mandates and specific curricular goals, but we must also ask how they connect with students' lives. In striving to form that connection, we might consider opening spaces in the classroom for students to discuss, question, and come to a better understanding of the music experience from myriad cultural perspectives, including their own. Discussions about music and personal experience may provide students with an understanding of music that is more relevant to their own lives (Dunbar-Hall 2005) and might lead to increased tolerance and acceptance of musics and cultural groups that are unfamiliar (Abril 2006b; Edwards 1998; Chen-Hafteck 2007). Pedagogical practices that open spaces for members of a given learning community to engage in meaningful classroom dialogues have the potential to provide a heightened understanding of music and its meaning (Abril 2009), as well as to create individual or even social transformations (Benedict 2006). Without focusing on *who* is being taught, multicultural educational approaches remain superficial and ineffective.

Noted education scholars have written about the importance of engaging a learning community through dialogues that give voice to myriad cultural perspectives. Maxine Greene (1995) believes that such classroom practices provide opportunities for perceptions, comprehension, and knowledge to be shaped and reshaped. She invites educators to "find ways of enabling the young to find their voices, to open their spaces, to reclaim their histories in all their variety and discontinuity . . . [with attention] paid to those on the margins" (120). Jerome Bruner (1996) contends that "interpretations of meaning reflect not only the idiosyncratic histories of individuals but also the culture's canonical ways of constructing reality. . . . Life in culture is, then, an interplay between the versions of the world that people form under its institutional sway and the versions of it that are products of their individual histories" (14). These forms of educational engagement move us toward reaching the highest levels of Banks's (2004) multicultural curriculum reform model, where pedagogy is transformed into something that enables "students to view concepts, issues, events, and themes from the perspective of diverse ethnic and cultural groups" while helping them "make decisions on important social issues and take action" (15). We must ask, Do our current music pedagogies do the same?

The traditional instrumental music education paradigm reflects a transmission model, where the teacher's or director's views dominate, while other perspectives are perceived to be "noise in the system." Pedagogical practices in instrumental music strive toward great efficiency in shaping a given musical product. These practices provide legitimacy, control, and comfort to the teacher, whereas "inquiry and problem posing . . . suggests discomfort, uncertainty, and disorder" (Allsup and Benedict 2008, 164). This dominant paradigm may explain why alternative approaches to teaching instrumental music have struggled to take root in U.S. schools.

Some music educators, however, have started to expand curricular structures beyond traditional offerings. Although this is still rare, some secondary schools offer courses in West African drumming, mariachi, popular music, and Celtic music (Abril and Gault 2008). It would be interesting to find out whether innovative couses are leading to alterative approaches to teaching music itself. Do courses that are considered to be culturally responsive or multicultural in nature lend themselves to connecting more closely with culture or students' lives? What challenges would these new structures and pedagogies pose?

In this chapter I take on some of these questions. More specifically, I examine how three tensions in a mariachi music program, as perceived by one of its members, can be mitigated by pedagogy that gives voice to diverse members of a learning community. We can view our teaching practices through the fresh lens of student perspective, which may then uncover taking paths less traveled in the instrumental music classroom—paths where members of a learning community delve beyond the surface of notes, rhythms, and fingerings to consider the sociocultural and political constructs that shape and are shaped by the musical experience. The hope is that the case study we examine here will provoke us to think critically about traditional practices in our own music classrooms.

THE CASE

This study builds upon a prior examination (Abril 2009) of the journey of the same teacher, Nancy, as she experimented with adding a mariachi ensemble to her music program at a suburban middle school in the Midwestern region of the United States. Her intent was to respond to Hispanic students' cultures and attract them to the school music program. However, Nancy, a white, non-Hispanic teacher whose formal training was in Western art music, had only basic knowledge of and minimal training in mariachi. That original study focused on broadly documenting and untangling her perspective of the classroom journey, with its concomitant challenges and outcomes. By way of contrast, this chapter examines how Nancy's pedagogical and curricular decisions impacted a particularly thoughtful, political, and articulate student in her class, a fourteen-year-old girl named Juli.

One of Nancy's typical mariachi classes included various combinations of rehearsing, listening, and discussing. Rehearsals focused on helping students learn to play the selected music for performance in formal concerts and in other more informal venues. Students listened to professional mariachi groups play the music the students were rehearsing or else listened to other, related, pieces. Nancy made an effort to engage students in discussions about the music they were performing, as well as about Mexican culture and traditions. She also worked to help her students make connections between the music and their cultures, ethnicities, and identities, both in and outside of school.

Juli was the unofficial student leader of the mariachi ensemble and claimed to participate in the class because she wanted to learn more about her Mexican heritage, expand her music repertoire, and improve her skill as a violinist. In my recorded observations and interviews I sought to examine multiple dimensions of Juli's experiences in mariachi.

I choose to give Juli voice because she was a second-generation Mexican American, knew about and practiced Mexican traditions at home and on trips to Mexico, and was knowledgeable about various styles of Mexican music. Furthermore, she was exceptionally articulate and willing to share her insights. In this chapter I will only focus on those aspects of the mariachi class that were sources of tension for her. I do so not to present a limited view of her experience or to criticize the music teacher's courageous efforts but because I believe that these tensions offer the greatest potential for learning. I will present and interpret these tensions in the order in which they arose. Finally, I will consider the implications for music teaching and learning practices.

TENSION 1: REPERTOIRE

The first tension arose from a song that the music teacher chose for the mariachi ensemble to learn and perform in a concert. Although Juli claimed it was "not a *major* issue," it was something that she remembered five months after the concert and discussed at various times during each of our three interviews. The song was "Las Mañanitas," a traditional song sung by many people of Latin American backgrounds when celebrating birthdays. It is completely different (melodically, rhythmically, and lyrically) from the U.S. birthday song.

Juli said that it was the only song in the year-long mariachi curriculum that she considered to be a part of her home culture. More specifically, she knew the song and sang it to celebrate family members' birthdays. She was quite enthusiastic about learning to play the song in the ensemble and felt that it was a piece that "was quite useful at home." She provided me with an example of how she used the song with her family: "I played the song for my *abuelita* [grandmother], who lives in Mexico. It was her birthday, and I wanted to play it over the telephone for her." While it was a song that she was pleased to have learned to play by memory, she was confused when her teacher decided to include it in a holiday concert program. This is what Juli had to say about the experience and her mother's subsequent response:

> Okay, the jazz band, they were playing, like, all of the "Jingle Bells," "Frosty the Snowman"—you know what they were playing! And here, we started playing "Las Mañanitas," okay? At least if we played "Las Posadas" [a traditional Latin American Christmas celebration, including seasonal songs] or something like that. But no, we played the Happy Birthday song at a winter concert! Okay? To me that made *no* sense! [she laughs] I was confused. My mom was like, "Okay, so why did she put that there?" . . . We were wondering whose birthday it was and why you'd be playing it in the concert anyway.

Nancy, the music teacher, was wise to select a song that was a part of many Hispanic students' cultures. The song was representative, respectful, and relevant, meeting most of the criteria for using music that validly represents a particular cultural group (Abril 2006b). However, its inclusion at the holiday concert didn't properly reflect the way the piece of music functioned in its culture. To Juli, playing the song out of context was inappropriate and demonstrated a lack of understanding on the part of the teacher and the ensemble. Intuitively, Juli understood what Alan Merriam (1964) had proposed many decades earlier in his seminal text, *Anthropology of Music*, writing that music "does not exist apart from its context; to the contrary, the context may well determine the conceptualization of music" (215).

Given the authoritative position of teachers in U.S. schools, it is not surprising that Juli did not object to the song's inclusion but merely accepted Nancy's concert program. In the pedagogical paradigm under which the class was operating, the teacher was viewed (and viewed herself) as the repository of knowledge and decision making. Perhaps a paradigm shift would resolve this tension, in a setting where the classroom operates as "a subcommunity of mutual learning, with the teacher orchestrating the proceedings" (Bruner 1996, 21). Had Nancy opened a space for dialogue in her instrumental classroom, would a new understanding of the music have emerged? Would the piece have been stricken from the concert program? Juli's consternation illustrates how developing a contextual understanding can impact musical practices and speaks to the value of using cultural diversity as a resource in the classroom.

Playing "Las Mañanitas" at the Christmas concert was a turning point for Juli. Thereafter she seemed to develop a more critical eye and ear in the classroom. She began asking an increasing number of questions during class time and said that at home she further engaged her mother and aunt in discussions about the things she was learning in class. The misunderstanding with the song selection became the first of several tensions for Juli in her mariachi learning community.

TENSION 2: CULTURAL EXPLORATION PROJECT

The second time Nancy's curriculum created tension for Juli was when the students were given a cultural-exploration worksheet to complete at home. Comprised of a series of questions students were supposed to answer, the purpose of the worksheet was to help them learn more about Mexican culture. While it seemed rather innocuous to Nancy and most of the other students, Juli thought otherwise. She told me, "Now *that* one got me a little mad!" She was frustrated by vague and overreaching questions on the worksheet, such as, "What are people like?" She also failed to see the connection between what they were learning in the mariachi class and the questions being posed. Juli said,

> I remember when we were going over our answers to this worksheet [a week later], I told the teacher exactly what I'm telling you. I'm like, "What are the people like? Well I put *normal*, Ms. Nancy." "They're normal. They are not really different from really American people or whatever." Then the worksheet asked, "What type of clothing do they wear?" and I'm like, "Well . . . for my thing, I said . . . they wear normal things." I remember when I shared my answer with my mom [while working on it] she said, "Well, we [meaning Mexicans] don't go out in our little *panchitos* and dress, or whatever, all the time!" and I said, "Ms. Nancy, we dress casual and normal . . . okay?"
>
> Another question was, "What languages do the people speak there in Mexico?" "That's Spanish!" Hello! [Juli laughs.] I'm like, I told her like that! And then I remember when Mom, she was like, "It's Mexico! What do you think they speak!? Like, Italian!?" And then, it says, "What kinds of foods are eaten there?" Okay . . . a little bit of a better question! And I was like, "Okay, Ms. Nancy, this question was a little bit better"; like, I told her, "It's kind of better than the other

questions, because that one you can actually say something about it."
And so that one I was alright with because we do eat things in my
family that are not typical here. . . . I would be fine answering questions about what we do in my family that is traditional.

Juli was concerned with the ways the worksheet seemed to es-
sentialize people of Mexican backgrounds. She seemed to recognize
the dangers in reducing all people of Mexican heritage (or any other
group for that matter) to a few simple statements. Fearing it had the
potential to propagate stereotypes and misunderstandings, Juli said she
would have preferred it if questions gave her more opportunities to
share stories about her family, rather than trying to reduce a huge national group into a few neat statements. She explained that Mexicans
are as diverse as Americans and so to say that all people from Mexico
are a certain way is problematic.

Clearly, the teacher was trying new ways to help some students
come to know more about their own heritage and others come to
know more about a less-familiar culture. It seems logical that a project
designed to get students thinking and talking about culture would be a
good starting point. Sure, but these project should also be constructed
in such a way as to move beyond discrete cultural elements that might
be somewhat limiting and seemingly irrelevant to students. To that
end, we teachers might take on Benedict's (2006) challenge to think of
ourselves as Other for a change. We could also consider Banks's (2004)
multicultural curriculum reform model, which shows teachers how
to move their pedagogy from the superficial study of discrete cultural
elements to transformative and social-action engagements, which are
more culturally responsive and meaningful.

TENSION 3: REPERTOIRE REPRISE

Juli became increasingly frustrated when Nancy selected the song "La
Raspa" for study. To Juli, this was the most problematic part of the
curriculum. She was incredulous that Nancy would have selected "La
Raspa," which is sometimes referred to as "The Mexican Hat Dance"
or "The Jumping Bean Song," and assumed her teacher would understand why. Curiously, none of her peers (both Latino and non-Latino)
were as vehemently opposed to the song as Juli. It was only through
dialogue that members began to consider the song from her point of
view. The following vignette, borrowed from a prior study (Abril 2009,
84–85), was constructed to provide a window into the classroom experience when Nancy opened up the floor for discussion:

After the ensemble read through "La Raspa," Nancy read some contextual information about the music that was included in the mariachi method book she was using. As soon as she was done, Juli exclaimed, "This song is so disrespectful to us." Ivana, another Mexican-American student standing next to her, nodded. Nancy and a few other students seemed befuddled by the comment. Connor, the violinist, sitting two stands away from her, said, "I've heard this song before, and I don't mind it." . . . Nancy asked, "Why is this disrespectful?" Juli replied, "It is because people make fun of us and it's like a joke about Mexicans. . . . They are making fun of it." Nancy, attempting to temporarily divert the tension, asked the students to think about it some more as they listened to a recording of the music.

As the music played, I noticed Juli furrow her brow and cross her arms, as possible indicators of resistance. Some students smiled; others studied the music on their stand; Ivana seemed to carefully observe Juli. When Nancy stopped the music, Brenda, the guitarrón player, said, "I've heard that song a lot of times on the radio and in *The Simpsons*!" Most of the students laughed and nodded.

Juli, seemingly frustrated that others did not see her point, said, "Hello, guys! It's like a big stereotype of Mexicans." The teacher asked students to define the term *stereotype*, and students did so by providing examples of common stereotypes. Juli said, "People laugh at us in a concert."

Nancy asked what others felt about programming it on a concert. Ivana said, "It depends how you play it." Nancy suggested the use of folkloric dancers to make it seem more authentic. Brenda said, "We could explain about it during the concert so they understand it better, and if people laugh, we stop playing." Juli immediately retorted, "Most of us are Mexican here! They'll be laughing at us, not you. It's worse for us!" Nancy offered that they might only play it for themselves in rehearsals. After discussing it, Nancy decided they should take a poll, so she helped students develop a survey to examine other teachers', family members', and peers' views. Students were asked to present their findings the following week.

The song itself is not what Juli objected to; it was performing it in a public forum that concerned her the most. She was highly attuned to possible criticisms from the audience, which would consist of her peers, teachers, and parents. If she believed that an audience would appreciate and be respectful of the music, she would have been pleased to perform it; but instead she worried that her peers would think the song was a joke or "something funny that they could just laugh at." Interestingly, the non-Hispanic students did not seem concerned about performing it for their peers. Juli even thought playing the song in concert might exacerbate what she said were existing tensions among ethnic groups (i.e., white and Latino) at her school. Juli had a nuanced understanding of the music and recognized it to be more than a series of sounds and silences. In fact, she recognized what the research has demonstrated—that music exists in a complex sociocultural ecosystem where it can incite behaviors that reflect cultural in-group loyalties and affiliations (Abril and Flowers 2007; Morrison 1998).

The tension, as perceived by Juli, prompted her to speak, which, in turn, sparked a dialogue that ended up helping students develop a more nuanced understanding of music's relation to culture. If Nancy had quieted Juli and tamped down the ensuing discussion, reverting instead to rehearsal, her students may never have had the opportunity to better explore how that song has been appropriated in the United States and its perception among various groups. The Latino peers in the class seemed to understand Juli's perspective a little more readily than the other students. Nonetheless, although some of her classmates never quite understood her position, they came to respect it.

From a pedagogical standpoint, this was a breakthrough for Nancy. Although she was somewhat uncomfortable with the discussion at the time—which is typical (Nieto 2004)—in retrospect she talked about it as an opportunity to move away from rehearsal mode to pedagogical space where understandings could be voiced and misunderstandings could be clarified (Abril 2009). Education scholars have stressed the need for teachers to provide classroom space for meaningful dialogues (Bruner 1996; Greene 1995; Haroutunian-Gordon 2009), and this case supports the need for similar engagements in the instrumental music classrooms. Music teachers should consider giving students a platform to discuss matters that relate to culture and music and to their perceptions and life experiences.

CONCLUSION: LESSONS LEARNED

We can find many lessons in examining this mariachi program from Juli's perceptive.

1. *Selecting repertoire:* Most music teachers take great care in selecting repertoire for their programs, as it often is the core to all the learning that takes place. Careful consideration ought to be given, especially when choosing music meant to be reflective of a given cultural group. When these musics are unfamiliar, it would behoove us to reflect on and examine the context before programming it and sharing it with the students. Also

use students as resources when considering musical selections, especially when they may be familiar with the music and its cultural contexts. Considering student perspective allows classroom discussion of song or piece of music, creating a valuable learning experience for you, the teacher.

2. *Connecting with culture and learners:* Consider how we situate students' cultures in the activities and projects we create: Are we playing into the exotic or essentializing cultural groups? We ought to refrain from normative behaviors and attitudes that consign students of certain cultural groups as Other. Teachers can help students make connections between the sociocultural, political, historical, and musical, as students might not automatically make these connections for themselves.

3. *Opening spaces:* Music teachers should open dialogic spaces for students to engage in meaningful discussions and debates about the music they are studying. This may offer the greatest opportunities for learning and social transformation.

In retrospect, Juli did not consider the tensions that arose in class to be negative. In fact, she saw them as a natural part of teaching and learning. I asked Juli how she became such a critical thinker. She said, "I always asked questions. I didn't see that as a bad thing. . . . I do that because I want to know more and help others to know too. It makes me feel like I make a difference. I would get angry [in class], but I liked to talk in the group, and I never, like, wanted to quit the whole time." Given the chance, she claimed she would have done it all over again.

REFERENCES

Abril, C. R. 2006a. Learning outcomes of two approaches to multicultural music education. *International Journal of Music Education* 24 (1): 30–42.

———. 2006b. Music that represents culture: Selecting music with integrity. *Music Educators Journal* 93 (1): 38–45.

———. 2009. Responding to culture in the instrumental music programme: A teacher's journey. *Music Education Research* 11 (1): 77–91.

Abril, C. R, and P. J. Flowers. 2007. Attention, preference, and identity in music listening by middle school students of different linguistic backgrounds. *Journal of Research in Music Education* 55 (3): 204–19.

Abril, C. R., and B. Gault. 2008. The state of music in secondary schools: The principal's perspective. *Journal of Research in Music Education* 56 (1): 68–81.

Allsup, R. E., and C. Benedict. 2008. The problems of band: An inquiry into the future of instrumental music education. *Philosophy of Music Education Review* 16 (2): 156–73.

Banks, J. 2004. Multicultural education: Historical development, dimensions, and practice. In *Handbook of research on multicultural education*, 2nd ed., ed. J. A. Banks and C. A. M. Banks, 3–29. San Francisco: Jossey-Bass.

Benedict, C. 2006. Defining ourselves as other: Envisioning transformative possibilities. In *Teaching music in the urban classroom*, ed. C. F. Campbell, 3–13. Lanham, Md.: MENC / Rowman & Littlefield Education.

Bruner, J. 1996. *The culture of education.* Cambridge, Mass.: Harvard University Press.

Campbell, P. S. 2002. Music education in a time of cultural transformation. *Music Educators Journal* 89 (1): 27–32, 54.

Chen-Hafteck, L. 2007. Contextual analysis of children's responses to an integrated Chinese music and culture experience. *Music Education Research* 9 (3): 337–53.

Consortium of National Arts Education Associations. 1994. *National standards for arts education: What every young American should know and be able to do in the arts.* Reston, Va.: MENC.

Dunbar-Hall, P. 2005. Colliding perspectives? Music curriculum as cultural studies. *Music Educators Journal* 91 (4): 33–37.

Edwards, K. L. 1998. Multicultural music instruction in the elementary school: What can be achieved? *Bulletin of the Council for Research in Music Education* 138:62–82.

Greene, M. 1995. *Releasing the imagination: Essays on education, the arts, and social change.* San Francisco: Jossey-Bass.

Haroutunian-Gordon, S. 2009. *Learning to teach through discussion: The art of turning the soul.* New Haven, Conn.: Yale University Press.

McCarthy, M. 2004. *Toward a global community: The International Society for Music Education 1953–2003.* Nedlands, Australia: ISME.

Merriam, A. P. 1964. *The anthropology of music.* Evanston, Ill.: Northwestern University Press.

Morrison, S. J. 1998. A comparison of preference responses of white and African-American students to musical versus musical/visual stimuli. *Journal of Research in Music Education* 46 (1): 208–22.

Nieto. 2004. *Affirming diversity: The sociopolitical context of multicultural education.* 4th ed. Boston: Pearson.

Reimer, B. 2003. *A philosophy of music education: Advancing the vision.* Upper Saddle River, N.J.: Prentice-Hall.

②

Guitar Class and the Popular Music Ensemble

Joseph Abramo

ABSTRACT

Popular music and the guitar classroom are fertile grounds for creating a music program that is inclusive to all students, regardless of their culture or ethnicity, musical interests, previous musical experiences, or future ambitions. It also proves to be a platform for the legitimate study of popular culture and provides an opportunity to explore alternative teaching and learning pedagogies. While there may be dilemmas regarding musical material selection, advice is provided for how music educators can navigate these potential difficulties to provide the maximum number of students a rich, diverse, and meaningful music education.

INTRODUCTION

As the vast majority of students in public schools choose not to participate in band, chorus, or orchestra, a guitar class that serves as a popular music ensemble might be a valuable tool to attract more students to join music programs. Popular music is an important part of many students' lives, and when it forms the core content of the curriculum, students are motivated to take an active role in learning. But popular music's worth does not lie solely in its ability to encourage students to perform; it also serves as useful repertoire for students to carry out theoretical analyses and form critical opinions of the music they experience in their everyday lives. However, because popular music sometimes has explicit language and controversial themes, a dilemma arises: do teachers help students understand these topics and media or do they eliminate popular music entirely from their classrooms?

It may seem strange to music education majors and practicing teachers that the majority of students do not elect to participate in band, chorus, or orchestra. Although for many or most music teachers performance in these ensembles was an important part of their youth and school experiences and is their inspiration to educate others in music (L'Roy 1983), this is not the typical experience for students in K–12 schools. Reimer (1989) suggests that roughly 15 percent of students enrolled in public schools participate in bands, orchestras, or choruses (182), and Williams (2007) says, "While exact statistics are hard to come by, we know that the percentage of secondary students not enrolled in music courses far exceeds the percentage of those who are" (20).

These trends seem to hold true in the local context of the high school where I teach. Of the 2,500 total students, only about 400 hundred participate in band or chorus, meaning that only 16 percent of the school population is involved in music learning during the school day. If, as the Consortium of National Arts Education Associations (1994) states, music education is a right of all students, our music program is abdicating one of its most important responsibilities. We needed to increase the number of students who participate and provide music education for as many students as possible. And so in the course of this study we asked ourselves, How do we maintain an intellectual and stimulating educational process while making music classes attractive to the 84 percent of students who do not participate in ensembles?

Some researchers have suggested that, generally, students from lower socioeconomic backgrounds and students with lower academic achievement join school ensembles less often than their peers (Nabb 1995), and African American students also participate in ensembles less frequently than white students (Watts, Doane, and Fekete 1994). In my school, the representation of minority students and students of color in particular in the traditional ensembles does not reflect the ethnic makeup of the school as a whole. In our school building, the population is evenly distributed among different ethnicities; roughly a third of the students are African American, a third are Latino/a, and a third are white, yet the vast majority of students in the ensembles are white. Due to this imbalance, our case study involved making changes that would allow our music department to reflect the general population of the high school and larger community.

THE CASE

Because the school was concerned with the music program participation statistics, the music department asked me to create a course
that would increase participation by students of varying ethnic and
cultural backgrounds; in order to do this, the class would have to
appeal to students who had shown no previous desire to perform in
traditional ensembles. As listening to and performing popular music is
an important part of adolescents' lives (Bosacki et al. 2006; Campbell,
Connell, and Beegle 2007; North and Hargreaves 1999; Williams 2007),
I thought including rock and similar styles of music to the coursework
would attract additional students to the music program. And because
the guitar is a versatile instrument that features in many different
genres of popular music, a course that focused on this instrument appeared to be a logical choice.

That said, I understood that using strategies commonly found in
traditional ensembles to teach guitar would not diversify instruction.
Recent research proposes that successfully incorporating popular
music into a classroom require a change in pedagogy. Green (2001,
2004, 2008), for example, suggests that popular musicians learn music
aurally, whereas classical musicians learn music through notation;
she goes on to say that popular musicians build up their technique
by practicing and performing songs rather than scales and exercises.
Green additionally found that rock musicians also learn music by
copying—or transcribing—recordings, being encultured (or immersed
in that musical culture), and receiving informal instruction from family members and peers.

It has also been suggested that popular musicians communicate
with each other differently than do other musicians. Jaffurs (2004)
found that popular musicians communicate informally and pick up
skills through encouragement and guidance from peers. She found that
they also exchange ideas through what she calls *doodling*, or the in-
termittent playing of licks that had nothing to do with the music they
were rehearsing. Similar to Jaffurs, Davis (2005), while studying a rock
band, found that popular music practices, in contrast to traditional
band pedagogy, have much to offer music educators. These practices—
playing by ear, using popular music that students like, and employing
collaborative composition—can positively affect music teaching and
learning. Allsup (2002, 2003, 2004) also found that popular musics,
like jazz and rock, fostered group composition and a sense of a mutual
learning community in the music classroom.

For my case study these writings, among others, served as the
models of the pedagogy I employed in my classroom and, to a degree,

created a shift from typical music instruction. When picturing a traditional rehearsal in a school ensemble, the classroom is typically a teacher-centered classroom (Allsup 2003): Students—led by the direct instruction of the teacher—work on a common goal at the same time. For example, everyone's effort in the room is simultaneously directed toward rehearsing a composition rendered in standard notation in preparation for a concert, sight-reading new music to develop reading skills, or practicing scales and exercises together. The director, who is ready to give the students personal instruction as to how they might improve their musicality, closely supervises all these activities.

In contrast to a traditional rehearsal, the popular music classroom is not always a collective effort, focused on notation, or completely directed by the teacher. Students are allowed—and even encouraged—to customize their learning and to study music that they find interesting. This might mean that they embark on individual or small-group projects that have little or no similarity to what other students are learning. In this situation, students may not learn the exact same concepts, but they are all engaging in music in ways that are relevant and useful to how they want to learn about music. It should be no surprise, then, that when students are allowed this flexibility their motivation to learn increases.

Because some researchers suggest that popular musicians learn through transcription of recordings (Green 2001; Björnberg et al. 2005), curricular units typically begin with students listening to, and playing with, recordings that share similar chords and keys. For instance, in one unit, students learn the G, C, D, and E minor chords by playing along to recordings of songs in G major, like "Brown Eyed Girl" by Van Morrison, "Disarm" by the Smashing Pumpkins, and "Good Riddance" by Green Day. By choosing among different activities ranging from strumming the chords, to learning to play the vocal melody, to improvising their own solos, to transcribing the solo performed on the recording, students tailor their educations to their individual interests and technical abilities.

While the songs I mentioned are music of my generation and generations before mine, students are encouraged to add songs to this list; consider more contemporary songs like "Your Call" by Secondhand Serenade, "Personal" by Fergie, and "Hey Ya!" by Outkast. When students add songs of their choice, the repertoire changes from year to year and helps to keep the content pertinent and interesting to the students' diverse and ever-evolving listening tastes. In addition, because students add music that is personally meaningful to them, they actively seek out compositions that have similar chords and begin to see that songs like "Brown Eyed Girl" and "Hey Ya!" have more in common than they would have noticed after just a casual listening.

In addition to collective group instruction, students are also able to create their own projects. I have, quite often, allowed students who are not interested in, say, playing "La Bamba" by Los Lobos, to independently work on more technically challenging music, like "One" by Metallica, for example. Students are also given the opportunity to form groups of three or four to rehearse songs together, or for one student to teach the others a song they are all interested in. In one unusual case, I had a student who signed up for the class and found that she was not interested in playing guitar. Because she wanted to be an English major in college, we created projects where she would write reviews of albums by her favorite artists. We looked at exemplar reviews in periodicals like the *New Yorker* and the *New York Times*, and this student learned how to think and write critically about music she liked and strengthen her writing skills.

This all goes to show that the freedom of choice afforded to students in this setting can eventually lead them to move away from the guitar to other aspects of music. Although the majority of students remain on guitar, some, through experimentation, choose to focus on other instruments. Some find the bass guitar more accessible, some would rather play the drum set, and others prefer the keyboard. But they are not required to remain on one instrument for the entire duration of the course and are, instead, encouraged to experiment. This allows students to experience the music in various ways, to cater to their strengths, and to tailor their education, as well as to make the instrumentation complete to form rock bands.

As can be imagined, an environment where students pursue different projects simultaneously provides challenges to classroom and sound management. Because of this, I found electric guitars to be more advantageous than acoustic guitars. Electric guitars can be plugged into headphones, providing relative ease for students to work individually or in small groups without the sound of other students' activities disturbing their own work.

As the electric guitar also provides a wider range of timbres than the acoustic guitar, students can use various effects—such as distortion, echo, and chorus—in order to sound more like the instruments on recordings they transcribe. Additionally, the electric guitar presents students a wider palette with which to experiment and compose, and they can begin to understand how the quality of a sound affects a composition and how an audience receives it. By experimenting with these different timbres with the electric guitar, students can also discover how timbre creates contrast in the songs they listen to. Many hard rock songs, for example, use a clean sound for the verses and distortion for the choruses, and when students use an acoustic guitar, the ability to try out and manipulate these different sounds is not available to them.

Students also attach complex meanings to different types of guitars because they associate certain types of music with acoustic guitars and other kinds with electric. Some researchers have suggested that the acoustic guitar is associated with femininity and the electric guitar with masculinity (Bayton 1997; Clawson 1999). Although some students—mostly girls—prefer the acoustic guitar, possibly because it is used more often in the music they listen to, the vast majority of students gravitate toward the electric guitar. Teachers need to consider the underlying meanings when students pick their instruments. A reductionist attitude viewing electric and acoustic guitars as equal because there is little technical difference in their performance misunderstands the cultural and musical meanings each instrument has for students and may dissuade them from performing on them (Abramo 2009).

Though the electric guitar has its advantages, it also has its drawbacks. Because they require amplifiers and wires, beginner electric guitars are more expensive than their acoustic counterparts. Also, the use of these amps and wires can quickly clutter up a classroom, and constant management is required to maintain a functional and organized learning environment. To establish a semblance of order in my classroom, students learn a consistent procedure for guitar storage. Despite the potential for disorder, allowing my students to learn on electric guitars, supplemented with some acoustic guitars for students who prefer them, has been most effective.

As I stated in the beginning, I created this class to attract "the missing 84 percent" of my school's student body, and the course has been successful in attracting a great majority of students who do not participate in traditional ensembles. Because of the limitations of my teaching load, the course—with an enrollment of eighty students in four sections—in its current incarnation can only accommodate half of the students that request to take the class. However, in addition to accepting more students into the overall music program, my course also has the added benefit of providing a different type of music education to the students who are already active in ensembles. In these traditional ensembles, students read notation, recreate music from the page, and are rarely, if ever, asked to play by ear and improvise (Kratus 2007; Williams 2007); but in a popular music setting, students are able to explore these types of musicianship.

BEYOND PERFORMANCE

Up to this point, I have only discussed the aspects of the course that involve musical performance. Indeed, performance is an important part of any music education, but in order for students to gain a multifaceted understanding of music and how it functions in their lives, they need to know how to listen, discover patterns, and question how music influences and is influenced by society (Consortium of National Arts Education Associations 1994). Because students, through performance, become familiar with the harmonic and melodic structures of songs they listen to everyday, a gateway opens for the class to conduct theoretical and cultural analyses of these compositions and their music videos. These types of in-depth investigations of the songs provide a richer and more comprehensive engagement with the music they perform and listen to regularly.

Tackling the song "Let It Be" by the Beatles, for example, allows students learn about form and variation. After they learn and perform the chord progressions with proficiency, they can begin to see patterns and repetitions in the song, and by using terms like *verse, chorus,* and *bridge,* students listen, begin to pick up on the patterns, and then start to think about the song's form. In addition, each repetition of the formal sections has different instrumentation. For example, the verse is performed first with piano and voice, but in the middle of the song the instruments have proliferated to include full band and orchestra. This allows students to explore how musicians balance the factors of repetition and contrast in music.

While "Let It Be" can teach form, the song "Imagine" can serve to study lyrics and show how tonalities change the mood of a piece. After students learn to play John Lennon's version of the song, I ask them to watch the video and discuss the use of imagery and words. Students often comment on the optimistic and utopian ideals of the lyrics. They commonly express that the wash of the color white in the video has a soothing and even optimistic effect. The students see John Lennon's "Imagine" as utopian, as portraying the hope of a perfect and beneficial society for all its citizens.

After this discussion, I ask students to watch a version of the song and video rendered in minor with stark vocal harmonies by the band A Perfect Circle. The video looks like a broadcast from a twenty-four-hour news station—complete with a ticker at the bottom of the screen—where images that look like those from the nightly newscast stand in ironic contrast to the lyrics. For example, the lyrics about greed and hunger are accompanied on screen with the image of a man in a food-eating contest, which then quickly switches to a picture of a boy in a famine-stricken land, perishing from hunger. Students often interpret the video as a statement that the world has not lived up to the ideals of John Lennon's lyrics. By changing the tonality to minor, A Perfect Circle turns John Lennon's utopia on its head into a dystopia.

As another example, the song "Personal (Big Girls Don't Cry)" by Fergie allows students to examine representations of gender in popular music. The video presents Fergie as a strong, independent woman who takes control of her life by leaving her drug dealer boyfriend. But perhaps contradictorily, the video also casts Fergie and the boyfriend in stereotypical gender roles: he has tattoos, fixes cars, and is tough and masculine, while she cleans laundry, writes in a diary, and engages in other soft, feminine activities.

It is possible to interpret the moment when Fergie leaves her boyfriend in the video as an act of female empowerment. Even so, Fergie presents herself as helpless and childlike through her musical gestures. On the signature line of the song, Fergie infantilizes her voice, singing the lyrics as if she were a helpless, disempowered little girl. The song and video, therefore, have an ambiguous message; couched in a storyline of freedom and empowerment, the images and musical gestures suggest a more confining representation of what it means to be feminine. Debating the positives and negatives of Fergie's depiction allows students to put a critical eye on media representations of gender without dismissing the work and on popular culture in general without condemning it all as bad or unmusical.

Studying these three songs alone covers a broad spectrum of topics. The formal analysis of "Let It Be" falls within traditional music theory content. Similarly, "Imagine" and its discussion of tonalities offers a somewhat typical analysis. Its interpretation of the use of imagery in the videos, however, begins to veer away from what is commonly thought of as traditional music theory, and the gendered analysis of "Personal" seems to venture far from what one might learn in music theory courses in high school or college. Although such analyses are not common in traditional theory, they have received attention in the fields of musicology (McClary 1991; Moisala and Diamond 2000), media studies (McRobbie 2000), and cultural studies (Leblanc 1999) and may help students understand music in ways that conventional music theory cannot.

In my guitar classes, I have tried to approach these types of analyses of the songs and videos as discussions, not lectures. Rather than dictating analyses or presenting interpretations as the only meaning of a song, I shift the focus from the teacher to the students, asking them to form their own opinions. Through these student-teacher dialogues, the class comes to informed and varying understandings. Some, for example, see the "Personal" video as a positive message, while some become critical of its representation of women. A classroom that welcomes and embraces a variety of sometimes-contradictory explanations allows for a heterogeneous and diverse community where members share different ideas (Allsup 2003; DeLorenzo 2003). In such settings students can think for themselves and form opinions, rather than simply memorize the interpretations of others.

When approached in this critical way, popular music has its own unique value. When I explain the guitar class to administrators, parents, and other teachers, a common response I hear is, "Whatever you need to do to draw them in; then you can teach the real stuff." But in a context where popular music is examined seriously, I contend that it *is* "the real stuff"; the coursework is rigorous and intellectually stimulating, not just an easy way to hook students, or as a gateway to so-called serious classical music. But valuing popular music in this way seems to be at odds with the way schools of music traditionally instruct future teachers. Courses in the history of Western classical music are required for all accredited music education programs, but popular musicology and performance courses, when they rarely appear, only serve as electives (Emmons 2004; Westurlund 2006).

THE DILEMMAS OF REPERTOIRE

When analyzing the last two examples I provided—"Imagine" and "Personal"—a dilemma arises with the use of repertoire in the classroom. Because of the sensitive nature of the content, the pedagogical uses of these songs and their videos must be approached with extreme care. The second version of "Imagine" by A Perfect Circle shows images of famine and war, and "Personal" by Fergie depicts images of femininity that might make some people uncomfortable. I believe it is fair to say that these types of analyses are not suitable for an elementary or middle school classroom. But whether this repertoire is appropriate for high school students is more ambiguous. We must ask, Should this type of music have a place in the classroom?

A teacher can ultimately decide not to include these types of analyses in her lessons, but while this might appear to be a neat and tidy solution to a potential problem, it creates its own difficulties. If students confront these media when they leave the classroom, which they do, is it preferable to ignore this repertoire altogether or to ask students to approach it in a critical manner? But whether videos belong in the classroom hinges on questions that only individual teachers in their unique communities can answer for themselves: To what degree ought a teacher approach the controversial themes students encounter in the media for the sake of teaching them to become better consumers? Should teachers censor "inappropriate" material, or should they help students learn how to listen and watch intelligently and perhaps even question what they are exposed to?

Some people might argue that it is not the job of a music teacher to tackle these issues, that teachers should instead teach the so-called building blocks of music—namely rhythm, form, harmony, melody, etc. But this is not how English teachers, for example, approach their discipline: Novels that address controversial issues, like *Catcher in the Rye*, *The Scarlet Letter*, and *The Adventures of Huckleberry Finn*, to name a few, are regularly used in high school English classes around the United States. Instructors have their classrooms read novels with explicit language, adultery, and racism in order to help teach the students to become better consumers of the English language and literature. Is it possible that the use of (sometimes controversial) music videos in the music classroom is analogous to the ways English classes use novels?

How teachers decide what is appropriate is ultimately based on their own position and the positions of their students. As a white, male teacher, I found discussions of the representations of race and gender difficult to engage in with students. I often wondered if I had the experience, or even the right, to talk about these topics. As a tenured teacher, who is a known member of the community and has job security, I have more flexibility to address somewhat contentious representations than I would have when I was a first-year teacher. Also, individual schools have different expectations of the curricula, and controversial ideas may be more acceptable in a liberal community than a conservative one. Teachers must consider these and other factors when choosing appropriate lessons that challenge and educate their students.

If a teacher does decide that it is valuable to use repertoire that includes controversial songs and videos, then she must make sure that she creates a serious environment. Many students approach the arts—both popular and, to a degree, classical—as entertainment divorced from intellectual rigor. (This is not to say that these students do not care deeply about their music or that they are not intelligent.) In fact, a culture of scholarly curiosity applied to popular culture is not available to students, and, hence, it never occurs to many of them to analyze a video or song. Consequently, they are sometimes more apt to avoid the occasionally uncomfortable task of analyzing the gendered meaning of a work by making jokes. It is the difficult but necessary duty of the teacher to help create a disposition in students to, when warranted, think about popular music seriously.

These problems do not arise to the same degree in band, orchestra, and chorus, perhaps making this a problem unique to popular music ensembles. Teachers of traditional ensembles sometimes wrestle with issues of appropriate repertoire when it comes to holiday music—like equal presentation of Christmas and Hanukkah songs, for example (Mirabal 2008)—and with ensuring that the selections are within the musical and technical skills of their students. But these teachers rarely, if ever, have to worry about whether the music itself is contentious or controversial. In a popular music classroom, teachers don't have editors and educational music publishers to select "school-friendly" content; that said, when they take on the responsibility of sorting through popular music for examination in the classroom, they can customize their instruction.

Regardless of all the dilemmas that the use of this repertoire entails, whenever I have studied each of these three songs in my classroom neither students nor adults have voiced concerns. Students have welcomed the discussions of "Imagine" and "Personal," and, with my careful guidance, they begin to see and hear the music in new and valuable ways. Only when the curriculum involves popular music and moves beyond the performance of songs are certain kinds of musical discovery available. So while the inclusion of this repertoire has, for me, created the added burden of sensitively surmising what students can maturely handle in the classroom and what they need in order to maneuver the contemporary musical world intelligently, the benefits have far exceeded the negatives.

It is perhaps typical to think that popular music is fine in the classroom, as long as the teacher makes sure the lyrics and the topics are appropriate. What I have struggled with, and what I have tried to show here, is that the word *appropriate* is not as obvious or commonsensical as one might think. It may be "appropriate" to include seemingly "inappropriate" materials for students to understand how to make sense of popular culture. How the teacher goes about determining how to help students engage with this repertoire should not simply be a matter of keeping students away from "the bad stuff"; rather, the teacher ought to help the students become informed listeners. Only individual teachers, taking into consideration their students and the culture of their schools, can ascertain the best way to proceed.

CONCLUSION

A guitar class and popular music ensemble as alternatives to more traditional ensembles have served my high school well by creating spaces where students can experience a different type of musicality than is traditionally offered, engage in genres they prefer, and participate in music in ways they find valuable. Teachers also exploit additional potentials of a popular music repertoire when they ask students to supplement their performing experiences by conducting theoretical and cultural analyses. How exactly it is appropriate to ask students to approach popular music dealing with controversial issues is not clear-cut, but when the teacher thinks it through carefully, this content may prove to be a valuable pedagogical tool. In this way, popular music becomes more than a way to grab students; it offers a unique, valuable interaction with the musical worlds they inhabit everyday.

REFERENCES

Abramo, J. M. 2009. Popular music and gender in the classroom. Ed.D. diss., Columbia University Teachers College.

Allsup, R. E. 2002. Crossing over: Mutual learning and democratic action in instrumental music education. Ed.D. diss., Columbia University Teachers College.

———. 2003. Mutual learning and democratic action in instrumental music education. *Journal of Research in Music Education* 51 (1): 24–37.

———. 2004. Of concert bands and garage bands: Creating democracy through popular music. In *Bridging the gap: Popular music and music education*, ed. C. X. Rodriguez, 204–23. Reston, Va.: MENC.

Bayton, M. 1997. Women and the electric guitar. In *Sexing the Groove*, ed. S. Whiteley, 37–49. London: Routledge.

Björnberg, A., et al. 2005. Can we get rid of the "popular" in popular music? A virtual symposium with contributions from the international advisory editors of *Popular Music*. *Popular Music* 24 (1): 133–45.

Bosacki, S., N. Francis-Murray, D. E. Pollon, and A. Elliott. 2006. "Sounds good to me": Canadian children's perceptions of popular music. *Music Education Research* 8 (3): 369–85.

Campbell, P. S., C. Connell, and A. Beegle. 2007. Adolescents' expressed meanings of music in and out of school. *Journal of Research in Music Education* 55 (3): 220–36.

Clawson, M. A. 1999. When women play the bass: Instrument specialization and gender interpretation in alternative rock music. *Gender & Society* 13 (2): 193–210.

Consortium of National Arts Education Associations. 1994. *National standards for arts education*. Reston, Va.: MENC.

Davis, S. G. 2005. "That thing you do!" Compositional processes of a rock band. *International Journal of Education & the Arts* 6 (16). http://ijea.asu.edu/v6n16/ (accessed November 12, 2006).

DeLorenzo, L. C. 2003. Teaching music as democratic practice. *Music Educators Journal* 90 (2): 35–40.

Emmons, S. E. 2004. Preparing teachers for popular music processes and practice. In *Bridging the gap: Popular music and music education*, ed. C. X. Rodriguez, 158–73. Reston, Va.: MENC.

Green, L. 2001. *How popular musicians learn: A way ahead for music education.* Cambridge: Cambridge University Press.

———. 2004. What can music educators learn from popular musicians? In *Bridging the gap: Popular music and music education*, ed. C. X. Rodriguez, 224–40. Reston, Va.: MENC.

———. 2008. *Music, informal learning and the school: A new classroom pedagogy.* Burlington, Vt.: Ashgate.

Jaffurs, S. E. 2004. The impact of informal music learning practices in the classroom, or how I learned how to teach from a garage band. *The International Journal of Music Education* 22 (3): 189–200.

Kratus, J. 2007. Music education at the tipping point. *Music Educators Journal* 94 (2): 42–48.

Leblanc, L. 1999. *Pretty in punk: Girls' resistance in a boys' subculture.* New Brunswick, N.J.: Rutgers University Press.

L'Roy, D. 1983. The development of occupational identity in undergraduate music education majors. Ph.D. diss., University of North Texas.

McClary, S. 1991. *Feminine endings.* Minneapolis: Minnesota University Press.

McRobbie, A. 2000. *Feminism and youth culture.* 2nd ed. New York: MacMillan.

Mirabal, L. B. 2008. Singing sacred songs in public schools: Perspectives of primary school students. Ed.D. diss., Columbia University Teachers College.

Moisala, P., and B. Diamond, eds. 2000. *Music and gender.* Chicago: University of Illinois Press.

Nabb, D. B. 1995. Music performance program enrollment and course availability for educationally disadvantaged versus non-educationally disadvantaged high school students in Texas. Ph.D. diss., University of North Texas.

North, A. C., and D. J. Hargreaves. 1999. Music and adolescent identity. *Music Education Research* 1 (1): 75–92.

Reimer, B. 1989. *A philosophy of music education.* 2nd ed. Upper Saddle River, N.J.: Prentice-Hall.

Watts, M., C. Doane, and G. Fekete. 1994. Minority students in the music performance program. http://music.arts.usf.edu/rpme/minority.htm (accessed January 1, 2009).

Westerlund, H. 2006. Garage rock bands: A future model for developing musical expertise? *International Journal of Music Education* 24 (2): 119–25.

Williams, D. A. 2007. What are music educators doing and how well are we doing it? *Music Educators Journal* 94 (1): 18–23.

3

Toward a New Conception of World Music Education: The Virtual Field Experience

Sarah J. Bartolome

ABSTRACT

The virtual field experience (VFE) is an immersive, multidimensional approach to world music education designed to provide students with meaningful, multisensory interactions with a selected musical culture. Students are engaged in listening, playing, singing, and moving activities in addition to learning about and discussing geography, history, and culture. Opportunities to explore visual media and cultural artifacts are integrated into the VFE, and a culture bearer lends a human face to the music of study. This approach presents world music within its cultural context and allows students to delve deeply into the lived and shared meanings of the musical culture.

INTRODUCTION

Even through the closed door, the sounds of African drumming fill the halls of Westlake Elementary School. In one corner of the music classroom, a small group of fourth graders experiment on Ghanaian drums, shakers, and bells. Across the room, another contingent of students watches a DVD of Ghanaian dancers, exclaiming gleefully as their music teacher, Miss Carlisle, dances into the frame. Yet another group of children is exploring a table full of Ghanaian artifacts: money, jewelry, carvings, cloth, woven baskets, and an album of pictures. The children move from station to station, experiencing these different facets of Ghanaian culture, before reconvening as a class.

Miss Carlisle fires up a slide show for her young students, full of colorful pictures of the Ghanaian countryside, people, instruments, food, cityscapes, festivals, and wildlife. Students ask questions throughout, curious about the lifestyles and customs of this foreign culture and Miss Carlisle's experiences among the Ghanaian people. After the presentation, the students take their places and practice the drum-and-dance selection they have been working on during weekly music classes. As the class comes to a close, Miss Carlisle thanks her students and reminds them that a Ghanaian xylophonist will be visiting their class the following week to give a musical presentation and answer questions. It will be a culminating experience to this eight-week virtual field experience in the music and culture of Ghana. The students buzz excitedly as they exit the room, clearly looking forward to the culture bearer's upcoming presentation.

WORLD MUSIC EDUCATION

Over the past several decades the evolution of a modern global society and the changing demographics of American schools have been catalysts for a strong movement among music educators promoting a more multicultural approach to music education practice. Although early efforts can be traced as far back as the 1900s (Volk 1994), the world music education movement began to gain momentum during the civil rights movement of the 1960s. Both the 1963 Yale Seminar and the 1964 Julliard Repertory Project called for the integration of non-Western and folk music into the school music curriculum. The 1967 Tanglewood Symposium culminated in a declaration that included a statement endorsing a multicultural music curriculum: "Music of all periods, styles, forms, and cultures belongs in the curriculum . . . including currently popular teenage music and avant-garde music, American folk music, and the music of other cultures" (Mark and Gary 1999, 312). The 1969 Goals and Objectives Project was organized by Paul Lehman to identify the responsibilities of MENC: The National Association for Music Education. One of the thirty-five resulting objectives of MENC was to "advance the teaching of music of all periods, styles, forms, and cultures" (Mark and Gary 1999, 313), an objective later identified as one of eight "priority goals" of the profession.

The next three decades saw a marked increase in multicultural music education articles (Elliot 1989; Volk 1993), publications (Anderson and Campbell 1989; Campbell 1991), and conference sessions (Volk 1993). In 1994, MENC published its landmark document, the *National Standards for Arts Education* (Consortium of National Arts Education Association), outlining benchmarks that comprise what the profession considered to be a comprehensive arts education. The ninth music standard, "understanding music in relation to history and culture" (Mark and Gary 1999, x), directly addresses the concept of world music education.

The sheer magnitude of research articles, (Elliot 1989; Volk 1993), resources (Anderson and Campbell 1989; Campbell 1996, 1991; 2008; Lundquist and Szego 1998), and philosophical writings (Campbell 2004; Reimer 2002; Volk 1998), published since the 1960s and its inclusion in the most important policy documents of our time, makes it clear that the profession has embraced the multicultural movement as an integral component of a comprehensive music education. The existence of such organizations as Cultural Diversity in Music Education (CDIME) and the International Society for Music Education (ISME), further illustrate this point. Patricia Shehan Campbell aptly stated that "musical cultures and styles must be studied for what they offer in the way of understanding music as a human phenomenon. In a democracy where every culture is meritorious and worthy of study, the presence of music in schools for its multiple sonic and cultural components is a natural outgrowth of such valuing" (2008, xv).

APPROACHES TO WORLD MUSIC EDUCATION

For some music educators, world music education might be equated with the inclusion of multicultural repertoire in music classes. This additive approach involves infusing the curriculum with musical selections drawn from a variety of the world's musical cultures. Students might sing songs, play musical games, and perform folk dances from a number of different cultures over the course of the year. While a sprinkling of multicultural music selections provides students with an opportunity to engage with diverse world musics, it does little to deepen students' awareness of cultural context. As Campbell stated, "Music is to be understood as it is manifested within its culture and for its comparative expression and use across cultures" (2008, xv). While an additive approach has its merits, in exposing students to diverse musical cultures, world music education might go deeper into the cultural context of the music, providing students with meaningful, multisensory cultural encounters through music.

Alternatively, some music educators employ a comparative approach to world music education, using musical selections drawn from a number of cultures to illustrate the musical concepts being taught. For example, students might learn and practice quarter notes and eighth notes by performing a Chinese folk song, listening to a Zimbabwean mbira piece, and playing an Anglo-American play-party game. This comparative approach, in which musical concepts are illustrated with musical selections from a wide range of cultures, has, at times, inspired controversy within scholarly circles. Dunbar-Hall posited that while

> any type of music can be used to demonstrate how music works . . . the ultimate aim of this type of music education is therefore structuralist, in that it focuses on methods for manipulating sounds and silences with little regard for the qualitative implications of such manipulations. . . . It teaches all music from an analytical perspective that imposes Eurocentric ways of understanding music that can be shown to contradict the ways music's creators may have of conceptualizing their music and meanings. (2005, 128)

A third approach to world music education involves a more immersive curriculum, allowing students to delve into a specific musical culture for an extended instructional unit. Students, for example, might engage with Turkish music and culture over the course of eight weeks, participating in listening, playing, singing, and moving activities and also learning about Turkish people, geography, and culture. It is upon this immersive curricular structure that the virtual field experience is based.

DEFINING THE VIRTUAL FIELD EXPERIENCE

A virtual field experience (VFE) is a multisensory, multidimensional instructional unit focusing on a single musical culture over the course of an extended period of time. Students are given the opportunity to listen to, play, sing, and discuss music examples drawn from the selected musical culture. Additionally, students engage with the culture visually, through photographic depictions of people, landscapes, food, and other cultural elements and through video presentations of music, dance, and theater performances. Students are also provided with kinesthetic experiences of the culture, as they touch and explore cultural artifacts, such as money, jewelry, art, crafts, and musical instruments.

Other aspects of children's culture, such as folk tales, riddles, or story-songs, might be integrated into the VFE to provide another perspective on the culture of study. Finally, a culture bearer adds a human element to the process, giving students the opportunity to interact with an expert and get an insider's perspective on the musical culture being explored. While it is often not possible to bring students to the field, for live engagement with diverse musics and musicians, through the VFE, educators might bring an approximation of the field into the classroom, weaving together rich and varied musical experiences embedded within cultural context.

VFE: DESTINATION GHANA

During a summer study expedition to West Africa, I spent four weeks studying drumming, dance, and local handicraft in Ghana. I came home from this experience loaded with instruments, artifacts, musical and dance repertoire, audio and video field recordings, and pictures. Upon my return, I developed a six-week virtual field experience using the materials and skills I collected in Ghana. A slide show presentation depicted Ghanaian people, landscape, and culture, the children learned and performed a drum-and-dance selection, I taught Ghanaian hand-clapping games, and we read traditional fables. The students learned about drum and shaker making and about kente and basket weaving. Video presentations of festival performances and audio recordings of traditional Ewe drumming provided additional aural and visual components to class engagement with Ghanaian musical culture. Students touched and explored authentic instruments, jewelry, carvings, money, cloth, and other cultural artifacts. Toward the end of the unit an African drum specialist joined our class to talk about his experiences in West Africa and to teach additional selections derived from the Ghanaian music tradition. Our VFE in Ghana culminated in a public performance for students and families, showcasing the musical skills and cultural knowledge gained over the course of the six-week intensive instructional unit.

Following the implementation of my first VFE, I asked my students to write down what they had learned from studying Ghanaian music and culture. The comments, a sampling of which are listed in box 3.1, were extremely rich and varied, addressing such issues as skill acquisition, geographical knowledge, general knowledge, and musical awareness.

Box 3.1   Students' Comments Following a VFE in Ghana

Geographical Knowledge:
- "Ghana is in West Africa."
- "They have beaches there!"

General Knowledge:
- "You have to use a mosquito net because the mosquitoes there carry malaria."
- "Making a basket or an *axatse* is hard work, but it's worth it!"

Musical Awareness:
- "I learned how the master drum made signals in the music to alert the other drums."
- "I learned how the drum patterns all fit together."

Skill Acquisition:
- "I learned to play the *axatse*."
- "I learned how to dance Gahu."

Used with the permission of Sarah J. Bartolome.

Perhaps most striking were the comments related to the living conditions in Ghana. One student remarked, "They are very poor, but they seem very happy. I am very proud of their heart and feelings, and they are strong to be living in such poor conditions." Another commented, "It really makes you think about how lucky we are." Several students made reference to the fact that "the life in Ghana is different than the life here," mentioning also the realization that "different people celebrate different cultures and dances." One boy gained a great deal of personal self-confidence over the course of the project, proudly stating, "I learned don't be afraid to dance or sing in front of lots of people." The range of skills, knowledge, and cultural awareness cultivated by the virtual field experience was truly impressive, and overall I feel the project was a valuable and meaningful component of these students' music education.

DEVELOPING A VIRTUAL FIELD EXPERIENCE

At first glance, developing a virtual field experience might seem a daunting and overwhelming undertaking, but a slight shift in perspective reveals several avenues through which one might find inspiration. Leisure travel provides endless possibilities for world music exploration: there are often opportunities to attend local concerts and music festivals, interact with local musicians, and purchase recordings, instruments, and other artifacts. Vacation photos provide an exciting and rich visual component to the developing VFE, making real and alive both the people and places associated with the musical culture. Upon return home, materials collected in the field might be supplemented with historical and geographical information, other world music recordings, books and fables from the library, and colorful maps. The resultant VFE will be a vivid, musicocultural mosaic of activities, grounded in teacher-collected resources.

It is also possible to explore musical traditions closer to home, connecting to musicians within the community and seeking out world music performances in local venues. Paired with Internet and library research, the development of a curriculum can easily be inspired by locally consumed world music performances. Interaction with local musicians might also facilitate access to musical communities and allow educators the opportunity to network with artists willing to aid in curricular development or visit classrooms as a culture bearer. The inclusion of a visit from a culture bearer in conjunction with world music study represents invaluable human interaction and adds saliency and immediacy to student experiences with recontextualized world musical traditions. The value of such human contact should be emphasized through a participatory encounter with such a guest musician. As Patricia Shehan Campbell stated, "Even their single visit to a classroom of students can be an occasion for making the human connection to the music and for allowing students to recognize its use and value by people within a particular segment of society" (2004, 219).

While there are issues and concerns related to the practicalities of arranging and facilitating such encounters, music educators should also recognize that culture bearers might aid them personally in preparing units of study, recommending repertoire, providing cultural and historical background, or helping with issues of pronunciation and diction, in addition to making class visits to perform for or interact with the children.

Music educators might also explore Internet and library resources as they piece together varied activities for their burgeoning VFE. Locating music examples online, finding storybooks and fables at the library, exploring visual media on websites such as YouTube, and utilizing existing textbooks and teacher references are all effective ways to find materials for integration into the VFE. Teachers should also consider the possibility of arranging listening examples for classroom instruments as a way to get students involved in the active performance of world music. Adapting marimba music for Orff instruments, transferring simplified African rhythms to hand drums, or learning a

Japanese melody on recorder or tone bells allows students to become creative producers as well as consumers of world music. Transcription and arrangement of listening examples provides an active and participatory component the VFE. In general, music educators might draw on their own experiences as world travelers, world music consumers, curriculum developers, and music arrangers as they develop and implement virtual field experiences based on their own interests, talents, and skills.

CHALLENGES AND STRATEGIES

One of the fundamental difficulties related to the development of a virtual field experience stems from a lack of quality resources. In the digital age, much of the research informing a developing curricular unit might be found online. The Smithsonian Folkways (SFW) website (www.folkways.si.edu) is an important source for music educators, providing not only an extensive and searchable library of world music tracks for download, but also featuring a growing body of educational materials designed with the music educator in mind. A collection of lesson plans highlighting SFW recordings provides easy access to a world of activities ready for immediate integration into existing curricula. An online library of video ethnographies provides free online access to performance videos and artist interviews organized by category.

The Seattle-based Experience Music Project (EMP) has compiled an extensive archive of oral histories and related educator resources that can be accessed freely on the EMP website (www.empsfm.org/index .asp). A wide range of artist interviews highlights such multiculturally oriented genres as Latino popular music, jazz, the blues, and African American musical heritage. Video footage of interviews is available on the website, and an extensive classroom-resource page provides lesson plans, curricula, and links to online and suggested print resources. Both the EMP and Smithsonian Folkways websites are treasure troves of resources and information for the music educator wishing to add a global perspective to the music curriculum while simultaneously showcasing the human faces of music-makers. These online resources provide educators with a plethora of educational materials that facilitate the integration of world musics into student-centered music learning experiences.

The Ethnomusicological Video for Instruction and Analysis Digital Archive (EVIA), a searchable, Web-based database developed and maintained by Indiana University and the University of Michigan, is available as a repository of video media collected and archived by ethnomusicologists. Since its inception in 2001, the project has archived more than three hundred hours of field-based recordings and will continue to expand its collection of video footage. EVIA "preserves video recordings with the intention of making them easily accessible for teaching and research" in an attempt "to create a functioning digital repository and delivery system of digital video and accompanying metadata" (www. indiana.edu/~eviada). The project is now available and free to scholars and educators, and may prove to be an extremely useful tool for educators searching for visual media to supplement world music learning activities.

Certainly, the Global Music Series published by Oxford is of tremendous value to music educators wishing to inform themselves about a wide range of diverse musical traditions. The development of Web manuals geared specifically for classroom use makes the books in the series particularly attractive to music educators. The volumes are thorough and yet fairly brief, what I consider to be a "manageable read," even for busy teachers. The accompanying CDs provide rich and authentic aural examples that can be imported directly to the classroom. The online resources, many designed by practicing music educators, offer activities and teaching suggestions that are easily implemented within existing music curricula. At the present, world music resources are more accessible than ever, both online and in print. As more and more world music recordings and videos are archived and print resources become more readily available, the development of virtual field experiences as an avenue for world music education will only become easier.

THE QUESTION OF AUTHENTICITY

Music educators often struggle with issues of authenticity related to world music in the music classroom. Some scholars are against the adaptation of traditional musics for classroom use, claiming that "music education and authenticity regularly have little in common" (Dunbar-Hall 2005, 129). Other scholars recognize the educational value of world music integration in classroom settings and accept the inherent limitations associated with such a recontextualization. While Trevor Wiggins (2005, 20) acknowledged that "it is virtually impossible for an institutional context to provide an appropriate method of handing down a tradition in respect of most musics," he went on to suggest that "the best we can aim for is a negotiation between and understanding of different methods of learning, and cultural knowledge about the music (not of the music) appropriate to the level of the learner."

Particularly in today's global society, musical recontextualization is a reality, and as global media allows music to be shared with astonishing ease, it is natural that fusion genres emerge. Huib Schippers (2005, 30) aptly stated that "contemporary performance and teaching practices demonstrate that traditions can be successfully *recontextualized*. The 'rerooting' of numerous traditions in new cultural settings challenges the idea that (particularly world) music should always be experienced in its original context."

Similarly, Patricia Shehan Campbell forwarded the idea that in an age of globalization and a proliferation of fusion styles, music, by nature, changes and adapts to its cultural contexts. She wrote, "Music can (and does) change its sound as it shifts from one context to another. . . . So be it! So long as the ears are open to the sounds of musicians at the source of a tradition, and those who wish to learn the music and musical style are listening with frequency to the recordings of the music, then a credible and musical performance can occur" (2008, xvi).

While a xylophone arrangement of gamelan music or a recorder ensemble piece based on a Chinese folk melody may not be authentic representations of the musical culture, students are involved in active music making that can enhance listening experiences and cultural discussions. Neither teacher nor student will become a master, but both teacher and student will experience and actively participate in the music of another culture.

CONCLUSION

The diverse nature of today's global society and the changing demographics of American classrooms necessitate the adoption of a more multicultural approach to music education practices. For music educators wishing to provide their students with meaningful, in-depth engagement with diverse musical cultures, the virtual field experience is an approach that strives to fuse authenticity and accessibility as it brings an approximation of the field into the classroom. Students have the opportunity to discover and explore music within its cultural context, gaining not only musical skills and knowledge but also geographical, historical, and cultural understanding. Through the integration of multisensory, multidimensional musical and cultural activities, virtual field experiences serve to broaden students' musical horizons, raise awareness of diverse lifestyles and cultures, and foster a more global perspective on music making as a human phenomenon.

REFERENCES

Anderson, W. M., and P. S. Campbell, eds. 1989. *Multicultural perspectives in music education.* Reston, Va.: MENC.

Campbell, P. S. 1991. *Lessons from the world: A cross-cultural guide to music teaching and learning.* New York: Schirmer books.

———. 1996. *Music in cultural context: Eight views on world music education.* Reston: Va.: MENC.

———. 2004. *Teaching music globally.* New York: Oxford University Press.

———. 2008. *Tunes and grooves for music education.* Upper Saddle River, N.J.: Prentice-Hall.

Consortium of National Arts Education Associations. 1994. *National standards for arts education.* Reston, Va.: MENC.

Dunbar-Hall, P. 2005. Training, community, and systemic music education: The aesthetics of Balinese music in different pedagogic settings. In *Cultural diversity in music education: Directions and challenges for the 21st century,* ed. P. S. Campbell et al., 125–32. Bowen Hills, Queensland: Australian Academic Press.

Elliot, D. J. 1989. Key concepts in multicultural music education. *International Journal of Music Education* 13:11–18.

Lundquist, B., and C. K. Szego. 1998. *Musics of the world's cultures: A source book for music educators.* Reading, UK: International Society for Music Education.

Mark, M. L., and C. L. Gary. 1999. *A history of American music education.* 2nd ed. Reston, Va.: MENC.

Reimer, B., ed. 2002. *World musics and music education: Facing the issues.* Reston, Va.: MENC.

Schippers, H. 2005. Taking distance and getting up close: The seven-continuum transmission model (SCTM). In *Cultural diversity in music education: Directions and challenges for the 21st century,* ed. P. S. Campbell et al., 13–22. Bowen Hills, Queensland: Australian Academic Press.

Volk, T. M. 1993. The history and development of multicultural music education as evidenced in the *Music Educators Journal,* 1967–1992. *Journal of Research in Music Education* 41:137–55.

———. 1994. Folk musics and increasing diversity in American music education: 1900–1916. *Journal of Research in Music Education* 42:285–305.

———. 1998. *Music, education, and multiculturalism: Foundations and principles.* New York: Oxford University Press.

Wiggins, T. 2005. Cultivating shadows in the field? Challenges for traditions in institutional contexts. In *Cultural diversity in music education: Directions and challenges for the 21st century,* ed. P. S. Campbell et al., 13–22. Bowen Hills, Queensland: Australian Academic Press.

4

Discovering World Music and Children's Worlds: Pedagogy Responding to Children's Learning Needs

Lily Chen-Hafteck

ABSTRACT

A total of 109 children from eight second- and fifth-grade classes in two schools participated in a world music program. Through exploring the children's responses to lessons presented on Chinese music and culture, children's learning needs were revealed and pedagogical implications are discussed. Children demonstrated their love of learning and need for self-expression of their ideas, musicality, creativity, and diverse learning needs. It was concluded that a world music program based on a sociocultural approach can be motivating to student learning. A world music program should provide ample opportunities to satisfy children's diverse learning needs through a balanced approach of varied activities.

INTRODUCTION

The study of world music opens the door to a new and exciting way of learning about music and culture. When the music is taught in relation to its sociocultural context, it provides novelty and interest in class and makes learning relevant and meaningful (Chen Hafteck 2007b). My previous study showed that my Chinese music and culture program had positive effects on students' acquisition of cultural and musical knowledge and attitude toward people from Chinese culture (Chen-Hafteck 2007a). In this chapter, I will discuss this program and my firsthand experiences as a teacher-researcher introducing the program to a varied group of children in a recent project.

THE PROGRAM

Basic Premises

A successful music education program is one in which students are motivated to learn and where they develop a positive, open-minded attitude toward music, even if the materials, activities, and information it provides are unfamiliar. For students to be motivated and receptive in class, the music presented needs to be relevant and meaningful. Music education that emphasizes music theory and musical skills without considering the role of music in its sociocultural context is inadequate (Campbell 2002; Dunbar-Hall 2005). Thus, this program adopted a sociocultural approach to multicultural music education in which music was learned together with its cultural background and significance.

Through studying the music and culture of unfamiliar cultures, students will develop understanding and appreciation of people from those cultures (Edwards 1998; Sousa et al. 2005; Chen-Hafteck 2007a). Through participating in musical activities such as games, folk dance, ensemble singing, and instrumental playing, students are required to work together and social skills can be enhanced. Therefore, this program also had the goal of equipping students with social skills that they need to become successful in society.

Music is a practical subject. It is an experience of sounds that we listen to and make. Thus, it has to be learned through hands-on activities. This program provided students with practical music experiences that were not only auditory but also visual, kinesthetic, and tactile. In this way, student learning was enhanced through the multiple modalities.

Content of Lessons

In this program, children learned about Chinese music and culture through listening to Chinese music, singing Chinese songs, performing Chinese dances, and seeing the images of people and sceneries in China. The focuses of the three lessons were as follows.

1. Lesson One:
   a. learning some useful phrases and words in Chinese through songs
   b. discovering where China is and how it looks through maps and images
   c. exploring the life of people in different regions of China through singing songs that describe them
2. Lesson Two:
   a. investigating the life of people in different regions of China through a regional Chinese dance
   b. examining the influential philosophies in China and music for self-cultivation
3. Lesson Three:
   a. learning about Chinese musical instruments and having the opportunity to play some of them
   b. observing the similarities in Chinese painting and Chinese music that portray sceneries
   c. introduction to Chinese festivals and music for celebration

THE CHILDREN

I taught three weekly lessons on Chinese music and culture to 109 students from eight classes of second-grade and fifth-grade children in two multicultural schools in New Jersey. A bilingual second-grade class with Spanish-speaking children and a special education fifth-grade class with children being diagnosed as "Learning Disabled" were included. In this way, I was able to observe responses of elementary children of different ages and linguistic and cultural backgrounds and varied learning abilities. School 1 has a high percentage of African American students and School 2 has a high percentage of Hispanic students.

CHILDREN'S RESPONSES TO THE PROGRAM

Children often find ways to do what they need. By carefully observing their responses in the classroom, we can learn more about these needs and how to adjust pedagogy to enhance their learning. In this section, the messages that children told us through their action as observed during the lessons (through field notes and video data) are used as the basis for reflections on pedagogical issues. This was the model used by Custodero and St. John (2007).

"We Love Learning!"

In this project, the love of learning was clearly demonstrated by the children through their excitement, curiosity, and engagement in class.

Excitement

On the whole, the children greatly enjoyed each of the activities, and they responded with enthusiasm and excitement. For instance, each class expressed excitement upon their first viewing of a picture of the scenery of the Great Wall of China, as evident through their exclamations. The exclamation continued with every picture that followed, like the constant cheers of spectators at a football game.

Beyond exploration of the geography and scenery through pictures, children were also excited by games and movement activities. When I asked children to locate China on a globe that was painted on a beach ball, the game of throwing it around in the classroom stirred up a high level of excitement. A Chinese dance and accompanying listening activity—in which the second graders jumped like frogs to the music of the "Frog Song"—also had similar effects. In fact, the children enjoyed these activities so much that they always asked me, "Ms. Lily, can we do that again?"

The excitement and eagerness to participate can be demonstrated through this description of, what was for me, an unforgettable moment, when I took out my Chinese drum for a demonstration.

After introducing the various Chinese musical instruments, I asked the children which one they preferred. "Who loves the *dizi* [Chinese flute]?" Only one or two hands went up. "Who loves the *erhu* [Chinese violin]?" A few more hands went up. "And *pipa* [Chinese guitar]?" "*Sheng* [mouth organ]?" "*Suona* [Chinese trumpet]?" Only very few hands were raised after I named each of these instruments. Yet I could feel that the room held its breath as if most of the children were waiting for something else. At the end, I said, "Who loves the *dagu*, the big drum?" All the hands went up before I could even finish my question. I then told the children, "I can guess this is your favorite instrument, and that's why I have brought you a surprise!" Everyone looked at me with their eyes wide open as I took the beautiful and shiny big red drum out from my bag. Immediately after they saw the drum, all the hands were up in the air once again. But this time, their hands were waving eagerly, hoping to draw my attention so that I would pick them to have a turn at playing the drum.

Curiosity

The children asked numerous interesting questions throughout the project. Many questions asked by the children, particularly the second graders, were often related to what they had just learned through an experience in the classroom. Here are some examples.

"Why didn't they put ShopRite, Pathmark, and Walmart in there?"

"Do you have Kentucky Fried Chicken in China?"

"Do little girls play musical instruments?"

"Can you walk on it [the Great Wall]?"

Likewise, I found two interesting comments that further support the notion that children learn through relating the unfamiliar to something equivalent that is known personally by them.

"That looks like a piñata," said John after seeing a picture of the colorful children's lanterns in the form of animals.

"It looks like a Chinese ukulele," said Brent after looking at a picture of *pipa*, the Chinese guitar.

Most of the fifth graders' questions showed their eagerness to learn more about the subject.

"How do you say *mom* and *dad* in Chinese?"

"How big is the Great Wall of China?"

"When they built it [dragon boat], what was it made of?"

"Does your [Chinese] name have a meaning?"

"Can you show how Chinese make their food?"

"Hong Kong and Philippines—do they speak different languages?"

"I wonder if there is any Chinese rock song."

The fifth graders also asked questions for verification of what they have heard about China in previous experiences, not directly related to the materials and information they were receiving in the music class.

"Is it true that the biggest wall is in China?"

"Do they [the Chinese] try to kill each other?"

"Is this real when you do this [showing the gesture of meditation], you could go up [while lifting himself up]?"

"Do they still show it down in China? It's a show on the robots."

Beyond the questioning, the curiosity of some of the fifth graders led them to do their own research after class. This was recorded in the field notes of my second visit to that school.

> That morning, Joe and Nick ran to me immediately upon entering the music room. They were very excited to show me a book about China that they had borrowed from the library. They told me that they had learned to speak Chinese with that book and wanted me to verify whether their pronunciation was correct. At that moment, I was very pleased because I felt that my first lesson was successful, leading them to become interested in learning about China.

Engagement

Most of the time, the children were engaged during the lessons. Some children had even brought their notebooks to the class meetings to take notes. They appeared to be very serious about understanding the information provided, even to the extent of not allowing me to change my slides until they had finished copying down all of the information. The notes taken by the children differed. Some were main points of the lessons, some were Chinese writings that I had placed on the board, and there was one second-grade girl who wrote some pronunciation guides that she created herself to help her remember how to correctly pronounce numbers in Chinese.

Interestingly, there were a few moments when all the students, including those who were overexcited or boisterous, suddenly became fully engaged, calm, and attentive. One of these times was when I showed the video of a Chinese boy playing a virtuoso piece of modern Chinese music on a musical instrument, the *yangqin*. Watching the accomplishment of another child appeared to be very attractive to the children. Meditation was another activity that had an effect of keeping the children totally absorbed and engaged. Surprisingly, I found the same result when I sang a Chinese song a cappella to the children. They just stopped whatever they were doing and listened. Perhaps reducing the stimulation from the sight and sound of the slide show, recorded music, and exciting activities to just the sound of one singing voice was what they needed at that moment. Thus, it shows that children are interested in calm and quiet activities in addition to the more energetic doings and thus need time for those as well.

Furthermore, on several occasions, the children were so engaged in an activity that they wanted to continue even when it was time to move on to something different. This is *extension,* one of the flow indicators illustrating engagement (Custodero 2005). For instance, in one of the lessons we had moved on to another listening activity after meditation. Yet one of the children continued to meditate to the music. In another second-grade classroom, a child was still singing the "Number Song" even after the rest of the class had moved on to the "Boat Song," our next activity. The fifth graders were so excited after the Chinese dance that even though they had returned to their seats, they kept doing the dance moves together. These are just some of the many examples observed indicating the high level of engagement among these children.

Pedagogical Considerations to Enhance the Love of Learning

The children's responses clearly indicated a love of learning and eagerness to learn when the teaching materials and approach were appropriate. In this program, the teaching materials on Chinese music and culture brought novelty, interest, and challenges that motivate learning. In addition, I chose songs that I liked, music that I enjoyed, and dances that I loved. When I was teaching, the children could feel my passion for the music and were affected by my enjoyment of the lessons. In terms of approach, varied activities were provided to maintain the children's interest. There were presentation, discussion, games, and musical activities, including singing, moving, and playing instruments. There were times when children had to listen and think quietly, and there were times when they had to participate actively. In short, world music taught through a variety of activities is a good way to enhance children's love of learning.

"We Need to Express Our Ideas!"

Merely listening to the teacher may not necessarily lead to the deepest level of understanding. In an interactive classroom, where students have opportunities to ask questions and voice their ideas, teachers can find out whether students have understood what they have been taught, and the children's voices become the foundation for future learning.

During my lessons, I saw the children's hands raised most of the time. It was clear that they needed to express their ideas and reactions to my presentation. They told me what they knew about Chinese food, movies, dragons, the Chinese New Year, and so on. Sometimes, they also told me about their concerns and worries. For instance, after I discussed Chinese philosophies and different views on life with the second graders, one of the children said to her friend, "I don't want to die." Another boy told me, "My mom said, 'Get out of my life!'" I was shocked when I heard these words while reviewing the video from class. In another second-grade class, during a discussion on meditation, a girl asked me, "What did it mean when they said *evil soul*? It's over there in the video." Before I could answer, another boy told her, "I think . . . when I heard of evil, I was like fighting somebody that chop my head out."

I realize how important it was in my lessons to allow children to express their experiences, feelings, and ideas. It was nice when they shared their pleasant experiences. However, it was even more meaningful when they shared something unpleasant that they had experienced. It is important for all teachers to slow down and listen to what their students have to say about issues and at least sympathize with the children. We need to assure our students that they are free to talk about concerns and worries, and, if possible, to guide the children through acceptance of their worries and help them overcome these issues.

It was unfortunate that I was limited by time and the format of whole-class instruction in this project. In School 1, I had three thirty-minute lessons, and in School 2, I had three forty-five-minute lessons to teach my Chinese-music program. So, although my lessons had piqued the children's excitement and curiosity, I didn't feel that I had enough time to allow all of the questions to be asked and all of the voices to be heard. This was particularly the case with the short sessions in School 1. In this setting, many of the children became restless and talkative among themselves because they were not given the time they needed to express their ideas in class.

Pedagogical Considerations to Enhance Children's Expression

When we have a noisy classroom, it may actually be a good sign! This can happen when the children are engaged and responsive in the lesson and in their own learning, which causes them to share their ideas with other children. Therefore, we need to provide opportunities for children to respond and express their ideas. If instruction time is too short, which it often is, children will need some extra time outside of the music classroom for discussion and questions. Moreover, providing only large-group instruction is often insufficient. Adding some small-group discussion time to the class can allow for all voices to be heard.

"You May Not Know What We Know!"

The children's responses to meditation were amazing not only to me but also to their classroom teachers who observed the lessons. Described below is one of the most remarkable sessions on meditation with the second graders that I observed. The surprise and unexpectedness that the classroom teacher and I experienced during the activity have been noted.

I showed the children a picture of a Buddha statue. One of the children asked, "Why is he being like that?" I said, "You know why? You know what this Buddha is doing?" Ann said, "He is meditating." I answered, "Ah, yes, you know that; he is meditating." The class teacher who had been observing quietly behind the children was stunned and showed a big grin.

Audrey then said, "Meditating means when you do this [showing the gesture of meditation]." "Exactly!" I said. After some more discussion on meditation, Ann continued, "Um . . . if you meditate, you will remember . . . um . . . you will remember . . . things?" I answered, "Oh, yes, you may remember something." More discussion continued until we decided to do a meditation. Then, we went to the carpet area and sat down on the floor. I asked, "Do you speak when you are meditating?" "No," everybody responded almost immediately except Neil. "Yes, in your mind," Neil said as he gestured with his right hand on his temple. Such an unexpected answer made me pause before I could respond. "Ahhh, that's a good idea."

Pedagogical Considerations to Unfold Children's Potential

We cannot underestimate what children know or do not know. Most of what the second-grade children already knew about meditation and spiritual matters were unexpected by their teacher and me. From this project, I also discovered that even the second-grade students were interested in learning about philosophy, as long as it was presented in a manner that was accessible to them. For instance, I discussed the idea of social hierarchy in Confucian philosophy through the story of Mulan, a Chinese folktale that has become well known through Disney's presentation in movie format. Due to their experiences with the movie, the children were able to relate the concepts discussed in the lessons to what they already knew. Therefore, as teachers, we need to provide ample and appropriate opportunities for children to express the things they already know, and we have a responsibility to add to that knowledge base with information we provide.

"We Are Musical and Creative!"

The children demonstrated their musicality frequently during the lessons. They showed that they understood the context of music, as some children responded appropriately to the Chinese musical style with certain movements that they had seen in Chinese dances. Moreover, the children's rhythmic abilities were evident. Their rhythmic movement observed during listening activities, and the beat and rhythm with which they played the percussion instruments, attested to this. Furthermore, children were able to identify the sound of some of the musical instruments that they heard in the music. On several occasions, I observed both the second and fifth graders pretending to play the flute and drum while listening to music featuring flute and drum. A fifth-grade girl had also visualized the melodic movement of a song, saying, "It [the music] has high and low, high and low," while demonstrating by raising and lowering her hands.

On the whole, all the children enjoyed singing and participated in singing activities. They particularly enjoyed learning the Chinese lyrics of the "Number Song." However, in terms of the level of singing skill, it varied from class to class. Many children sang with their low speaking voices and did not match my pitch at the beginning. After some practice with their singing voice, they sounded better. Thus, singing skill is something that needs to be practiced and worked on with the teacher in class, yet vocal remediation was beyond the scope of this project.

Children's creativity was evident during musical activities. When everybody rowed their boats forward while singing the "Boat Song," a second-grade boy rowed his boat backward. While the children were jumping like a frog to the "Frog Song," a second-grade girl stuck out her tongue just like a frog trying to catch an insect. The fifth graders were very good at improvising movements and dances.

The verbal responses that I collected from the children after listening to Chinese music also demonstrated a combination of their musicality and creativity. I considered the responses musical because they showed that the children experienced and responded to the musical characteristics such as styles, rhythm, timbres, as described above. I also found them creative because these responses were both personal and unique.

Below is a listing of some of the fifth graders' comments after listening to the "Frog Song."

"It's very nice, the way that background music kind of blend with the voice."

"Reminds me of flowers."

"It's soothing."

"Soft and pretty."

"It sounds like a river with pond where the frogs are."

Here are the comments of some of the second graders after meditating to the music of *guqin*, an ancient seven-string instrument.

"I was sleeping in my mind."

"I felt like I was flying."

"I felt I was in space like an astronaut."

"I saw a lion, and the dragon takes me to the eyes, and it turns so fast, and then a big explosion."

Pedagogical Considerations to Enhance Children's Musicality and Creativity

My experience with the children convinced me that the children have considerable potential for musicality and creativity; thus it is important for teachers to provide adequate time and space for children to express their musicality and creativity.

In this program, I used a sociocultural approach to music education, teaching music in relation to its cultural context and not as an abstract, unconnected subject. Although musical concepts were not presented as the focus of the lessons, during the music activities, the children's musical learning was pronounced. Specialized music instruction was provided only when there was a need for it and as time allowed. However, it should be cautioned that children naturally enjoy singing, playing instruments, listening, and movement, regardless of the accuracy. Music teachers should encourage their development in each of these activities, while maintaining confidence and enjoyment.

"We Need a Break!"

Although the children enjoyed the program and were excited and engaged most of the time, there were times when they showed clearly that they needed a break. However, a break does not mean that they need to stop and rest. A break is simply a break from paying full attention in class. The children are often paying a certain degree of attention, even though that may not be readily apparent. This downtime might have actually given them an opportunity to recharge and to be able to focus on the next element of the lesson more enthusiastically. Below is an example to illustrate this point.

During a slide show of Chinese festivals, Sue suddenly said in an excited and fast voice, "I wish I could go to China!" Kathy said to herself, "It's so pretty in China." Next, Sue scratched her desk with her hands and then smelled her desk. She said to Andrea, who was sitting next to her and writing notes, "You should smell my desk." Andrea put her nose on Sue's desk and smelled. Then she said, "Cool!" After this, they returned to the slide show. Kathy, who was sitting in front of Andrea, nudged Neil. When she got his attention, she opened her eyes wide with a smile and looked into his eyes. Neil turned around and continued to write his notes. But then Kathy called him again. She did the same thing once more. Neil said something that was inaudible from the video and continued with his notes. Soon I played some Chinese music and started to talk about the Chinese New Year. Everybody paid full attention once again.

Pedagogical Considerations to Give Children the Space They Need

Children need spaces of their own. They may not be attentive all the time and need a break. However, this does not mean that they do not want to learn. On the contrary, they will return to the class when they are ready. Therefore, I do not think that an absolutely quiet and well-disciplined classroom is a natural environment for children. Of course, teachers still need to be observant and maintain some degree of order and structure to ensure that the environment is conducive to meet the learning needs and styles of all the children. It is clear that a teacher has to be sensitive to children's learning needs and allow them the space they need.

"We Are All Different!"

The observations above came from a combination of all the students involved in this project. They gave an overall picture of children's responses to the Chinese-music program. However, it should be noted that among the eight classes that I taught within each class there were individual responses that were different from the majority. For instance, during the Chinese dance, I often found one child in the class not wanting to participate at the beginning. However, after observing the other children having a lot of fun, that child invariably joined the other children at a later stage. I also saw a fifth grader who became very upset when his classmate took the globe away from him. He wanted to take a close look at the geography of China. So he needed more time than the others, who had been happy just to have a quick glance at the globe.

The children's attention spans varied greatly. A good example is Jack, a second grader. He talked about a cupcake sale in the middle of a heated discussion of Chinese New Year. In another lesson, he asked if we could play the game Duck Duck Goose while we were talking about Confucianism. Obviously, his attention span was much shorter than his fellow classmates'.

The children's preferred learning modalities also differed from child to child and class to class. The contrasting responses of two fifth-grade classes in School 1 are a good illustration. In one class, the children loved discussion. They were thoughtful and expressed their ideas very well verbally. They remembered nearly everything I had taught them and could sing the entire "Number Song" by themselves by the third lesson. It was a rewarding experience for a teacher to teach a class like this. On the other hand, the children in the other fifth-grade class were more restless and could not sit long without given instruction. They needed to learn through their bodies, and so movement activities worked well for them. Interestingly, they had the most creative movement and dances than I had observed among all of the classes.

The children in the bilingual class were not very verbal, and their attention span was short. This appeared to be due to the language barrier and possibly cultural differences. I do not speak Spanish, and they had to respond to me in English, adding to some moments of silence and general trepidation on both our parts. I found that short-ening the discussion time and providing more movement activities for this class appeared to break these barriers and facilitated student involvement.

Children with special needs were present in many of the classes I worked with. In a second-grade class, I witnessed a special needs child sitting at the back with his special teacher; and one of the fifth-grade classes contained a child with hearing loss. There may have been other students with special needs, but they were not readily identifiable to me. I found that in activity-based music lessons, these children often participated and enjoyed the activities in the same ways as the children without disabilities. This demonstrates that musical activities are good for all children, regardless of abilities or disabilities, and a well-prepared and diverse world music project can be engaging to all children.

Pedagogical Considerations to Respect Children's Diverse Learning Needs

Presentation through a combination of music, pictures, and videos can appeal to children's auditory and visual learning modalities. Practical music activities including singing, playing instruments, moving, and dancing can satisfy children's kinesthetic and tactile learning modalities. Thus, a balanced teaching approach that includes varied activities can ensure that children have the opportunities to learn through different ways and to satisfy their learning needs even if they have certain preferred learning modalities.

CONCLUSION

World music brings a whole new realm of experiences to the music classroom that can motivate children's learning. Children are excited, curious, and engaged in learning about world music through varied activities that satisfy their diverse learning needs.

Children love learning. As teachers, we have an important but challenging responsibility—to help children realize their learning potential. In our classrooms, we need to be sensitive to children's needs. We need to look at the learning processes very carefully and not make judgments based on assessment of children's musical performances only. In this way, we can ascertain what the children's needs are and provide every child with the opportunities they need to learn and grow. World music is a natural fit for these ideals.

REFERENCES

Campbell, P. S. 2002. Music education in a time of cultural transformation. *Music Educators Journal* 89 (1): 27–32.
Chen-Hafteck, L. 2007a. Contextual analyses of children's responses to an integrated Chinese music and culture experience. *Music Education Research* 9 (3): 337–53.
———. 2007b. In search of a motivating multicultural music experience: Lessons learned from the Sounds of Silk project. *International Journal of Music Education* 25 (3): 223–33.

Custodero, L. A. 2005. Observable indicators of flow experience: A developmental perspective on musical engagement in young children from infancy to school age. *Music Education Research* 7 (2): 185–209.

Custodero, L. A., and P. A. St. John. 2007. Actions speak: Lessons learned from the systematic observation of flow experience in young children's music making. In *Listen to their voices: Research and practice in early childhood music*, ed. K. Smithrim and R. Upitis, 2–18. Toronto, Ontario: Canadian Music Educators Association.

Dunbar-Hall, P. 2005. Colliding perspectives? Music curriculum as cultural studies. *Music Educators Journal* 91 (4): 33–37.

Edwards, K. L. 1998. Multicultural music instruction in the elementary school: What can be achieved? *Bulletin of the Council for Research in Music Education* 138:62–82.

Sousa, M. D. R., F. Neto, and E. Mullet. 2005. Can music change ethnic attitudes among children? *Psychology of Music* 33 (3): 304–16.

5

The Lakewood Project: Rockin' Out with Informal Music Learning

Megan Clay Constantine

ABSTRACT

The Lakewood Project is a rock orchestra that combines traditional string instruments, electric string instruments (vipers), and rhythm section instruments. The first of its kind, the Lakewood Project fosters creativity, musical communication, and collaboration through incorporating informal music learning into a school music ensemble. Informal learning aspects—such as composition, arranging, and improvisation—are what make this group distinct from traditional ensembles. Incorporating rhythm section instruments also creates an opportunity for informal musicians not already enrolled in other school music programs to participate. Because of the repertoire and instruments offered, this group is also contextual and relevant to students' everyday lives. The Lakewood Project is an example of how music educators may combine contemporary techniques with a traditional classical program. Ensembles such as the Lakewood Project could possibly provide a more accessible musical experience to a wide range of students.

INTRODUCTION

Informal music learning generally refers to the manner in which amateur or popular musicians learn, and it is how I learned music when I was young. I began playing piano by ear, and I was able, through guidance from music teachers, to build upon what I had learned on my own and could already hear. As a music learner, I combined elements of informal learning with formal music instruction. The way in which I learned music led me to examine the work of Lucy Green, one of the leading researchers in the field of informal music learning.

While reading Green's literature, I began to wonder if informal music learning, which Green believes may provide a more meaningful experience for students (Green 2004a, 2004b, 2005, 2008), could be incorporated into the secondary ensemble experience. Although some of Green's research focuses on incorporating informal learning techniques in the classroom, those studies mainly pertain to the general music setting (2004a, 2005, 2008). Exploring the incorporation of informal music learning into the secondary music ensemble is equally important because high school–level musical course offerings are often limited to participation in traditional instrumental and choral groups. Upon the recommendation of a music education professor at Case Western Reserve, I observed the Lakewood Project, a rock orchestra incorporating some informal music learning elements into a secondary school ensemble. This group also interests me because I am a graduate of Lakewood High School, and I participated in the music program prior to the start of the Lakewood Project.

The Lakewood Project was started by director Beth Hankins in 2002. In 2001, she met Mark Wood of the Trans-Siberian Orchestra, a prominent performer, composer, instrument maker, and producer, at the Rock and Roll Hall of Fame. At this meeting, Hankins inquired about an original composition for her high school orchestra students and about acquiring some of Wood's viper instruments (electric violins, violas, and cellos) (Mark Wood Music Productions 2009b). Presently, the Lakewood Project, the first of its kind, consists of four viper violins, two viper violas, two viper cellos, four acoustic violins, two acoustic violas, two acoustic cellos, two acoustic basses (one bowed, one pizzicato), electric guitars, electric bass, electric keyboards, and percussion. The acoustic instruments are amplified through electric pickups. This group also incorporates a crew of student technicians who learn and assist with operating sound and lights.

All musicians in the Lakewood Project must audition for the director. String players are required to take private lessons to be in the ensemble. The members audition in the late spring for the following year, and rehearsals begin in the summer. The rehearsal and performance schedule is rigorous, requiring a tremendous amount of dedication on the part of the students and director.

ASPECTS THAT MAKE THE LAKEWOOD PROJECT A UNIQUE ENSEMBLE

The Lakewood Project, one of only a few rock orchestras in the country, is different from the traditional ensemble because it incorporates informal learning practices within a school ensemble. Research suggests that the actual process of informal music learning, the manner in which most popular musicians learn, is important to music education; it is not simply a matter of incorporating popular music (Green 2004a). Popular music has been incorporated since the Tanglewood Symposium (Choate 1968), but only within the context of formal music learning. In general, educators incorporate pop music within formal education but overlook the way in which pop musicians learn to make music.

Throughout the informal learning process, musicians often integrate listening, performing, improvising, and composing. Students in the Lakewood Project regularly engage in all of these processes. Recorded music is used as a viable learning tool in informal music learning; musicians use an aural and oral approach, as opposed to formal musicians, who significantly depend on notation and try to copy it exactly without any change or improvisation (Bowman 2004). In the case of the Lakewood Project, rhythm section members learn their parts from recordings, while leaving room for creativity and interpretation. For instance, while observing one rehearsal, I noticed that the drummer added his own half-time feel and double bass-pedal beat to one of the pieces. The important aspect here is that the director allowed the drummer to add his own creative dimension to the song.

Students in the Lakewood Project have the unique opportunity to create music, arrange, improvise, and "get down" with the feel of nontraditional repertoire. Many music educators may assume that a rock orchestra is simply a traditional orchestra that performs watered-down arrangements of pop tunes. This is certainly not the case with the Lakewood Project. Their ever-expanding repertoire, which encourages creativity and musical growth, spans from unique arrangements of classical literature to contemporary rock styles.

The group also performs original compositions, some by students, which may incorporate traditional blues forms, Arabic scales, and funk styles with plenty of opportunities for students to improvise. The incorporation of creative elements is especially unique to school string programs. Many band programs have jazz bands, which offer students opportunities to improvise, but ensembles such as these are not normally available to string players within the school setting.

Musical communication is another aspect that distinguishes this group from traditional music ensembles. Through involvement in the Lakewood Project, students may gain a deeper understanding of harmony and musical structures through communicating in informal ways. Many of the rhythm section students are informal musicians and do not read music or rehearse with charts. This often causes the string players (formal musicians) and rhythm section students (informal musicians) to communicate through nontraditional means during rehearsals.

Formally trained orchestral musicians are accustomed to using letters and numbers for rehearsal purposes. This system does not work when an entire section of the ensemble does not have printed music, however. This has ultimately led to the kind of communication between the string section (formal musicians) and rhythm section (informal musicians) that is found within informal music making. Students may say "Let's start at the bridge" or "Let's start on the five chord" during rehearsal, which is not common in traditional ensemble rehearsals, where a conductor or director starts, stops, and makes adjustments based on rehearsal numbers. In a conversation on May 27, 2008, Ms. Hankins expressed that this type of communication has ultimately led the rock orchestra students to a deeper and more meaningful understanding of harmony and musical structures. The understanding gained from these communication skills has carried over and benefitted the other traditional orchestras at Lakewood High School.

The Lakewood Project is also unique because it incorporates electric guitar, electric bass, and keyboards, which are more commonly found in informal settings. This provides an opportunity to include informal musicians, who do not typically participate in school music ensembles. In a study of nine male musicians, aged fourteen to sixteen, in the Seattle area, Campbell (1995) examined the transmission of information and learning within rock or garage bands and the participants' experiences with formal music education. All but two of the participants had been involved in school music ensembles in the past, but none of the participants were enrolled at the time of this study. Their primary reasons for dropping out of school music programs were the slow pace of rehearsals, the simple repertoire, and not liking the sound of concert or marching band music (Campbell 1995). Based on my observations of the Lakewood Project, I could honestly say that the rehearsals are fast-paced, the repertoire is varied with room for creative interpretation, and the students are generally enthusiastic about the pieces.

Research also suggests that informal musicians may turn away from school music or have a negative perception of school music. Green (2004b) studied the perceptions formal music education and musical learning practices of fourteen popular musicians in England. Nine out of the fourteen participants took classical lessons in schools; seven reported that formal music study was not worthwhile. In general, the participants in her study found that school music was boring, slow, and not contextual to their lives. None of the participants in the study linked the information they learned in classical lessons to what they did in their rock bands. The nine oldest participants in the study felt alienated and bored during school music classes. They also felt that their instructors did not recognize their enthusiasm for music making, learning, and musical accomplishments outside of school. Ensembles such as the Lakewood Project may help to change these perceptions about school music over time.

Through the Lakewood Project, informal musicians have a place in the school music program, where their enthusiasm, achievements, and love of music can be recognized and rewarded. In general, course offerings in high school are limited to participation in traditional ensembles such as band, orchestra, or choir (Jones 2006). Students who may wish to play an instrument in high school must choose a traditional band or orchestra instrument. A small number of high schools offer additional ensembles, such as show choirs and jazz bands. Due to the lack of standardization in this area, music instruction in high school is often limited to participation in traditional band, orchestra, and choral ensembles.

Ensembles such as the Lakewood Project correspond to both Vision 2020 (Madsen 2000) and the National Standards for Music Education (Consortium of National Arts Education Associations 1994). The Housewright Declaration, a culminating statement of Vision 2020 (Madsen 2000) asserts that by the year 2020, students in middle school and high school will have opportunities to participate in diverse ensembles other than formal traditional ensembles (Lehman 2000). The National Standards for Music Education (Consortium of National Arts Education Associations 1994) include improvisation and composition, which may be overlooked by traditional ensemble directors (Byo 1999; Strand 2006). Ensembles such as the Lakewood Project could help music educators follow these recommendations by providing alternative course offering and transforming the traditional ensemble into a modern and creative experience for students.

By including rhythm section and electrified instruments, the Lakewood Project is contextual and relevant to students' lives. Jones (2008) did a study on music course offerings and found that the instruments being taught in schools are not connected to the rhythm section instruments that are being sold in stores. Current school music classes may not be relevant to students' lives outside of the classroom (Allsup 2003). Many high school instrumental ensemble courses are outdated, and the rehearsal rooms resemble those of the 1920s, despite the changing times.

The group is also distinct from other traditional ensembles through its use of technology and sound equipment, which is another aspect that makes the ensemble contextual to students' daily lives. Students in the group utilize technology and are responsible for setting up their amplifiers, cords, and ear monitors for performances and rehearsals. The acoustic instruments used in the group are also amplified, so those students may gain knowledge about electronic sound equipment as well.

The high volume level of the ensemble is also another component that makes this ensemble relevant to students' lives. The performances are on par with modern rock concerts: they are spectacular, high-energy, multimedia events with lights, cameras, and enthusiastic crowds. This group has performed sold-out concerts at the Rock and Roll Hall of Fame and the House of Blues in Cleveland for thousands of people. This is different from high school marching bands that perform for thousands of people at a professional football game or the Rose Bowl Parade. In the Lakewood Project's case, thousands of spectators were present and bought tickets to see the Lakewood Project itself, not a professional football team or big parade. "They strut around the stage, yelling to one another, and expressing themselves in heady teenage rock star postures. Watching them perform, you get the feeling that these are the cool kids rather than the 'band geeks' or 'orchestra dorks'" (Besenyodi 2006, para. 5).

The Lakewood Project is the premiere string ensemble of the Lakewood City Schools' orchestra program. Adjacent to Cleveland, Ohio, Lakewood is the city's second largest suburb. Lakewood High School is the only high school in the suburb, with an enrollment of 1,956 (Ohio Department of Education). There are four traditional orchestras, which correspond to student skill levels and include approximately 160 students at Lakewood High School.

The Lakewood Project answers the question how to combine contemporary techniques with a traditional classical program. It opens creative pathways for students, especially the string players. Through involvement in this group, they learn how to play different repertoire and utilize creative techniques on their string instruments. At the same time, this group includes informal musicians in the rhythm section who may not be enrolled in school music. This group encourages student creativity through improvisation and composition with positive results. Within the first few weeks of starting the Lakewood Project, the director noticed a change in some of her students; they seemed more engaged with music in rehearsal and outside of school. For example, students reported that they were jamming with other family members on blues scales. Other students in the Lakewood Project wanted to play different scales (minor pentatonic, blues scales) and transpose those scales during traditional orchestra warm-ups (Mark Wood Music Productions 2009b).

The Lakewood Project has taken the high school and community by storm and has also been useful for recruitment purposes. Involvement in this group, which is very visible and popular in Lakewood and the surrounding communities, may be a goal of many elementary and middle school string students. Ms. Hankins revealed in conversation to me that some of those younger string students have viper stickers and drawings on their orchestra folders and method books. These younger students also have the opportunity to participate in a music camp dedicated to the creative techniques used in the Lakewood Project.

The success of this group can be attributed to the support of the school and the community. This project was started through a generous alumni donation to purchase the vipers (electric violins) and sound equipment. This group is also very successful because of the vision of director Beth Hankins. Like most music educators, Hankins was classically trained. Rock music, sound equipment, and rhythm section instruments were not a part of Hankins's preservice preparation at Oberlin Conservatory, as is the case with most music education preparation programs. Although the research suggests that music teachers are generally not prepared to teach popular music styles or rhythm section instruments (Boespflug 1999; Jones and Clements 2006), Hankins forged ahead anyway, calling on community musicians and experts in the field for pointers. Mark Wood and members of the Trans-Siberian Orchestra, Julie Lyonn Lieberman, Wish You Were Here (a Pink Floyd tribute band), A Hard Day's Night (a Beatles tribute band), Neil Zaza, and Matt Turner were among the experts with whom she consulted and collaborated. The Lakewood Project has been as great learning experience for the director as well as the students.

Beth Hankins's experiences in developing the Lakewood Project can serve as an example for music teachers who may be hesitant to incorporate nontraditional or often ignored components such as composition, improvisation, and pop and rock repertoire. Hankins was willing to jump in and start this project even if she wasn't a rock musician herself. By doing this, she built upon her excellent training and exceptional musicianship and learned new repertoire and teaching techniques. From this sort of experience, music educators can learn to trust in and enhance their own musicianship skills as they continue learning new things for the benefit of their students.

Although Ms. Hankins is the director of the Lakewood Project, she has more of a peripheral role in the ensemble than that of a traditional director. Hankins is more of a moderator and facilitator than conductor. Students actively participate as leaders in rehearsals. They start the songs in rehearsal and performance and perform without a conductor. The structure of the rehearsals appears very loose compared to those of traditional ensembles, but the Lakewood Project students are also very engaged and enthusiastic during these practices. At times, Ms. Hankins may stop the group to work on a specific section with a few players. During that time the other students can turn their electronic sound off and silently practice, which is a benefit of electronic equipment. By relinquishing control of the podium, Hankins has allowed room for student leadership and creativity, possibly leading to a more meaningful musical experience. The students are in the spotlight in the Lakewood Project. They are taking the bows. They, and not the director, are the rock stars.

CONCLUSION

The Lakewood Project, the first rock orchestra of its kind, fosters creativity and collaboration through incorporating informal music learning into formal music education. Informal learning aspects, such as contemporary repertoire, composition, arranging, and improvisation, are what distinguish this group from traditional ensembles. Incorporating rhythm section instruments also creates an opportunity for informal musicians who are not enrolled in school music to participate. Because of the repertoire and instruments offered, this group is also more relevant to students' lives. Through initiatives such as the National Standards (Consortium of National Arts Education Associations 1994) and Vision 2020 (Madsen 2000), music educators are encouraged to incorporate improvisation and composition and to offer alternative music courses in order to provide a more meaningful experience for their students. Ensembles such as the Lakewood Project can help music educators accomplish this. While watching the Lakewood Project perform at the Rock and Roll Hall of Fame in 2003, I heard Hankins encourage the educators in the crowd to "set your students free." Setting students free through groups like the Lakewood Project may lead to a meaningful, inclusive, and relevant musical experience for a wider community of students than traditional ensembles alone.

Music educators could start their own rock ensembles by trusting in their own musical abilities, having the courage to try new things with their ensemble, and having the courage to ask the school and community for assistance in starting such a unique project. Educators could also seek assistance from community rock musicians and experts in the field. There are resources available to music educators who are interested in starting a rock orchestra on Mark Wood's website (www.mark woodmusic.com). His electric violin method book *Electrify Your Strings* (2008) is now available for sale and comes with an accompanying CD. Wood also offers special programs and in-services to electrify string programs (Mark Wood Music Productions 2009a, 2009c). Information about these programs can be found at www.electrifyyourstrings.com.

REFERENCES

Allsup, R. E. 2003. Transformational education and critical music pedagogy: Examining the link between culture and learning. *Music Education Research* 5:5–12.

Besenyodi, A. 2006. The Lakewood Project. *PopMatters Concert Review* (January 27, 2006). www.popmatters.com/music/concerts/l/lakewood-project -060127.shtml.

Boespflug, G. 1999. Popular music and the instrumental ensemble. *Music Educators Journal* 85 (6): 33–37.

———. 2004. The pop music ensemble in music education. In *Bridging the gap: Popular music and music education*, ed. C. X. Rodriguez. Reston, Va.: MENC.

Bowman, W. 2004. "Pop" goes . . . ? Taking popular music seriously. In *Bridging the gap: Popular music and music education*, ed. C. X. Rodriguez. Reston, Va.: MENC.

Byo, S. 1999. Classroom teachers' and music specialists' perceived ability to implement the National Standards for Music Education. *Journal of Research in Music Education* 47:111–23.

Campbell, P. S. 1995. Of garage bands and song-getting: The musical development of young rock musicians. *Research Studies in Music Education* 4:12–20.

Choate, R. A. 1968. *Documentary report of the Tanglewood Symposium.* Washington, D.C.: MENC.

Consortium of National Arts Education Associations. 1994. *National standards for arts education: What every young American should know and be able to do in the arts.* Reston, Va.: MENC.

Emmons, S. E. 2004. Preparing teachers for popular music processes and practices. In *Bridging the gap: Popular music and music education,* ed. C. X. Rodriguez. Reston, Va.: MENC.

Green, L. 2004a. Popular music education in and for itself, and for "other" music: Current research in the classroom. *International Journal of Music Education* 24:101–18.

———. 2004b. What can music educators learn from popular musicians? In *Bridging the gap: Popular music and music education,* ed. C. X. Rodriguez. Reston, Va.: MENC.

———. 2005. The music curriculum as lived experience: Children's "natural" music-learning processes. *Music Educators Journal* 91:27–32.

———. 2008. *Music, informal learning and the school: A new classroom pedagogy.* Hampshire, UK: Ashgate Publishing Limited.

Jones, P. M. 2006. Returning music education to the mainstream: Reconnecting with the community. *Visions of Research in Music Education* 7. www-usr.rider.edu/~vrme.

———. 2008. Preparing music teachers for change: Broadening instrument class offerings to foster lifewide and lifelong musicing. *Visions of Research in Music Education* 11. www-usr.rider.edu/~vrme.

Jones, P. M., and A. C. Clements. 2006. Making room for student voice: Rock and popular musics in school curricula. Unpublished paper presented at the MayDay Group Colloquium. Princeton, N.J., June 22–25.

Lehman, P. R. 2000. How can the skills and knowledge called for in the National Standards best be taught? In *Vision 2020: The Housewright Symposium on the future of music education,* ed. C. K. Madsen. Reston, Va.: MENC.

Madsen, C. K. 2000. *Vision 2020: The Housewright Symposium on the future of music education.* Reston, Va.: MENC.

Mark Wood Music Productions, Inc. 2009a. *Electrify your strings!* www.electrifyyourstrings.com/index2.html100027 (accessed March 20, 2009).

———. 2009b. *The Lakewood Project.* www.markwoodmusic.com/cgi-bin/gallery/gallery.cgi?Category=100027 (accessed March 15, 2009).

———. 2009c. *Wood violins.* www.woodviolins.com/html/contact.html (accessed March 21, 2009).

Ohio Department of Education. n.d. *Interactive local report card.* Ohio Department of Education. http://ilrc.ode.state.oh.us/default.asp.

Strand, K. 2006. Survey of Indiana music teachers on using composition in the classroom. *Journal of Research in Music Education* 54:154–67.

Wood, M. 2008. *Electrify your strings.* New York: Cherry Lane Music Company.

6

Music Tech, Adaptive Music, and Rock Band 101: Engaging Middle School–Age Students in General Music Class

Mary L. Cohen and Cecilia Roudabush

ABSTRACT

Finding a place for those students who do not choose to enroll in band, orchestra, and choir at the middle school level can be a daunting yet very necessary task for music educators. This case study is based on the creation of a meaningful musical alternative for middle school–age students in the Iowa City Community School District. Through the dedicated work of two middle school music teachers, a vivid alternative program that meets the needs of these students has been developed and implemented.

INTRODUCTION

> Everyone can make music. It's up to me to figure out *how* they can.
>
> —Cecilia Roudabush

Middle school–age students who do not want to enroll in band, orchestra, or choir need a meaningful alternative for their school music class. Two Iowa City Community School District (ICCSD) middle school general music teachers have created a curriculum that engages youth who are not interested in choir, band, or orchestra. This chapter details the background, issues, curriculum, and evaluation of this alternative program.

This alternative general music program has three components: (1) Music Tech (short for Music Technology and Electronic Instruments), (2) Adaptive Music, and (3) Rock Band 101. Students may also participate in the Garage Band After School Club. Adaptive Music is a course for students receiving special education services, although these students have the option to enroll concurrently in Music Tech. Eighth graders may take Rock Band 101 to fulfill the district's fine-arts requirement, which is that all middle school students take an entire year of a music ensemble or one trimester of a general music elective. The philosophy of all three general music courses is that every student, even the unmotivated adolescent, can make music if given the right opportunities and appropriate guidance.

With an amazing collection of equipment and instruments, originally purchased through a grant, and an extended collection furnished by fundraising money and Parent-Teacher Associations, all three middle schools, Southeast, Northwest and North Central, have as many as thirty acoustic guitars, fifteen electronic keyboards, four electric basses, eight electric guitars, and one or two electronic trap sets (see photos 6.1, 6.2, and 6.3). The classrooms also have a computer lab

Photo 6.1. North Central Junior High School general music classroom

Photo 6.2. Northwest Junior High School music lab

Photo 6.3. Northwest Junior High School music-lab guitars and drums

used for composing, working with software, and listening activities. In addition, each school has at least one piece of music technology that is different than the other schools' resources. For example, North Central has a Clavinova, while Southeast and Northwest Junior Highs each have a DJX beat machine.

ISSUES AND BACKGROUND

In 2006, the Iowa City Community School District, similar to many districts across the United States trying to meet No Child Left Behind criteria, created a year-long literacy class at the seventh-grade level. This additional literature requirement reduced time in students' schedules to take a general music class if they were enrolled in a musical ensemble. Starting in August 2006, only students who were not taking band, orchestra, or choir would take general music; whereas previously every middle school student had participated in this class.

Middle school general music instructors Terri Finger and Cecilia Roudabush used the 2006 school year to evaluate the needs of their new student populations and then restructured the class for students who most likely identified themselves as nonmusicians. The typical student had never played an instrument, while some others had started an instrument but later quit. Some played an instrument, usually the piano, but were not interested in school performance ensembles. Most of these students did not fluently read traditional music notation. Students in band, orchestra, or choir had permission to take the class if they could accommodate it in their schedule; however, only three of these students have enrolled in general music since 2007.

Cecilia Roudabush's perception that every student can make music, if only she can determine what they need to be successful, proved to be a factor in the new curriculum's success. Her background in music therapy and counseling served her well with this new student population.

Roudabush received her bachelor's of fine arts degree from the University of Iowa, completing in 1989 a major in music education and music therapy with a minor in counseling. In 1998, she earned a master's degree in music education, specializing in music therapy. She began her career teaching general and adaptive music at Iowa City's Hoover Elementary and Southeast Junior High for thirteen years before teaching seventh- and eighth-grade students in starting 2001. Roudabush is currently a general music and adaptive music teacher at Northwest Junior High in Coralville and at North Central Junior High in North Liberty (both areas are part of the Iowa City Community School District). She also teaches seventh-grade personal development classes. Through her training and teaching experience, she has developed a keen awareness of student needs, skills, strengths, and weaknesses.

Roudabush has found that the key to helping students become successful musicians is to diversify materials and activities based on their skills and ability levels. Music Tech assignments do not require the same amount of diversification as Adaptive Music or Rock Band 101, because most of the students in Music Tech are beginners. However, in Adaptive Music, Roudabush may be working with students with severe or profound mental or physical disabilities in the same class as a student with an identified behavior disorder who has otherwise normal intellectual and gross/fine motor skills.

Rock Band 101 may have students that need adaptations to be able to play even one instrument as well as students who can play every instrument in the room. Individualized teaching strategies for this wide range of abilities could include using color-coded or simplified music for the student unable to read standard notation and tablature, as well as alternative activities for more advanced students during beginner units.

Roudabush and Finger wrote the new curriculum in the summer of 2006 with the framework of diversification for their new student population. Both realized that by creating diversified levels within their curriculum while writing it they could immediately respond to students' needs with ready-made materials. They focused on the most popular songs and materials from previous experience and continue to add to their collection of diversified materials.

MUSIC TECH

Starting in the fall of 2007, students who take Music Tech learn musical elements through technological tools. They study music theory with Music Ace software, work with a voice processor (a device that alters the voice electronically), learn to read guitar-chord diagrams and tablature while playing acoustic or electric guitar, play the electric bass and electronic trap set, and examine the rules and controversies surrounding copyright and illegal file sharing and downloading through a unit on Mozart.

Additionally, Roudabush spends the trimester emphasizing multiple musical styles, such as crossover country, blues, classic rock, old school hip hop, world and Latin (Tejano), and every style Roudabush discovers that exists in contemporary media outlets. This particular circuit is one of her favorites, because she hooks her students with what they like while encouraging them to listen to a broader range of musical styles.

A highlight of the Music Tech class is Rock Central, a concept created by Larry Knipfer and Janice Shields, the former general music teachers at Northwest and Southeast. Students rotate through three circuits for the last fifteen days of the twelve-week trimester, bringing together much of the information they have learned. The unit is named for the most popular circuit, Rock Central, which allows the students individual time on the electric guitar, electric bass, electronic trap set, keyboard, DJX or Clavinova, and voice processor. Roudabush and Finger added two different circuits to Rock Central that Roudabush calls Mozart Central and Discovery Central.

In Mozart Central students individually write a composition in the computer lab using Hyperscore. Hyperscore, a software product from Harmony Line Music, uses color, sound, and length as compositional tools in an easy-to-use format that allows anyone to compose melodies, rhythmic accompaniments, and combine them into a composition. This tool allows the students to focus on the creativity of composing rather than the details of standard notation.

The Discovery Central circuit exposes students to music technologies. Students at each school make use of technology devices such as the Zoom 1204 voice processor, a Clavinova or DJX beat machine, recording devices (i.e., a Tascam), the Doodle Pad compositional tool of Music Ace, other software such as Sibelius Instruments or Microsoft Musical Instruments, and Internet websites such as DJ Rick, a sample and loop program on the Internet.

STUDENT'S HYPERSCORE COMPOSITION
PERFORMED BY YING QUARTET

In 2007, the Education Department at the University of Iowa's Hancher Auditorium invited the ICCSD and West Branch Middle Schools to participate in a composition project at the middle school level with the Ying Quartet and Tod Machover, the creator of Hyperscore. Students created four-part compositions for strings. The Ying Quartet performed five student compositions at a workshop at Hancher. Machover explained the program during the workshop.

Three of the five composers were Roudabush's students. One had a learning disability, and another had discipline problems, but all wrote interesting and lively pieces of music. The Ying Quartet played one of the student's compositions at the professional evening performance. The quartet recognized the student on stage in front of the audience and his proud family. Hyperscore continues to be an important component of the Music Tech program and is an attractive activity for students attending Garage Band Club.

ROCK BAND 101

Rock Band 101 students study the history of rock and roll from 1954 to the present day, focusing on the blues and African Americans artists. Students extend their learning of guitar, electric bass, and trap set; learn to play the electronic keyboard using automatic bass chords; use Music Ace software to learn music theory; compare the characteristics of their favorite songs to classical rock from the 1950s to the present day; and test their skills to qualify for positions within the class's culminating small-group bands. Emphasis is on meeting the students at their level and taking them a step further. Students may test out of a unit and pursue alternative assignments using headphones. If students take the class more than once, Roudabush encourages them to specialize in a different instrument in their small-group bands.

In Rock Band 101, students practice reading standard notation through an electronic keyboard unit where they learn to play treble clef melodies in the right hand and coordinate that with bass chords in the left. Before choosing a beginner, intermediate, or advanced melody from a set of prepared materials, Rock Band 101 students review standard notation using specific lessons in Music Ace. This allows students to write note names into the score of their chosen melody using a diagram of the treble clef staff and to play the melody in the correct octaves. This unit allows many more of the students to read standard treble clef notation in the small-group rock bands.

ADAPTIVE MUSIC

If students receive special education services, they may take Adaptive Music. The class size ranges from two to fourteen students. Adaptive Music meets in the General Music room so that students have supervised access to the same materials, instruments, and pieces of equipment as their peers. The curriculum of Adaptive Music is designed around the specific needs of the students in each class. Activities may be based upon features of Music Tech or Rock Band 101, such as learning to play the electronic instruments, or be specific to Adaptive

Music, such as exploring units on categorizing rhythm instruments, hand drumming, or singing folk songs. Students perform a concert for their peers, parents, and teachers. They may take Adaptive Music for one trimester or throughout their middle school years.

GARAGE BAND AFTER-SCHOOL CLUB

Students have an opportunity to participate in a one-hour after-school club on Tuesdays at North Central and Wednesdays at Northwest. As an informal club, attendance is not taken and students can stay for the entire hour or leave as needed to complete homework, catch a bus, or participate in another club. After an orientation to the equipment in the room, particularly important if they have not taken the general-music classes, students are allowed to, alone or with others, use any of the instruments, equipment, or computers and keyboards in the music lab. If a group of students forms a band, the teacher supports the band using free online tablature and arranges opportunities for the band to play at school events such as dances and assemblies. Band, orchestra, and choir students make up about 75 percent of the participants in this club at Northwest and about 50 percent at North Central.

INTENTIONS OF THESE PROGRAMS

These programs were devised to provide successful music-making activities for every student, regardless of any mental or physical disability or other learning challenge such as behavior problems. Because Music Tech is the last required music course in the Iowa City Community School District for students not participating in choir, band, or orchestra, it was imperative to engage student interest for continued involvement with music. Such involvement could include playing nontraditional school instruments such as a guitar—a portable instrument that one can play for personal enjoyment. Involvement could also occur simply through supporting performing musicians by purchasing (not illegally downloading or file sharing) recordings. A combination of these types of musical involvement is an intended outcome.

ASSESSING STUDENTS IN MUSIC TECH

During the presentation of the American Music Styles unit in Music Tech, students learn to talk intelligently about the music they are hearing. Students take a written assessment that evaluates how well they describe six musical elements (style, meter, tempo, dynamics, instruments, and vocals) in six different musical selections. They conclude the assessment with a thoughtful review of each piece. One purpose of this activity is to increase their willingness to give genres of music a first or second chance as a listening choice.

For the Elements of Music unit, students alternate days of instruction on a concept such as melody with a day of practice creating and manipulating the same concept using Hyperscore. Students learn and review the elements of rhythm, meter, melody, form, tone color, dynamics, and harmony. At the end of the entire unit, students take a vocabulary test (multiple choice, fill in the blank, and matching). The students use the vocabulary throughout the rest of the trimester in all of the units.

For the unit on acoustic guitar, students write a daily goal and then self-evaluate their effort and process, journaling about their daily experience at the end of the class period. The unit ends with a playing test done in pairs (the rest of the class is using Music Ace), a written test about the parts of the guitar and holding and playing techniques, and a self-evaluation of their overall progress in the unit. For the playing test, partners demonstrate the ability to (1) read tablature for the playing positions on the first, second, and third strings, (2) play the G scale as written in tablature, (3) perform a one-string song, a song using the first and second strings, and a song using the first three strings of lead guitar, (4) show correct finger position for the C and G7 chords, (5) switch between the C and G7 chords in a folk song, and (6) use rock strum-and-picking techniques.

The students begin the Mozart/Illegal File Sharing and Downloading unit by taking notes on a biographical documentary on Mozart and then comparing their notes to the PG version of the film *Amadeus*. The students tend to empathize with Mozart's burial in a pauper's grave and make transfers between Mozart's alleged problems with his finances and the need for copyright and royalties today. They play a role in a presentation regarding copyright and filesharing (one student may be the artist, another the copyright officer, while another may be an agent paying a royalty to use the artist's music in his or her latest movie). The students' learning culminates in a paper they write that brings together the information they learned about Mozart and examines their understanding of why a composer deserves to be paid for his or her work.

After an introductory unit explaining the electric bass and electronic trap set, students earn process points for demonstrating their abilities to play the electric guitar (both chords and melody), electric bass, and electronic trap set for the teacher at the end of the Rock Central rotation.

Roudabush awards forty out of fifty points to students who practiced but can only play beginner patterns, forty-five out of fifty for students who can play the intermediate patterns, and a full fifty points for students who can play advanced patterns.

In the Mozart Central rotations, students have the option to spend the entire rotation perfecting one composition or to dabble in multiple compositional strategies with defined parameters for whichever choice they make. They earn a score out of fifty points for their effort and process as defined by a rubric. Students complete a packet that guides and shows their work at each technological center as their assessment for the Discovery Central rotation. Discovery Central is also worth fifty points.

ASSESSING STUDENTS IN ROCK BAND 101

Similar to Music Tech, Rock Band students complete skills testing at the end of the instrument units. They are graded on being able to play the beginner-, intermediate-, or advanced-level patterns. At the end of the unit, the student bands are assessed on their ability to stay together and play an entire song or, if time allows, more than one song. Students earn points for participation during each in-class activity and complete one homework assignment worth fifty points. This assignment prepares them to talk intelligently about their musical preferences during the listening lab exercise.

ASSESSING STUDENTS IN ADAPTIVE MUSIC

In Adaptive Music, Finger and Roudabush assess students on their participation in activities. These students are graded on their individual effort to progress from their individual starting points rather than meeting a standardized level of achievement. Students earn up to fifty points for each in-class activity. Homework is not a component of Adaptive Music.

WERE THE ORIGINAL ASSUMPTIONS CORRECT OR INCORRECT?

Finger and Roudabush assumed, in the initial implementation of the program, that most of the students would have varied interests in music or musical instruments, with some identifying themselves as nonmusicians. They thought it would be essential to connect with the students at their current level of motivation and attempt to increase their interest through the activities and instruments. These assumptions proved to be true. The program has shown benefits such as increased interest in taking the eighth-grade elective Rock Band 101 and increased attendance at Garage Band Club, with as many as twenty-five students attending one session.

Finger and Roudabush have been extremely lucky to start with a wonderful classroom set of equipment at both schools. The school district continues to support the program. In 2006 they purchased the same materials and equipment for the new middle school, North Central, and continued funding repairs and replacement materials at all three schools. Parents' comments are supportive of the program. Some parents express amazement at their children's opportunities through the general music program.

Roudabush has noticed that parents' attendance at parent-teacher conferences has lessened dramatically since the general music population changed. Parents often only check in to make sure their children are behaving. Roudabush is pleased that the average grade in Music Tech, Adaptive Music, and Rock Band 101 is an A, although this may account for parents not stopping in to conference. Perhaps with continued education through newsletters, back-to-school nights, newspaper articles, presentations at PTA meetings, and word-of-mouth, parents may begin to champion nontraditional approaches to music education. An initial fear in calling the eighth-grade elective Rock Band 101, a decidedly nonscholarly ("fun") name, has not ended up deterring parents from letting their children take the class. The classes are always full at all three schools, and often students must be turned away due to class-size limits.

POTENTIAL LONG-TERM BENEFITS

One of the best parts of the new program is hearing from parents whose children come home using musical words to describe songs on the radio, talking excitedly about pursuing an interest in guitar or bass, sharing information they learned about illegal downloading, and even telling their parents about Mozart! In the first three years of the new program, five of Roudabush's students have joined choir, while two students have joined the concert band. One group of highly motivated students created their own band, took Rock Band 101, played at the school's ending-day celebration, and participated in the Weekend Warriors program. Weekend Warriors is an eight-week guided program, created by local music store West Music, where participants prepare songs for a gig. Then, if ready, the ensemble performs at a downtown Iowa City establishment.

Roudabush challenges all students in her classes to find a way to make music a part of their lives forever. Students have been much more appropriately challenged by the new curriculum. Most students are surprised at what they are able to do with the right set of tools. It is not surprising to find that in Roudabush's classrooms there are fewer behavioral problems because of the hands-on nature of the coursework and the mutual respect developed between teacher and students. Roudabush loves to tell the story of the eighth-grade Rock Band student who said, "You can't make me play that keyboard" and then went through the unit and ended up playing the keyboard for his band. She also believes that if she had a penny for every electric guitar sold after the class's guitar unit, she would be rich! It is too early in the general music program to examine its long-term benefits, but the interest and motivation is sufficient to create stories to tell for years to come.

ROAD BLOCKS FOR INITIATING A SIMILAR PROGRAM

Funding

Money to purchase the initial equipment may be the largest hurdle for initiating a similar program. In 1996, Larry Knipfer and Janice Shields, the Iowa City middle school general music teachers at that time, convinced the ICCSD that they could procure the electronic equipment at little or no cost to the district as a compliment to the thirty acoustic guitars each school already owned. They wrote a grant and received $10,000 to purchase one set of electronic instruments and equipment. Knipfer and Shields traded use of this equipment for six weeks of each trimester. They received computers for the music laboratory from a company that was upgrading its office computers. They purchased additional instruments and equipment using gifts from the student's yearly fundraising dollars. In 1999 the district purchased a second set of equipment so that each school had its own set.

When Finger and Roudabush became the general music teachers in 2001, each experimented independently with what to do with the equipment. Roudabush has found that rotating the students through equipment allows everyone to have a chance to use a single piece of equipment, and both Roudabush and Finger employ rotation stations to facilitate equipment use. Over the years, each school has added to their basic instrumentarium and technology through the school's magazine sales fundraising dollars. Each school also has a small yearly budget for the general music program that covers the cost of broken strings or headphones, small repairs, and, if funding is left, new books and musical scores.

Differentiating Levels of Success

Another roadblock to implementation may be the teacher's level of experience or motivation to differentiate levels of success for students. If a student is unable to coordinate reading the score while playing the keyboard after multiple sessions of individual practice time, Rouda-bush has adapted the keyboard using color or pitch names on the keys written on sticky notes that can be easily removed. Roudabush has created templates that she places in the gap behind or below the keys that can delineate only the keys used in a particular piece or target a key note, such as middle C. She encourages students to use these props only until they are able to find the notes on their own and then discard the templates.

With the emphasis on differentiation, Roudabush has developed the materials in all three classes to fit multiple levels of success. At the simplest level, Roudabush has created a system she refers to as *beat boxes*, where she writes the score as a single-row table with fixed-width columns representing the beat. She labels and color-codes the notation so the student can successfully follow the beat with his or her peers without any of the traditional symbols one has to understand to follow standard notation such as repeats or first and second endings. She may also simplify the standard notation to contain only whole, half, or quarter notes that mimic the melody or bass line of the piece (simplified level), while students at the middle level may also use quarter or eighth notes in a simplified score.

Roudabush recalls the trimester a student from the Severe and Pro-found Disabilities program took Rock Band 101. Because the student loved the keyboard, Roudabush assigned her to the keyboard for the final band. Roudabush used the bass line of the band's chosen song and cre-ated colored-coded beat boxes, laying out a simplified pattern of the root, fourth, and fifth. The student was able to read this simplified notation and participate along with her peers in the regular-education track.

In Music Tech's Rock Central rotation, students read simplified, middle-level, and actual patterns written in tablature paired with standard notation and choose the one they are best able to perform. They have the opportunity to move to harder material throughout the rotation. In the final band portion of Rock Band 101, students receive the original composition but can request simplified patterns once they have attempted to read the standard notation for one or more practice sessions. Roudabush has been astounded that most students will learn to play the standard notation paired with tablature if they are required to spend one to two practice sessions reading this paired notation. She has broken down the patterns to even simpler levels for Adaptive Music. Students may use headphones and work at their own pace and ability level as they progress through the increasingly difficult material.

As stated before, task analysis is the key to assessing what needs to get done at its simplest level. In Rock Band 101, Roudabush started with "Another One Bites the Dust," creating levels of difficulty for every instrument. Another favorite request caused her to write out levels for "Iron Man." Once Roudabush had more experience and the desire to use different material, more songs followed. Both teachers have learned to use books that have parts written out to guide their construction of simplified parts. At this point, Roudabush is learning to use Finale but writes out parts if needed. Finger uses Print Music to publish musical examples and completed scores.

One key to making differentiation workable is to create three levels of difficulty for the students within one song so that the students are more motivated to learn. Begin with the original arrangement (most difficult), then create a moderately difficult arrangement, and then add a simplified arrangement. In the first year or two, the teacher might think it too repetitive if she has to listen to "Another One Bites the Dust" ever again, but that provides motivation to expand the student repertoire!

IMPLEMENTATION IDEAS

Finger and Roudabush discovered early on in their first year with the nonperformance students that twelve weeks (one trimester) was not enough time to teach everything students need to know about reading traditional notation and still allow time to use the equipment. Keeping this in mind, Finger and Roudabush reduced time reviewing musical concepts to about two weeks of the trimester. They began to include tablature, paired with standard notation, as a vehicle for reading musical scores. Many of today's music books feature standard notation paired with tablature, but tablature can often be found free online. However, most copyright-free online tablature does not pair with standard notation, requiring the user to know the song well enough to play the rhythms without overt delineation.

If a teacher is interested in using any of the curricular ideas presented in this chapter, Roudabush suggests starting with a classroom set of acoustic guitars. Because electric guitar–playing technique is similar to acoustic, students will be able to learn skills on the acoustic and easily transfer skills to the electric if given the opportunity. Many of Roudabush's students comment that the electric is easier because the neck is not as wide and the strings are lighter weight. Students can also learn techniques to play electric bass using the acoustic guitar's third, fourth, fifth, and sixth strings.

Roudabush suggests after acquiring the classroom set of acoustic guitars to add an electric guitar, electric bass, and electronic drum machine or electronic trap set. In a Rock Band 101 setting, it would be ideal to have the next instrument be an electronic keyboard, but it would also work for both classes to have a second electric guitar instead (one would be used for rhythm, or chords, while the other would be lead). Students could be grouped in corners of the room according to the part they are practicing and then rotate to the actual equipment while wearing headphones.

Roudabush has created a lesson that seems to successfully teach students to learn a standard drum pattern for the electronic trap set. After presenting the lesson, she suggests that students go home and practice on the kitchen table or a desk (but not on their desk in social studies class!) so that when they get their turn on the actual trap set they are more likely to be able to perform the "three-things-at-the-same-time" pattern on the pads and kick pedal.

When Roudabush started at the middle school, Rock Band 101 students moved the electronic instruments to the orchestra and choir room when they needed to play out loud so as to not disturb the math classroom next door to her general music room. Since then, her schools have purchased the Yamaha LC2 Listening Lab, allowing her students to use headphones and practice in isolation or, through LC2 (mixer), in small groups. They perform aloud on Performance Day, the only day when math class has to rock along with the bands or move to an alternative space.

Roudabush would again urge other teachers to be creative in the use of stations and to add instruments and equipment as funding allows. She has found that having instruments in increments of four is the perfect grouping for facilitating supervision and keeping everyone actively involved in class work, although she suggests that the music lab should have fifteen keyboards and computer stations as an ulti-mate goal (enough for a class of thirty).

CONCLUSION

The general music program at the Iowa City Community School District's middle schools has provided alternative opportunities for adolescents to develop musicianship skills. Many of the students originally identified themselves as nonperformers. Through diversi-fication of tasks, learning opportunities that they deemed interesting and meaningful, and encouragement, these students have cultivated a deeper personal interest in music. Some of these students have chosen to continue performing on guitars or in school-offered performance groups, many have improved self-confidence through composition and learning to play an instrument, and all have explored a broad range of musical styles.

Music teachers can incorporate elements and strategies of this pro-gram into their classrooms. For example, teachers who connect with students when choosing activities and musical styles build positive rapport with their students. Because students learn in such diverse ways, teachers need to be able to adapt tasks to meet individual learn-ing needs. Careful assessment of student learning along with gentle and encouraging guidance facilitate students' successful completion of musical tasks. This strong alternative program provides a promis-ing model for preservice and current teachers in the complex world of adolescent music education.

7

Rock 'n' Roll High School:
A Genre Comes of Age
in the Curriculum

Robert Gardner

ABSTRACT

This chapter profiles an active rock-and-roll curriculum in place at a public high school in State College, Pennsylvania. The course titled Rock Ensemble is an academic class provided during the school day, and enrollment tripled over its first three years. The majority of students in the classes do not take the traditional music ensemble courses also offered at the school. The students learn to perform rock music in a structured yet informal setting as they work together as teams in standard rock group instrumentation.

INTRODUCTION

Concert band? No. Chorus? No. Orchestra? No. Chamber ensemble? Jazz ensemble? Folk ensemble? World music group? None of the above. This was Jim Robinson's dilemma as he was filling out the application form for his group to be included as a featured performance ensemble at the upcoming 2009 Pennsylvania Music Educators Association (PMEA) in-service conference. After reading all of the other options, he came upon the final entry on the list. Naturally, it was the ubiquitous *other*. This is the category into which the group from the State College Area

High School course Rock Ensemble (Y415) inevitably fit, so Robinson wrote a short description in the provided blank line.

THE CASE

The State High Rock Ensemble is extraordinary because it is a credit-bearing course in a high school music program that meets during the regular school day. It is not an extra-curricular program or an extension of any of the existing traditional music ensemble classes. Previous musical experience is not necessary to participate, although an audition and/or interview with the instructor is required before students can sign up for the class.

In many school jazz or contemporary-music ensembles, the majority of the students are also members of one of the traditional ensembles. This is not the case with the State High Rock Ensemble, so the class is generally serving a different sample of the overall school population. There was one section of Rock Ensemble the first year the course was offered (2007–2008) and three sections the second year. Each section included an average of fifteen students, but the students were not organized by ability level. Students who ended up with a flex period during one of the other sections, however, were invited to attend during other periods but were not promised the opportunity to play, as the students signed up for that section would be given priority during that rehearsal.

During a later visit, Robinson reported to me that there were already sixty students signed up for Y415 for the upcoming third year that the course was offered, which he speculated might be enough to justify four sections. Robinson appreciates this because it will further justify his full-time schedule at the high school and, more importantly, because the class not only seems to be viable but is still growing year to year.

The life cycle of a typical rock band is infamously short. Many of the issues that eventually cause the dissolution of bands are often centered on conflict between personalities as they attempt to negotiate the learning and creating processes. This is where Robinson's leadership eliminates much friction, although it certainly doesn't completely eliminate the need to mediate frustration, conflict, and tension between students. He reports, however, that once the routines of the class are established in the beginning of the school year, such conflicts are not generally a problem in the class.

Although the class utilizes a different learning style than a traditional ensemble, Robinson insists that his expectations are not lower for achievement in Rock Ensemble than in his orchestras. He has strongly encouraged several students to drop the course when it became apparent that they were not interested in actively participating in the class and were negatively affecting the progress of the other students.

In general, Robinson believes that students are more engaged in the learning process partly because the music is more relevant to their everyday lives. He feels that the skills and knowledge the students develop in the class are those that will contribute to the students being active musicians throughout their lives. The popularity of classical music and even jazz has been declining over the years, and this raises the question of how well music ensembles that perform these genres can continue to provide meaningful musical experiences for the current generation of students.

There were many obstacles to overcome in order to make Rock Ensemble a reality. Although most administrators and other music teachers were supportive of the idea, a few were skeptical or inhibiting. It took much time and effort for Robinson to lay the groundwork for the creation of the course. He had to demonstrate that there existed significant student interest in the course to make it viable and sustainable. His work with the annual State High Battle of the Bands greatly contributed to his being able to demonstrate this interest. A majority of the students who participated in this event actually did not participate in the traditional music ensemble classes. Nonetheless, all of these students had a strong interest in performing, and many already had well-developed musical abilities.

Robinson also had to work with the music faculty and administration to demonstrate that the course was even logistically feasible. He had to determine how the course could fit within in the overall high school class schedule, which experienced educators know can be a monumental task. There were most likely many other concerns about the course that had to be addressed before implementation. For example, the class could be seen as redundant with the many other classes offered by the well-respected State College music program, or it could conflict with too many other courses to allow students to actually sign up for it.

In addition, although the administration was supportive in the creation of the course, Robinson stated that there was virtually no budget available to help with related expenses. One reality of being in a rock group is that the electronic equipment necessary to even participate can be expensive. Being able to use and maintain all of the equipment effectively requires a unique set of skills and knowledge. Robinson reports that he expended a lot of time and energy at the early stages securing enough equipment to get the class up and running.

Much of the equipment being used to this day, in fact, is Robinson's personal gear. Although most students bring their own guitars or basses, he does have a couple instruments that he allows students without their own to use. Other creative methods were explored to get his hands on as many instruments, amps, recording devices, microphones, cords, and all the other things needed for the class. Several pieces were donated by generous parents or community members, and others were acquired for very little cost through instrument exchange programs or from online auction services.

The class meets in the choir classroom, which has a stage area on the south side of the room where the equipment resides. The working environment is now very functional, with enough good-quality equipment to accommodate two guitarists, one bassist, one drum set player, one electric keyboard player, and multiple vocalists. It also includes a sound system as well as equipment for audio and video recording. Of course, the need to maintain and upgrade the equipment will never cease, so Robinson will continue to look for frugal ways to do so.

MY, MY, HEY, HEY

Personal expression is a central tenet for many genres of music. Early rock-and-roll musicians sang about the unspeakable sides of life, within insinuated contexts of racial tension. Later rock music facilitated songwriters to take on any topic, whether social, political, or philosophical. Millions of fans have sung along to many a youthful anthem about the invisible citizens just trying to get by and have fun in an unfair world. And whether they are rock fans or not, the human need to express our perspective knows know stylistic bounds.

Traditional school music ensembles are sometimes maligned because of the one-sided learning style they often involve. In other words, the conductor interprets the score, imparts the needed information, and dictates how the students should perform the music. Some suggest that music instruction should employ a much more democratic learning process, such as that used by semiprofessional original rock bands (Ferguson 2002). They argue that the learning process should be more of a collaboration between musicians (teachers and students) with common goals, whereas most, if not all, members of the ensemble participate in the decision making (Allsup 2007; Green 2008).

Traditional performing ensemble classes are focused on developing technical and musical abilities, and they sometimes facilitate interaction among the students in the learning process, although probably not as much as one would hope. It is difficult for individual musicians to connect with the music on a personal level when they are but one of many trying to reproduce someone else's (e.g., conductor or composer) interpretation of a piece. Of course, many ensemble directors do involve their students in the decision-making process and also provide opportunities for individual creativity. Alternatively, rock groups can sometimes be dominated by overbearing leaders or songwriters, thereby making for a more dictatorial process.

Although the garage-band model may have many positive implications for K–12 music education, it may not always translate well. For example, rock bands are most often formed for recreational purposes, even though a few may hold aspirations for unlikely future financial success. Therefore, the process of writing and rehearsing tunes is often the main objective instead of a means toward the procurement of profitable gigs or desirable grades. Therefore, all of the many decisions that are made in the process are made free from the pressure of eventually reaching a grander goal.

Rock music has historically been challenged "in achieving widespread acceptance in American music education" (Hebert and Campbell 2000, 14), which may be attributed to several factors. These include the fact that rock music is considered aesthetically inferior to other genres of music, that it encourages rebelliousness and could be unhealthy for adolescents, and that teachers do not have adequate experience or training in rock music to design effective curricula for teaching it in an authentic manner.

Performing rock music has generally been a male-dominated activity throughout its history (Clawson 1999), and this trend seems to be continuing in the State High Rock Ensembles. I did not have the opportunity to solicit Robinson's thoughts on how students of different genders experience the class or if they might function differently than one other, or in different environments, although it would certainly be an interesting topic to explore with someone with significant experience teaching rock music to adolescents. In fact, the Rock 'n' Roll Camp for Girls (www.girlsrockcamp.org/main/), a summer workshop started in 2001 in Portland, Oregon, is designed to provide just such a setting.

Nonetheless, K–12 students studying rock music in the schools is not a new phenomenon. Over the years it has been used as a medium to teach other subjects besides music, such as literature, history, and social studies. Support for learning to perform rock music began to emerge in the late 1960s, partially inspired by the culminating reports from the Tanglewood Symposium (Mark and Gary 2007), and has continued over the years (Woody 2007). Many school jazz ensembles do not actually limit themselves to the performance of jazz repertoire and, in fact, are often mislabeled or glorified rock or funk groups.

Extracurricular rock ensembles have increased in recent years, taking their place alongside existing jazz bands, fiddle groups, and show
choirs. In addition, and although still not common, there have been
examples of successful programs with rock band classes in the regular
school curriculum (Newsome 1998).

In addition, independent entities such as community-based rock
schools have provided workshops and after-school programs for students to perform contemporary music. Examples include the Blue
Bear School of Music (www.bluebearmusic.org/index.php), which
started in San Francisco in 1971, and the Paul Green School of Rock
Music (www.schoolofrock.com/index.php), which has many locations
around the United States and is said to be the inspiration for the 2003
movie *School of Rock* (Webb 2006).

MOVE IT ON OVER

Rock Ensemble (Y415) began the same way each time I visited. The students gradually entered the room as the start of the hour neared. Most
of them sat in chairs at one of six tables in the center of the classroom.
Each table holds six people, so most sit in groups of four or five. Robinson sits in a chair at the head of a table on the end. Some students talk
with Robinson before the class starts. A couple students in each class
enter after the official starting time but generally either had a pass from
another teacher or received a firm but friendly reminder to arrive on time
from the instructor.

This was an example of Robinson's subtle yet effective interaction
with the students, which was a juxtaposition of a laid-back demeanor
and clearly communicated high expectations for participation. He reported to me that when the classes first started, he used a more directive
and heavy-handed approach to classroom management, more like what
he would use in his orchestra classes, but he found that it just didn't
work in this setting.

Once all the individual business is addressed, Robinson starts the
class. He begins with announcements. He has a clipboard. Half of the
lights in the room are off. He speaks in a well-projected voice as he announces details about upcoming events on the calendar or reviews the
work they did in previous classes. He takes attendance. He talks about
the schedule of rehearsals for the week and what tasks need to be done
for upcoming trips and performances.

Everything Robinson does to begin class is deliberate. He discovered
that if he made the students sit and listen quietly for a short period of
time at the beginning of class it helped them to calm down and become

more focused when they got up onto the stage and had the instruments in their hands. As many veteran teachers often recommend, one would assume that it would be better to start a class with action or music making rather than with lecture or verbal explanation. On the contrary, Robinson said it was usually a disaster when he had the students set up immediately after they arrived to the class, because he had trouble getting them to stop noodling (practicing riffs) as he was trying to give instructions. It is important that music teachers remember that some students will have different styles of learning than others and that we must be able to adapt our teaching style to be effective in the specific social context of our classes.

Once Mr. Robinson finishes the announcements, including which tunes will be practiced that day, he announces the first tune and who is playing which instruments for it. Once plans are reviewed, the students move to their various assignments. Some move to the stage and prepare their instruments or test their microphones. Three other students sit down at the recording equipment and begin to check volume levels. A couple others go to the video equipment and check the camera and recorder. The majority of students are active in an assigned position at any one time during the class, and all students will participate at some point eventually. The only exceptions are a couple students who have chosen to attend the class during one of their flex periods, so they know beforehand that students signed up for the current section of the class are prioritized.

Those that are not active sit to the side of the room and generally practice their instruments, look over tab charts, read, or study for other classes. Robinson never had to ask students to not interrupt during any of the classes I have observed. He reported, however, that he focuses on discipline in the early part of the school year to send the message that this is not a goof-off class, and several students have dropped the class due to their inability to participate appropriately. Robinson realizes that he is working with a broader sample of the student body and that he needs to be flexible with some students who have not been successful in more traditional academic classes. It seems that he does a nice job allowing for second chances while maintaining high expectations for behavior and effort. The end result is a casual learning environment where students know they will be expected to give their best effort but also know that they will have fun and be praised by the teacher when they do.

The songs to be rehearsed in this particular class include "Don't Take Me Alive" by Steely Dan, "Behind Blue Eyes" by the Who, and "Babe" by Styx. On this day there are nineteen students in the class, including sixteen boys and three girls. After the initial discussions, Robinson instructs the students to take their positions. The instrumentation of the group for the Steely Dan tune includes two guitarists, one bassist, one drummer, and one keyboard player. Normally there would be at least one vocalist, but apparently none of the students had learned the lyrics well enough to give it a go as of yet. So Robinson grudgingly assumes the role of the lead vocalist, but not without first giving the class a pointed yet jovial ribbing about how someone should have learned the vocal line by now.

Two other students sit down at the main mixer for the sound system, and a third sits at a computer used for recording the rehearsals. There is also a video camera set up and attached to editing equipment, although the group is not using it in this class. Robinson reported to me, however, that they sometimes video-record practices so that students can review their progress and plan what to work on in future rehearsals. They also video-record more polished performances of songs for posterity's sake or to provide footage to submit with applications for performing at various locales, festivals, or conferences.

As the group begins to rehearse the Steely Dan tune, Robinson asks one of the guitarists if he has learned the middle section with the different chord progression. The other guitarist objects, stating that Robinson had told him before that he didn't have to learn the part. Mr. Robinson confirms this by reminding him that only one of the guitars plays the part. With no one in the group having learned it, the keyboard player states that she would be willing to figure it out. She noodles around a while, with Robinson interjecting occasionally when she hits upon one of the chords. She eventually comes up with something that is probably close to the actual part, and the group decides that it is good enough to move on and rehearse the tune.

This is a good example of a learning moment with many implications: First, the situation demonstrated that, even with orderly and efficient rehearsals, it is always necessary for students to practice on their own in order for things to move forward in group practices. Even young rock musicians understand this, and it is fairly common for them to spend many hours outside of rehearsals working on technical exercises or learning tunes from recordings or tablature. Of course, it is probably just as common for musicians to come to band practice without doing the necessary work on their own. The result is a meandering rehearsal in which the players try to figure out important riffs from memory, come to close approximations of the actual parts, and end up with sloppy and inaccurate performances that contribute to their eventual lack of fulfillment or success.

Another implication of this situation is that all members play an important role in contributing to the overall sound of the band. It is not correct to say that all members play an equal role, because that can depend on which instrument the play or what repertoire they are performing. It is true, however, that each member must play his or her part to the best of their ability in order for the overall sound to be accurate and cohesive. This can certainly be said about traditional music ensembles as well, although I believe it is more obvious and demanding in a rock band where the individual parts contribute in a way more similar to a chamber ensemble than a symphony orchestra. In general, each instrument plays a unique part and in a different frequency range or timbre, which requires more musical awareness and independence than playing the same second violin part among a section of thirteen other violinists.

One of the culminating objectives for the course is a final concert in the spring. Robinson enjoys the cooperative learning environment employed in Rock Ensemble, and several aspects of the concert demonstrate how the class is different than other ensemble courses. The set list for the concert includes twenty-five tunes, and all students in the class are required to learn how to play all tunes on their particular instrument. In reality, some students are stronger than others on certain songs, but Robinson emphasizes the need for active participation in the class so that everyone contributes to the final performance. The concert lasts over two hours, and all of the music is memorized and performed without reading music notation. Robinson pointed out that it would be quite a challenge to have similar expectations for a typical high school concert band or symphony orchestra.

Learning music in such an exploratory manner is consistent with how rock musicians have functioned over the history of the genre. In fact, most of the music in the world is learned and passed on through oral transmission, and many rock musicians do not know how to read Western classical-music notation (Lilliestam 1996). Nonetheless, the creative accomplishments of many highly talented and accomplished rock performers have greatly influenced the evolution of contemporary music and our society as a whole. It is an exciting thing to witness a teacher reaching out to students, many of whom had never before participated in school music classes, to provide the opportunity to be musical in a setting that was previously unavailable to them, and through a genre that they appreciate and relate to in their everyday lives.

WISH YOU WERE HERE

One of the reasons why Rock Ensemble has been successful so far is that Robinson has a special talent for providing constructive criticism to students in a way that allows them to accept it without becoming defensive. He sometimes gives the students a hard time in a sarcastic manner for making mistakes or failing to remember things. At the same time, he makes obvious efforts to give students praise when they do something well or make noticeable improvement. His process is effective because the students are aware that he takes his role of providing critique very seriously, but the humorous manner in which he does it shows them that they should not take it personally. The students obviously know that everyone in the class has an equal chance at finding themselves at the business end of one of his sarcastic comments. They also know, however, that he only does it to make a point and that he cares about their progress and would never do it to embarrass them or make them feel like a failure.

Robinson hopes that more opportunities for school rock bands will arise in the future, similar to those currently available to traditional ensembles. These could include events such as MEA-sponsored performance contests, small-ensemble contests, or large-scale music festivals such as Music in the Parks. This may eventually happen, although perhaps not until rock band courses are more prevalent in school curricula. Nonetheless, its progress into the curriculum may turn out to have a similar evolution as jazz, as it became institutionalized in the last half of the twentieth century (Marquis 1998).

Robinson hopes that the different sections of the course can be organized by ability level in future school years. This would allow him to form groups with student musicians of more-similar abilities, thereby facilitating more-effective instruction that provides rewarding musical experiences that appropriately challenge all of the students involved.

Rock music has had a long history, and the genre encompasses a variety of subcategories of music. It has transformed over time and has interacted with and been influenced by other contemporary styles along the way. How popular rock music will remain, how it will evolve as a style, and how prevalent it will become in K–12 school curricula cannot be predicted (Fornas 1995). Past experience has shown us, however, that it will most likely continue to influence our overall society and our educational institutions for many years to come.

REFERENCES

Allsup, R. 2007. Democracy and one hundred years of music education. *Music Educators Journal* 93 (5): 52–56.

Clawson, M. 1999. Masculinity and skill acquisition in the adolescent rock band. *Popular Music* 18 (1): 99–114.

Ferguson, H. 2002. In search of bandhood: Consultation with original music groups. *Group* 26 (4): 267–82.

Fornas, J. 1995. The future of rock: Discourses that struggle to define a genre. *Popular Music* 14 (1): 111–25.

Green, L. 2008. *Music, informal learning and the school: A new classroom pedagogy.* Aldershot, UK: Ashgate Publishing.

Hebert, D., and P. Campbell. 2000. Rock music in American schools: Positions and practices since the 1960s. *International Journal of Music Education* 36 (1): 14–22.

Lilliestam, L. 1996. On playing by ear. *Popular Music* 15(2): 195–216.

Mark, M., and C. Gary. 2007. *A history of American music education.* 3rd ed. Lanham, Md.: MENC / Rowman & Littlefield Eduction.

Marquis, L. 1998. Jazz goes to college: Has academic status served the art? *Popular Music and Society* 22 (2): 117–24.

Martinez, T. 1995. Where popular culture meets deviant behavior: Classroom experiences with music. *Teaching Sociology* 23 (4): 413–18.

Newsom, D. 1998. Rock's quarrel with tradition: Popular music's carnival comes to the classroom. *Popular Music and Society* 22 (3): 1–20.

Webb, M. 2006. Rock goes to school on screen: A model for teaching non-"learned" musics derived from the films *School of Rock* (2003) and *Rock School* (2005). *Action, Criticism, and Theory for Music Education* 6 (3): 51–73.

Woody, R. 2007. Popular music in school: Remixing the issues. *Music Educators Journal* 93 (4): 32–37.

8

Lead Lines, Licks, and Everything in Between: Popular Music in a Preschool Music Classroom

Beth Gibbs and Mark Ross

ABSTRACT

Mark Ross's preschool music classes at the Penn State University Child Development Lab are anything but typical. Just like the teacher, these classes are innovative and include an alternative content, approach, and intention. Instead of conquering the plethora of familiar children's repertoire, these children are immersed in popular musical styles from blues and bluegrass to funk and rock and roll. They explore these genres through instruction grounded in developmentally appropriate practice and activities that include singing, movement, and improvisation. Mark's mission was born of a desire to make music accessible to all children and the recognition that he could teach far more than musical skills in his classes. Teaching strategies used within the classes reflect the necessity of being responsive to the needs of young children. With a flexible repertoire of materials and expert facility on the guitar, Mark has created a stimulating music-learning environment for young children.

INTRODUCTION

When we think of preschool music classes, it may bring to mind images of bustling children engaged in listening to, singing, or moving to musical selections from the vast array of traditional children's and folk songs. We may think of children engaged in exploration of music through "simple songs" or those typically thought to be "age appropriate" based on our traditions and preconceived notions of what children in this age group can do. We don't typically think of presenting or, even more the point, creating an entire curriculum, based on popular music, improvisation, and identification of licks and lead lines. This is exactly what Mark Ross has done as preschool music teacher at the Penn State University Child Development Lab.

THE TEACHER

With a musical background as a successful performing blues guitarist, Mark Ross is not a typical music teacher, though his facility with guitar has become a gateway to making music with children and introducing them to a wide variety of popular music genres. Mark's teaching is not limited to musical content and knowledge. He uses songs and musical games to facilitate children's mental and emotional development in his classes.

In sharing his philosophy of teaching, Mark Ross says that "music is accessible to the whole world. Music isn't this special thing that only some people can reach up out of the air and grab. It's up there for everybody, and everybody's use of it will be different." He encourages teachers to find ways to use music to their own benefit and the benefit of their students. Mark feels that one of the best things about making music with children is the joy they bring to the experience and his interactions with the students. Of teaching music he says, "If anyone's going to do this, if they don't like that [interacting with children], it doesn't matter how much they know about music—nothing's gonna happen."

Mark Ross began working with children as an aide, teaching and counseling special-needs children at the Rainbow School where he had the "luxury of learning about special-needs children" from Patty Hild, who he credits as "the most talented special-education teacher I've ever seen." Knowing that Mark played in a band, Patty decided to find a way to use his guitar in the classroom. In working with special-needs students, Mark soon realized that he could use his guitar to teach far more than music. He found that he was using his guitar 60 percent of the day with children to work on their cognitive skills, gross-motor and fine-motor coordination, and emotional development. Music was a vehicle through which students could experience their environment in different ways, and it allowed Mark to build connections with special-needs students.

After his group Queen Bee and the Blue Hornet Band received a record deal, he left his teaching position to go on tour. During his fifteen years on the road, he frequently found preschool teachers coming to his gigs and inviting him to visit their classes the next day. This allowed him to continue using his music skills to teach young children. When he finished touring, Mark returned to his roots in State College, Pennsylvania, and enrolled his son in classes at Penn State's Child Development Lab (PSCDL). A significant part of the PSCDL experience is involving parents in the teaching and learning process. After seeing Mark perform one evening, an intern at the school asked him to come in to the preschool with his guitar. Linda Duerr, the director of childcare programs at Penn State, observed his class and recognized the value of his interactions with the children. After speaking about his past experiences working with children, he was offered a job on the spot. Mark says that Linda "is beyond reproach in her knowledge and willingness to explore music and use it in any manner that myself and the other teachers in the room felt was beneficial to the children."

THE PENN STATE CHILD DEVELOPMENT LAB

Penn State's Child Development Lab operates under the auspices of the Department of Human Development and Family Studies on campus. The program operates on a full-day, full-year schedule, serving children from six months to six years of age. Children at the lab learn through play and exploration as they interact with peers and adults. The curriculum evolves from the children's development, exploration, and curiosity. Teachers provide learning opportunities through appropriate materials, engaging questions, and a variety of choices (Penn State Department of Human Development and Family Studies 2009, section 2).

Three large classrooms house the mixed-age groupings of children at the Child Development Laboratory. According to the Penn State Department of Human Development and Family Studies (2009, section 3), the infant and toddler room "is known for its inviting environment where low platforms and shelving, cozy caves, safe climbers, and accessible materials offer the opportunity for our youngest children to actively explore their surroundings. Low partitions create a sense of comfort and intimacy while allowing for easy adult supervision." The classrooms for three- to six-year-old children "are alive with activity in areas designed to encourage dramatic play, construction, creative art, music, literature, sharing, and small- and larger-group encounters."

In 1996, the National Association for the Education of Young Children (NAEYC) released a statement outlining the principles for *developmentally appropriate practice* (DAP) that reflect a synthesis of theoretical perspectives on children's physical, social, and cognitive development (Miranda 2004). NAEYC recognized that the domains of children's development—physical, social, emotional, and cognitive— are closely related and that development in one domain influences and is influenced by development in other domains. The PSCDL adopted these guidelines, which have become a guiding force for all curricula, included in the school building.

Mark teaches a variety of age groups within the school building, focusing primarily on children in the three-to-six-year-old classrooms. The Golden Rule takes on new meaning in this setting, where it tends to mean, If they're out of diapers, they can come to music class. He is the sole music teacher in this facility and sees all students in the upper-age-level classrooms and the younger students when his time allows or there is a need for his particular musical skills.

MUSIC LESSONS AT THE CHILD DEVELOPMENT LAB

The learning atmosphere at the Child Development Lab reflects the DAP principles as it allows children to explore their environments, interact with peers and adults, and experience learning in a variety of ways. Mark's music classes play an important role in helping children to socialize musically, learning through musical play. Children in the program are actively involved in music through listening, movement, singing, playing instruments, and improvising musical responses. At the same time, Mark organizes activities that require the students to make decisions, expand their vocabularies, and develop physical awareness of their surroundings. I offer the following vignette as an example of Mark's music classes.

Entering the Child Development Lab classroom, Mark pushes a cart of classroom instruments. With his guitar strapped to his back, he gathers the children around him for music time. The atmosphere is lively as the children greet him. Smiles and chatter fill the classroom. The classroom teachers and aides join the children on the rug area for music. He doesn't require students to sit still. They may move around the area as long as they are respectful of those sitting around them. There are eleven young children in the room with their attention fixed

---

Box 8.1. "Good Morning"

Good morning, everybody. How are you?
  (Children shout, "Rock 'n' roll!")
Good morning, everybody. How are you?
  (Rock 'n' roll!)
I'm happy I came.
I hope you feel the same
Good morning everybody, how are you? (Rock 'n' roll!)

Created by and used with the permission of Mark Ross.

---

squarely on Mark. Encouraging students to move and strumming the guitar, he begins with the "Good Morning" song, which he wrote himself. The lyrics are written in box 8.1 above.

The children have already identified that Mark is playing the song in a rock-and-roll style, which caused them to respond with "Rock 'n' roll." In subsequent verses, Mark changes the riffs and feel of the song as he plays, switching from rock, now moving on to funk. Noticing the change in style, the children spontaneously change their response to "Funkafied!" The next verse changes style once again, this time to bluegrass, and the children change their response to "Bluegrassed out!" Mark's style transitions are seamless, and the children are able to recognize the various genres of music immediately. In addition to the change in genres and responses, the children clap their hands, stomp their feet, and demonstrate different ways to laugh. Some children are standing, and some are sitting, but all are involved in the song.

Maintaining the momentum of the children's involvement, Mark segues into the next song, which has a country-western feel, and asks the children to stand up. The lyrics are written in box 8.2.

As he continues the song, Mark adds different movements for the children to listen for and follow. Some of his directions are used to assess the children's listening and error detection, as when he asks for the girl with two eyes, one nose, and two mouths to move, the students are delighted to correct his mistake and allow him to try again. To finish the song, he asks the children to name the different song endings he plays on the guitar: He plays multiple licks from famous musicians as well as musical elements common in popular musical styles. As he begins each new ending, the children gleefully shout their answers: "Count Basie!" "Shave and a Haircut!" "The blues!" "Les Paul!" "B. B. King!" "John Lee Hooker!" "Descending chromatic

---

Box 8.2. "Take Your Hands"

Take your hands
Raise 'em up high
Make 'em go around in circles
In a big blue sky
Twist your waist
Twist it round and round
Open your mouth
And howl like a big old hound!
   (Children howl as prompted)

Created by and used with the permission of Mark Ross.

---

chord ending!" The children have a little trouble with the last ending, and he takes the time to play it again to work on their aural perception and their pronunciation.

He continues the lesson with songs composed by Hap Palmer and Ella Jenkins. It should be noted that these songs rarely are performed as they were composed. He commonly rearranges them to accommodate what he feels the students need to work on. For example, Hap Palmer's "Flick a Fly" was altered into a "sesquipedalian" version, using alternate names of body parts to work on developing the children's vocabularies. The altered lyrics are provided in box 8.3.

Transitioning to his next song with a blues accompaniment on his guitar, Mark sings the lyrics printed in box 8.4.

Mark encourages the students to recall the lyrics to the song as he continues and has them join in to sing the horn lick. The students give Mark suggestions on how to recreate the song for his "Mixed-Up Morning Blues" and once again identify the ending of the song as a "descending chromatic chord ending" to reinforce their previous experience with the riff.

The class continues with a rhythmic echo activity inspired by Ella Jenkins's "I Wonder Who's Outside My Door," using different instruments for students to hear and play. Mark reviews each of the instruments used with the children, who correctly identify the lollipop drum, the maraca, and the guiro. Mark plays a "shave and a haircut" rhythm on the drum and asks a boy in the class to play it back. The boy performs the rhythm complete with the "two bits" ending. Continuing with the activity, Mark alternates the instruments used, allowing several children an opportunity to play.

Box 8.3. "Flick a Fly"

Out in the barnyard forkin' up hay
Bzzz, bzzz, flies, get away!
When flies in your eyes drive you crazy
Flick those flies away
Flick a fly off of your cranium
   (That's your head!)
Flick a fly off of your baby cow
   (What is that? There it is, your calf!)
Flick a fly off of your pork string
   (Yes, that's your hamstring.)
Flick a fly off of your collarbone
A flick is quick, sharp, and light
A flick can get those flies alright
Flick a fly off of your patella
   (That's your knee.)
Flick a fly off of your abdomen
   (Good job!)
Out in the barnyard forkin' up hay
Bzzz, bzzz, flies, get away!
I've got flies in my eyes driving me crazy
I flick 'em all away

Originally performed by Hap Palmer; adapted by Mark Ross.

Box 8.4. "Mixed-Up Morning Blues"

When I woke up this morning
My dog was wearing my shoes!
My cat was brushing his teeth with my toothbrush
What am I gonna do?
I got the . . . What do I got?
   (Children shout, "Mixed-up morning blues!")
Horn section!
   (Singing horn lick)
When I woke up this morning
I got the mixed-up morning blues

Created by and used with the permission of Mark Ross.

The class continues with several more activities using classroom instruments, including a washboard and rhythm sticks. Mark gives the children frequent positive reinforcement for their participation and creates multiple opportunities for informal assessment of student progress, such as when the students play the rhythm sticks using different dynamic levels to the song "I've Got a Rhythm Groove": over half of the students perform on the beat, and several are given the opportunity to improvise their own rhythms.

CLASSROOM STRATEGIES AND CURRICULAR INFLUENCES

When discussing his classroom strategies, Mark emphasizes the importance of being able to read the room to find out how ready the children are to participate and being flexible enough to meet their needs. For example, if the students are "all fired up" when he enters the room, he might begin right away with a movement song and then bring them down to a calmer focus with the next song or activity. Alternately, he might choose to sing a song that requires their attention to detail in order to focus their participation. He says, "It's up to me to be more creative every time. Sometimes the best things come from what happened that day and working with it." His flexibility as a teacher allows him to adjust his instruction throughout class to keep students engaged musically.

Mark's musical repertoire is influenced by the works of children's folk musician Ella Jenkins, as well as by children's songwriter Hap Palmer, whose work includes many songs written to teach broader educational concepts such as math and literacy. In addition, Mark's own experience as a musician plays a key role in creating musical experiences for his students. The children learn different musical "bags," such as bluegrass, funk, blues, and swing, when he leads songs in different styles. This helps to develop the children's aural perception and familiarity with popular musical genres. Mark will often ask children to "name that ending," playing guitar riffs in different styles, or to "name that blues artist" as he plays licks from B. B. King, Otis Rush, and Magic Sam. He uses these moments not only to teach children about the blues but also to help develop their listening skills.

Mark also feels it is important to work on extramusical skills within the framework of his songs. For example, he will use his chant "One, two, three, four, I wonder who's outside my door" to stimulate open-ended responses from children about different topics they may be learning about, such as their addresses and phone numbers or identifying their current moods and favorite colors. It is not unusual for him to take well-known songs, such as tunes from Ella Jenkins or Hap Palmer, and adjust the lyrics to include different forms of movement or kinesthetic awareness and counting skills. Depending on the cognitive development of the children, he will increase the complexity of these skills, such as additive counting or reverse counting.

CONCLUSION

Although at first glance Mark's music classes differ from the norm because he uses a rock, bluegrass, and blues repertoire, his teaching and interactions with children evince a more important distinction: his commitment to teaching with an awareness of social, physical, and cognitive development clearly demonstrates several principles of DAP. He introduces students to multiple musical cultures and ways of engaging in music as a means of socialization. His classes are active, allowing students to manipulate lyrics and improvise songs and rhythms, helping them to construct their own musical meanings. Finally, of primary importance, he creates a classroom environment in which students feel nurtured and valued and are safe to explore music with their peers and the adults in the room. Teachers wishing to follow Mark's model should keep in mind that his success as a teacher is founded on his skill as a musician, his awareness of child development, his flexibility as a teacher, and his genuine care for his students.

It is important for those in the music education profession to realize that there is a lot more out there than we typically bring into the music classroom, and these different styles of learning and teaching and diverse materials can have a place in music education at all age levels. It's also imperative that we begin to realize that the definition of *music educator* needs to be expanded to include those who may not have music education degrees but nonetheless have rich musical lives coupled with a passion for teaching.

REFERENCES

Miranda, M. 2004. The implications of developmentally appropriate practice in a kindergarten general music classroom. *Journal of Research in Music Education* 52 (1): 43–63.

National Association for the Education of Young Children. 1996. *Developmentally appropriate practice in early childhood programs serving children*

from birth through age 8. www.naeyc.org/resources/position_statements/
daptoc.htm (accessed March 6, 2009).

Penn State Department of Human Development and Family Studies. 2009.
HDFS children's programs: Child development laboratory. www.hhdev.psu
.edu/hdfs/cp/cdl/index.html (accessed March 6, 2009).

9

Starting Young: Developing a Successful Instrumental Music Program in Kindergarten

Elizabeth M. Guerriero and Matthew Hoy

ABSTRACT

Public school instrumental music programs often delay starting string instruments until third, fourth, or fifth grade. The North Penn School District, however, provides students the unique opportunity to begin instrumental string lessons on violin in kindergarten and continue the lessons through sixth grade. In third grade, the school district simultaneously initiates a traditional string program with students who have chosen not to participate in the early-start program. Benefits of running two concurrent programs include building a greater sense of musical community, emphasizing the importance of music within the school, and engaging the students with more class time in a musical setting. Students in the early-start instrumental violin program receive two lessons per week in a small-group environment with the parent in attendance. Teachers in the program, however, find that scheduling can be complicated with two lessons each week and that students progress at different rates, which can make lesson planning difficult. Yet with support from parents, teachers, and administrators, this unique model could be implemented in many school districts.

THE CASE

The atmosphere of the school right before winter break is one of excitement and bustling energy. I wait in the lobby to meet Mr. Matthew Hoy, instrumental music teacher at Knapp Elementary School in suburban Philadelphia. As Mr. Hoy approaches to greet me, two students wave and enthusiastically shout, "Hi, Mr. Hoy!" As we make our way down the hall to his classroom, students greet Mr. Hoy at almost every door.

As Mr. Hoy and I enter the school's instrumental music room, Mr. Hoy mentions that the room is shared with the band teacher as well. The room is simply furnished with a desk, piano, a few chairs, and music stands. I find a seat toward the back, and four second-grade students enter the classroom with their parents. The chairs are positioned in two semi-circles facing Mr. Hoy. The students find a seat in the front row, while the parents situate themselves in the row directly behind their child. The parents have been instructed previously to sit behind their child so that they may observe what they are doing physically and assist Mr. Hoy when necessary.

Mr. Hoy begins tuning the students' violins. As he tunes, he explains the lesson plan for that day. The students stand with their instruments in rest position and then say "Hello, feet!" as they take a bow. The students are very focused on the songs they are playing and on Mr. Hoy's directions. Parents sit quietly in the back and take notes, occasionally whispering to each other. There is a great sense of community in the classroom because the parents and children are comfortable with each other, engaged in the learning process, and everyone appears to be having fun.

Mr. Hoy listens as the students play "Allegro" by Shinichi Suzuki (2007) as a group. He helps the students make small corrections to their posture and then comments on what a great job they are doing. There is much positive reinforcement in Mr. Hoy's classroom. Mr. Hoy then works with the students on "Perpetual Motion" by Shinichi Suzuki (2007). As the students work on the first part of the piece, Mr. Hoy emphasizes that students should always perform with the proper posture and produce a beautiful tone quality when playing the violin. Most of the teaching is done by rote for the kindergarten, first-grade, and second-grade students in North Penn School District. A cornerstone of the Suzuki philosophy is that children learn music the same way that they learn how to speak language, by listening (Suzuki 1981). In second grade they will begin a note-reading lesson in addition to the Suzuki lessons.

During the last part of the lesson, the students participate in a mini-concert. Each student stands up and performs a small solo with Mr. Hoy accompanying on the piano. The other students and parents sit quietly and observe. After each student plays, the group claps enthusiastically for the students and parents comment on the great progress made since the last lesson. The parents support all children in the learning environment, not just their own child. The students are rewarded with stickers as they pack up their violins and then depart back to class to finish the school day. The parents leave for home or work for the rest of their day.

"How is it that these parents are able to take time from their day to come to school and make time for music lessons with their children?" I ask. Mr. Hoy responds that it is a tough commitment but that the parents consider it a worthy investment. Suzuki's commitment to parents' involvement in education is evident, and he says that "the fate of the child is in the hands of the parents" (Suzuki 1981). Hoy (2006) found that for a Suzuki program to be successful, there must be equal participation and commitment from three people: teacher, student, and parent. The parents have the important responsibility of assuming the role of the teacher when the student is practicing at home.

The responsibility and requirements of the parents are clearly communicated by Mr. Hoy. In fact, before the students' formal lessons begin in January of the kindergarten year, parents have already had several meetings and educational sessions with Mr. Hoy.

They first receive a letter in September, which explains the program.

Welcome to Kindergarten! *Talent education* is a term used in Japan to mean *the education of the whole child through music.* It has come to be known as the *Suzuki Violin Method* and is being offered to kindergarten students in the North Penn schools. Dr. Suzuki believed that ability is not an inherited trait and that anyone can learn to play the violin the same way in which one learns his native language, by imitation. Lessons are provided by the school district during the school day. Students who are enrolled receive two lessons each week. The students first learn by rote, making it necessary for a parent to attend the violin lessons with the child until he or she reads music (usually third grade). This parent also then becomes the "home teacher." . . .
If it is not possible for you to attend lessons this year, please keep in mind that there will be other opportunities for your child to learn to play the violin. Third through sixth graders take lessons during school and do not require a parent as a home teacher.

A second contact is made in November for parents interested in enrolling their children in lessons. This next letter also emphasizes that lessons are during the school day, underscoring the parental commitment. A third letter is sent home in December, and parent classes begin in the next week in preparation of the students' January start. During these parent sessions, they learn important aspects of the Suzuki method—listening, learning by rote, and how the parent becomes the home teacher. The parents also learn how to play the Suzuki variations on the violin, which is an important step in the process for several reasons: By learning the basics of the violin, the parents gain firsthand experience with the learning process, which helps them to become better home teachers. Also, when the children see their parents learning to play the violin, it motivates them to want to learn themselves.

A few days after my visit to Knapp Elementary, I stop by Gwyn-Nor Elementary School to observe an early-morning orchestra rehearsal for the school's winter concert. The orchestra, which includes students from Gwyn-Nor Elementary School and Knapp Elementary School, consists of both Suzuki violin students who started in kindergarten and the traditional students who began in third grade. There are about thirty-five students on the stage, ranging from fourth to sixth graders. Of particular interest to me is the integration of the Suzuki students with the traditional students. One of the Suzuki students has been appointed concertmaster for the group, and three others help lead the second violins. The students playing second violin are strong on the harmony parts and very independent. Because the Suzuki students have been taking note-reading lessons since second grade, their music reading is very strong. Playing in the orchestra gives the Suzuki students the opportunity to combine the skills they have learned in their Suzuki lessons and their music-reading lessons.

THE IMPORTANCE OF THE PROGRAM

The North Penn School District Suzuki violin program is considered a unique program, as there are very few public schools that offer this teaching method. It is available to all students in the district starting in kindergarten, as long as a parent or guardian can attend the lessons. Suzuki believed that young children relate easily to movement and sound and that a nurturing environment is created when parent and child learn together. Dr. Suzuki once said, "I tell how to develop a person's aptitude, how a mediocre child was turned into a noble human being and an excellent musician" (1983).

John Kendall (1985), a prominent American string educator who studied with Suzuki, believed that the Suzuki method could be effective in a public-school setting. He contended that if teachers could keep the core of Suzuki's principles and creativity, then the Suzuki method would "undoubtedly make a tremendous contribution to musical and humanistic education in American life."

The North Penn School District also considers the nonmusical skills enhanced in learning instrumental music. A school-district flyer passed out to new parents and students joining the program emphasizes that instrumental music encourages a higher level of thinking, develops the ability to focus, and employs multiple sensory development. A study (Scott 1991) has even found that students involved in the Suzuki method develop increased attention spans and perseverance. Also, the nature of the method, which includes small groups in a nurturing and safe environment, provides an opportunity for students to increase their self-esteem, develop socially, and feel like they are a part of the community (Collier-Slone 1991; Hoy 2006).

Within the North Penn elementary schools, the program's long-term benefits are obvious, from the sense of musical community to the quality of the concerts. These benefits extend through the district's middle and high schools, as the Suzuki students become leaders in the orchestra, as well as in various vocal and band ensembles. Students from North Penn also place in the District, Regional and All-State Orchestras. The school-district music supervisor regards the retention of students from year to year to be one of the program's highest measures of success.

A PLAN OF ACTION

Implementation of a plan similar to the North Penn School District Suzuki Violin Program would require a commitment from all of the people involved to provide quality music education at a young age. Administrators would have to provide teachers the time and funds necessary to start and sustain the program. Kindergarten, first-grade, and second-grade teachers would have to allow students out of class time.

Elementary instrumental music teachers in public school would need some background training in the Suzuki violin method. Though Mr. Hoy has never undergone the formal training through the Suzuki Association of the Americas, he studied violin with the Suzuki method as a child and has researched all aspects of the Suzuki method (including its use in public schools) for his master's thesis.

Another essential element to a successful public-school Suzuki violin program is the commitment of the parents. The teachers in the North Penn School District work hard to communicate with students' parents about the level of involvement required in this early-start program. Parents must be willing and able to attend lessons on a consistent basis for the program to be successful.

With some careful planning and commitment from administrators, teachers, and parents, a successful program like the North Penn School District Suzuki Violin program could be implemented in any school district and could greatly enhance the overall quality of music education.

REFERENCES

Collier-Slone, K. 1991. The psychology of humanistic life education: A longitudinal study. Ph.D. diss., The Union Institute. *Dissertation Abstracts International* 53:580.

Hoy, M. 2006. An ethnographic study of the creation of a Suzuki culture in an elementary school string program. Unpublished master's thesis, Temple University.

Kendall, J. D. 1985. *The Suzuki violin method in American music education.* Rev. ed. Miami: Summy-Birchard.

Scott, L. 1991. Attention and perseverance behaviors of preschool children enrolled in Suzuki violin lessons and other activities. *Journal of Research in Music Education* 40 (3): 225–35.

Suzuki, S. 1981. *Ability development from age zero.* Miami: Summy-Birchard.

———. 1983. *Nurtured by love: The classic approach to talent education.* Rev. ed. Miami: Summy-Birchard.

———. 2007. *Violin method.* Vols. 1–10. Rev. ed. Miami: Summy-Birchard.

⑩

Music in Cyberspace: Exploring New Models in Education

Sheri E. Jaffurs and Betty Anne Younker

ABSTRACT

This chapter explores Music in Cyberspace, a music education course focused on the integration of the software programs Moodle and Blackboard and the virtual-world game Second Life. Using these three programs, students were encouraged to exchange ideas, download assignment information and lessons, blog, create wikis, and otherwise generally participate in what is increasingly becoming a traditional online learning experience. Students used the Teen Grid, a segment of the Second Life multiuser virtual environment, to develop the skills and processes necessary to becoming a musician in a multimedia world. Projects were developed specifically to encourage the development of musicianship and include songwriting and film-score composing. Portions of the class were conducted in the virtual 3-D classrooms in Second Life, which meant that both live- and recorded-streaming of student compositions were possible.

INTRODUCTION

Students have been making music outside of school-based music programs for years (Green 2008, 2002). It could be suggested that there has been a surge in such music making as musical styles and genres have multiplied in popular culture. In addition, multicultural music has experienced an increased presence in school and university-based music programs. As a result, students and music educators have begun to embrace diverse music-making traditions in their classrooms and have sought venues in which an understanding of these traditions can be acquired and practiced.

Opportunities for making music exist both in and outside of school, in formal and informal settings. One kind of nontraditional music ensemble increasingly popular with young people is the garage band (Jaffurs 2006). In such a group, students learn music in the aural tradition: knowledge about the music generates through the practice of making the music, and often times the roles of teacher and learner are interchanged as students with varying levels of knowledge guide or receive guidance (Jaffurs 2006). The interchange can consist of multiple voices guiding musical decisions and informing or being informed. The resultant experience is characterized by democratic principles of voice, ownership, and responsibility. In the absence of a teacher, group members are each motivated to engage, lead, and be led. They identify themselves as musicians who are members of a community with a shared value—making music of a chosen style or genre (Younker and Hickey 2007).

One instrument that has contributed to the proliferation of nontraditional music making is the personal computer, along with its accompanying music software. In addition to engaging in garage-band experiences with acoustic and electric instruments, students are increasingly using technology as the instrument itself. Using technology to make music is finding an increasing presence in music-technology labs and virtual environments at home and at school. The technology is available, students are engaged, and music continues to be made in nontraditional ensembles. It would behoove the profession to build on the work of researchers who have examined students who make music outside of traditional school-based ensembles (e.g., Green 2002; Jaffurs 2006) so that informed decisions can be made when expanding on existing music programs.

As Younker and Hickey (2007) noted, we are ethically bound to examine what we do well—that is, our traditions—and evaluate and transform accordingly (Bowman 2002). We have strong traditional-music ensembles in our schools that nurture students' musicianship; these ensembles will continue to thrive. We must acknowledge, however, that there are many ways to experience music, of all styles and genres, and as public music educators it is our responsibility to engage students in all of the possible musical experiences whenever possible. Through examining students' experiences in nontraditional settings we can begin to be informed about and generate reasons for broadening the offerings of existing school-based music programs. The following is an in-depth examination of such a setting.

THE COURSE PROPOSAL

During the 2007–2008 school year, a course targeting nontraditional music students either currently participating in school-based music programs or not was proposed to a large school district in the Midwest of the United States. The instructor's research interests and informal music training along with the discovery of virtual-education settings inspired the course. A series of presentations to the district's administration, curriculum committee, technology committee, and high school principals resulted in the launching of the pilot course Music in Cyberspace.

For the class, student participation would take place entirely in a virtual environment with Moodle, an online course-content management system, providing the delivery system. The Moodle software was chosen because it was created from a social constructivist's perspective that cohered with the instructor's beliefs about learning and pedagogy. Another content-management system, Blackboard, was investigated as a choice for the course, but its fees were prohibitive, whereas Moodle is freeware. In the online class, participation would mirror that of a traditional setting, with students engaging in classwide discussions and exchanging assignment information, but they also blogged and created wikis, elements of what has become a traditional online learning experience. The course was instituted in the fall of 2008 and is the first online high school program offered in the district.

VENUE DESCRIPTION

The course venue is a virtual multiuser platform sponsored by Linden Lab's Second Life. The district purchased a private, virtual island in a protected sector of the Second Life world created just for teens, called the Teen Grid. It is on the Teen Grid and Moodle that students can have access to course content. The Moodle shell was launched from the county school district. This accessibility was provided because originally the plan was for the course to be a collaboration between two districts within the county, with each sponsoring Moodle and the

intermediate school district sponsoring the course. This would have allowed students from both districts to access the program from one joint
location. Teacher Sheri E. Jaffurs developed the Moodle shell over the
summer of 2008, and the course was ready to launch it in the fall.

CLASS ENVIRONMENT

A multiuser virtual environment enables all participants to experience a virtual face-to-face. Synchronous meetings in virtual worlds
allow for instant text messaging and audio communication in real
time. There is an embodiment of the people attending the course at
the same time, talking to each other, and even watching the interaction between each other's avatars. This encouraged a kind of student
collaboration that more closely resembled traditional, face-to-face
courses while maintaining the advantages of online instruction. Using
a virtual environment minimizes the sense of distance between students, specifically enhanced through the virtual platform and the capability to view an avatar—or a virtual 3-dimensional version of each
participant. Through the avatar, students can stream live music onto
the island, schedule shows, perform via Internet broadcasting, and
create and play music with other avatars. With Moodle, students can
discuss their performances and music using blogs, wikis, and discussion forums. This environment provides similar experiences to those
one would have in a classroom, with the only difference being that
this environment is virtual. While the concept of online learning is of
concern to some educators (Norton and Hathaway 2008), its strength
is in allowing students from across the district to learn from the one
teacher who oversees the course. The setup's strength has less to do
with its being online and more to do with the interactions it facilitates
among students and between students and the teacher. The result is
a learning environment as described at the beginning of this chapter,
in which democratic principles of voice, ownership, and responsibility
are valued and practiced. Furthermore, in this setting students are active agents in their learning, involved in choices made, and accounting
for these choices (Bruner 1996; Dewey 1938; Woodford 2005).

THE HARDWARE, SOFTWARE, AND PLATFORM

For the program the district loaned midi keyboard controllers, head-
sets, and a digital audio program. Due to the fact that students owned

different computers, the equipment and resources needed to work on both Apples and PCs. The company supplying the keyboard controller provided a free digital editing and recording program that was PC compatible. The software was chosen because of editing capabilities and its looping library. Apple computers users already have access to a program that has digital editing and recording capabilities and an extensive looping library.

The content management system, Moodle, was selected as the platform for course delivery. Moodle supports thematic lessons that are project-based. Students gain an understanding of the skills and processes necessary to becoming a musician in a multimedia world. Projects are presented in units that encourage the development of musicianship—like songwriting and film scoring. Portions of this class were available in virtual 3-D classrooms on Second Life's Teen Grid and offered possibilities for streaming both live and recorded music.

THE PARTICIPANTS

The online music course targeted nontraditional music students between the ages of thirteen and seventeen who had access to a computer, were from any of the four participating district high schools, and had been recommended to the program by high school counselors late in the 2008 school year. The district is located in a large suburb with a diverse population of about one hundred thousand residents, and the approximately twelve thousand students are of diverse ethnic and socioeconomic background. When the course first opened, in the fall of 2008, five male students enrolled.

THE CHALLENGES

Recruiting students for any new course that reaches across four high schools has its own challenges. Offering the course online only compounds the challenges. For one, while online courses are increasingly available in university environments, they are not as utilized in high school settings, particularly in urban areas, as this district is. Furthermore, some feared that offering an online music course would decrease enrollment in the traditional music ensembles.

But music educators have an ethical responsibility to examine tradition, maintaining what works and transforming the rest (Bowman 2002). It became clear that the virtual course could very well increase the enrollment of students in district music programs and diversify the musical experiences typically encountered in school-based music programs (Woodford 2005). The program, it was hoped, would teach the students about composing and other elements of music, which in turn would encourage some to pursue performance, others to compose and orchestrate, and others still to edit. Even so, fears about the new course were understandable, especially since it would satisfy the state's high school arts requirement, which previously could only be met through a school performance-based ensemble.

Finally, another challenge was whether students could maintain their academic focus in the virtual environment. Though the teacher would be in consistent virtual contact with the class, the motivation at the individual level differs because of the solitude in which the work is completed. This requires a certain kind of discipline and motivation that is fueled by the task at hand. Discussions and personal interactions would be virtual and few, with the exception of any face-to-face meetings required by the teacher. A related challenge is maintaining the motivation to find solutions to problems encountered because of the technology. While technology becomes more accessible with each passing year and students' understanding and ability continue to increase every year, there are still challenges to find solutions as issues arise.

CONCLUSION

In sum, online music-technology courses for nontraditional students can offer a diversified music education that goes beyond the traditional performance tracks found in most school programs. The very nature of composing, sharing the compositions, and responding to peers' compositions in such a setting widens the class's dialogue. While such idea exchanges can happen in ensemble-based programs, particularly ones in which students are involved in chamber groups on a regular basis (Allsup 2003; Younker 2004), studies indicate that the role of the teacher and student differs in composition-based environments—both with and without technology (Reese 2003)—from that experienced in performance-based ensembles. Such settings improve a student's opportunity to share their knowledge and provide validity to their music practices. Additionally, it provides an opportunity for schools to offer other kinds of music making, representing a wider gamut of what music has to offer and what music education can, and possibly should, be. And finally, this course can reveal characteristics of successful student-directed collaboration in a nontraditional music-making environment. These opportunities can allow for transference of music learned in school to the music students currently value and make. Giving our students the opportunity to participate in a course such as this may prove to be a powerful advocate for music in the schools.

REFERENCES

Allsup, R. 2003. Mutual learning and democratic action in instrumental music education. *Journal of Research in Music Education* 51 (1): 24–37.

Bowman, W. 2002. Educating musically. In *The handbook of research for music teaching and learning*, 2nd ed., ed. R. Colwell and C. P. Richardson, 63–84. New York: Oxford University Press.

Bruner, J. 1996. *The culture of education*. Cambridge, Mass.: Harvard University Press.

Dewey, J. 1938. *Experience and education*. New York: Collier Books / Macmillan.

Green, L. 2002. *How popular musicians learn: A way ahead for music education*. Aldershot, UK: Ashgate Publishing.

———. 2008. *Music, informal learning and the school: A new classroom pedagogy*. Aldershot, UK: Ashgate Publishing.

Jaffurs, S. 2006. Lessons from a garage band: Informal venues for music making. Ph.D. diss., Michigan State University.

Norton, P., and D. Hathaway. 2008. Exploring two teacher education online learning designs: A classroom of one or many? *Journal of Research on Technology in Education* 49 (4): 475–95.

Reese, S. 2003. Responding to students' compositions. In *Music composition in the schools: A new horizon for music education*, ed. M. Hickey, 211–32. Reston, Va.: MENC.

Wiggins, J. H. 1992. The nature of children's musical learning in the context of a music classroom. Unpublished Ph.D. diss., University of Illinois at Urbana-Champaign.

Woodford, P. G. 2005. *Democracy and music education: Liberalism, ethics and the politics of practice*. Bloomington: Indiana University Press.

Younker, B. A. 2004. Communities of singing: A democratic approach. In *Share the voices: The phenomenon of singing*, ed. A. Rose and K. Adams, *Proceedings of the International Symposium, St. John's, Newfoundland, Canada*. Paper presented at The Phenomenon of Singing International Symposium II, 235–47. St. John's, Newfoundland, Canada, June.

Younker, B. A., and M. Hickey. 2007. Examining the profession through the lens of social Justice: Two music educators' stories and their stark realizations. *Music Education Research* 9 (2) (July): 1–13.

❿

Exploring the Creation of Music through Film Scoring

Douglas C. Orzolek

ABSTRACT

Helping our students explore the creative process through music is often daunting and frightening for both the music educator and his students. In the following chapter I discuss a film-scoring experience I offered students who were participating in musical ensembles at the high school level. The aim of my project was to engage students in an entry-level composition or arranging experience that would pique their desire to further pursue the creation of music.

INTRODUCTION

In 1995, as a part of the performing-ensembles curriculum at Thomas Jefferson High School in Bloomington, Minnesota, all of the students participated in a general music component that was intended to expand their musical understanding and experiences outside of their band, choir, and orchestra classes. The objectives of the general music course included acquiring foundational musical knowledge, skills, and contextual understanding, as well as creating, responding to, and performing music. The course was primarily grounded in the Minnesota Standards for Arts Education, which is based on the artistic processes of creating, responding, and performing. The course creators felt that students who completed the general music component would also partially fulfill the National Standards for Arts Education.

The development of the Absolute Musicianship for Performers course (AMP) in 1995 resulted from the need to address two major concerns regarding music education at the high school level: First, block scheduling of courses for students in following the performing-ensembles curriculum had reduced the number of periods in a high school day to only four, each lasting approximately ninety minutes. Considering the attention span and physical demands required of such a lengthy rehearsal, advocates for restructuring felt that students weren't able to play or sing for a full hour and a half every day of the school year. And so the development of the revised general-music class was to offer another way to manage time effectively and improve the quality of music education the students received.

Second, it was felt that that students who participate in musical ensembles still lacked fundamental musical knowledge and listening skills. Introducing and honing such skills would not only enhance musical performance but also increase the likelihood that the students would go on to develop a lifelong love and understanding of music. Few schools offered classes addressing these fundamentals, partly because few students were able to fit such electives into their schedules already crowded with core-requirement classes. But as the school's mission was to foster the maximum musical growth of each student, the importance of addressing fundamental music knowledge and listening skills in the classroom became of critical importance (Orzolek 2004).

And so AMP was designed as a general music course for the high schooler and aimed to integrate music appreciation, music listening, music history, and music theory. It was determined that a class with a broad range of topics and discussions would be most appropriate. The general goals of this class were (1) to enhance and improve musical understanding, knowledge about music, and individual musical skills; (2) to develop and improve an awareness of how music is reflective of life and the human experience; and (3) to foster and develop a lifelong appreciation and love for music (Orzolek 2004).

By breaking down the standard ninety-minute class block throughout the school and adding the AMP course to the roster, teachers continued to meet performance goals while providing their students with the type of music education that they deserved and needed—an education that would last a lifetime. And while the debate continues about the future of the block schedule, one thing is certain: the general music portion of the high school curriculum has been deemed a success and will remain in place for many years to come (Orzolek 2004).

The history of the general music program at Thomas Jefferson High School has been researched and outlined in a master's thesis by Daniel Fretland, *Comprehensive Musicianship in High School Instrumental Music: A Historical Study of the Thomas Jefferson High School Band Curriculum* (2007). In addition, the program has been replicated in several other schools across the country and has been recognized as an outstanding music program by the Minnesota Music Educators Association.

Although the original plan for the course did not include composition and improvisation (due mainly to the size of the classes and the limited skills of the teacher and students), those components were eventually added. Students now complete projects outside of the class and present them by means of an electronic portfolio (Orzolek 2004). In the following section I address the early course's initial attempts to provide the students with experiences in the creation of music.

INITIAL ATTEMPTS

Engaging students in the process of creating music was a mystery to me primarily due to my inexperience. Knowing where to start was daunting. The initial request to include more coursework addressing the creation of music actually came from a student in the AMP course. We had been studying and listening to the works of Igor Stravinsky when a student said something to the effect of, How does a composer come up with this stuff? The student had made a terrific point (although she didn't know it)—how could I expect them to understand this music if they didn't have any experience with composition themselves? That started my quest to find a way to help the students learn about the creative process.

After researching and thinking about how to implement some sort of composition experience into the AMP course and feeling as if I hadn't made sufficient headway, I nonetheless jumped into the experience feet first. An article on the topic suggested that it was extremely important to establish some guidelines for the compositions. With that, I asked the students to compose a piece including what I considered to be the primary concepts of music: melody, harmony, rhythm, timbre, and form. We had been discussing these terms for months so I had naively assumed that the compositions would be stellar. Nothing could have been further from the truth.

Among the generally disappointing compositions, one stood out, as unusually good. A group of percussionists had decided to use a variety of nontraditional instruments to composed a piece in binary form that included hand drumming on filing cabinets, music stands, chairs, and a sousaphone. Their score consisted of a pictograph with symbols that roughly indicated when things should be struck over an ostinato. It was the strongest composition of the bunch, and the students were quite excited about it.

Although I was well intentioned in my desire to provide the students with a composition experience, I had neglected to take into account the factors that could have made it more productive. The students had had very limited exposure to notating music. In fact, the only time any of them had been required to notate music was for a written quiz or if they lost their score and had to quickly transcribe it from someone else's stand. In addition, I met with nine sections of forty-five students each, twice a week for twenty-five minutes. That amount of time was barely enough to begin a *discussion* about a piece let alone compose it. Finally, the students' ages, abilities, and skills were far ranging. Several students later went on to attend some of the nation's best conservatories and music schools and were classmates with students who couldn't read a line of music or name the notes on their octavo.

Upon later reflection, I identified some positive outcomes from the experience besides the lone percussion piece. As I had wandered through the room to check on my students' work, I heard some wonderful discussions among the groups: Students were asking one another about the definitions of *melody* and *harmony* and sharing in a back-and-forth of ideas. In effect, they were teaching each other. These interactions caught my attention, and I prompted the students to share even more with one another. Furthermore, I noticed that several students found it easier to compose their pieces if they worked with a program or story. And while I had thought I had set enough time aside for this project, it ended up taking twice as long as I had anticipated, and the students always asked for more time to work on their pieces. In the end, I noticed they had taken a strong pride in their work—no matter how poor *I* felt they were. While it was important, of course, that I critically assess these pieces, I knew it was also important to maintain the students' sense of pride in what had become a very personal project for them.

PROFESSIONAL DEVELOPMENT

With a desire to learn more about teaching creativity, I focused on my professional development over the next year. That spring I was nominated and invited to join the Minnesota Arts Best Practice Network (BPN) sponsored by the Perpich Center for Arts Education. The BPN brought together arts educators to consider and discuss our work in our classrooms as well as consider some of the difficult things facing our profession. In particular, the BPN spent a great deal of time considering the artistic processes of creating, responding, and performing. It was in this setting that I learned about the various stages or steps of creativity (Perpich Center for Arts Education 1997):

1. imagine/generate
2. plan/prepare
3. explore/incubate/focus
4. develop/make
5. evaluate/refine
6. present/perform
7. reflect/refine

The BPN helped us experience every aspect of these stages through a variety of art forms. In particular, I learned a great deal from a project in which we created a self-portrait, which had an assessment piece where rubrics were developed to help guide our work as well as our reflection. The BPN truly shaped my thinking and teaching of music.

Later I attended a workshop session presented by the well-known composer Libby Larsen. She was speaking at a band director's conference on teaching creativity to students in an ensemble setting and was sharing all kinds of ideas about how to begin the process. Libby spoke of music as *art in sound* and suggested that students should begin their compositions with an exploration of a *sound palette*. She encouraged us to allow students to play around with their own instruments in order to discover what sounds (traditional and nontraditional) were available, share them with others, and then decide which ones to use in a group piece. She also spoke of the value of program and stories as a means to explore the creative process. This confirmed some of my thoughts from my first attempts at letting my students compose.

I attended many other sessions over the years, and from them I've learned many things; but these two sessions had a direct impact on this first film-scoring project I undertook. And so I encourage anyone reading this to take advantage of as many professional-development opportunities as possible, as there is always more to learn!

THE FILM-SCORING PROJECT

Armed with these new ideas, I felt much more prepared for my next attempt at teaching creativity. This time I felt as if I had a frame for guiding the students through the process. One question remained: what kind of compositions should I ask the students to create?

In latter half of the 1990s, the Twin Cities were in the midst of a theater and musical revival. Many Broadway shows and musicals were traveling to our revitalized theaters. Most notably, *The Lion King* was being staged and premiered here prior to its opening in New York. It was also a time when musical shows like *Riverdance* and *Blue Man Group* were becoming popular. Influenced by the creativity around them, the students were greatly taken by soundtracks for these shows and movies and were constantly bringing in soundtracks to share with me and with their fellow students. In this I had found the doorway—I decided to work on a film scoring.

The project idea certainly seemed to suit the criteria that I had established for a creativity experience. Scoring a film would provide the story that would give the students a point of reference. In addition, I could easily picture and lead the creation steps that I had learned from the BPN. Scoring a film would also require students to consider the sound palette that I had learned about. Obviously, some sounds would work better than others, and the exploration of those sounds would surely cause great conversation between the students. Finally, the fact that students were deeply interested in soundtracks, movies, and shows would certainly help.

To prepare students for the project, I developed a series of lectures, listening experiences, and readings related to film scoring. We listened to examples with and without the video, and, likewise, we watched many videos with and without the accompanying music. We considered two major questions: How does the music support the action in the scene? And how can you describe the musical elements of that supportive music? With this their attention was keenly focused: Throughout the lectures, students maintained a notebook of ideas and questions that emerged as we considered different examples. As an aside, recently I rediscovered many of the soundtracks that we had studied during this class. I remembered that I had also used a video recording of Sergei Eisenstein's movie *Alexander Nevsky*, which at that time had just been rereleased with a new recording of Prokofiev's score. It's a terrific example of film scoring, and I would encourage readers to familiarize themselves with it.

Following several days of this preparation, I began to explain the creative process outlined in the Perpich Center for the Arts Education's publication, *The Minnesota Framework of Arts Curriculum Strategies* (FACS). So as to not stifle their creative instincts, I decided to share the stages as a suggestion rather than a requirement. In addition, I shared the rubric that would be used to assess their projects. I also explained that the goal of the project was to create and perform music to accompany a short film clip. At this point, the students seemed eager to being the process, and I was encouraged by the discussions and questions that emerged.

With the help of the school's media specialist, I prepared three different one-minute VHS clip loops: a fast horse-riding scene from an old Western, a scene from the *War of the Worlds*, and a television commercial where a student returns home from college for the holiday break. None of the clips included any speaking parts. We made about seven copies of each video loop so that several students could be working on the same example at the same time. We also ended up making several additional copies for students to take home. (Of note, music educators should carefully review copyright restrictions and seek appropriate permissions when beginning this type of project. Fortunately, our media specialist was well versed in that area!)

Students were permitted to break into their own groups of four or five students, and we ended up with ten groups per section of the class. I encouraged the students to choose their groups carefully, with special consideration given to instruments and voice parts. Once settled, they watched the clips several times and made their choice as to which they would score. I had borrowed several TVs and VCRs from all over the building so that each group could have its own. The tape loops were extremely helpful, allowing the students to just let the clip run over and over again.

The guidelines for the scoring project were rather broad and ambiguous, owing to the varied skills of the students in the class—they were to create a score to accompany the sound clip. The groups were given the freedom to choose traditional or nontraditional instruments and were permitted to notate the score in any fashion that they desired; some chose traditional notation, others used verbal descriptions, and some used nontraditional symbols. I did remind the groups that the purpose of the score was to not only note their musical choices but also do so in a way that others might replicate it. Throughout the development of their scores, each group's scribe maintained a journal of their process, their discussions, and any problems encountered.

These proved quite helpful to the groups and to my assessment of their work.

As the groups began their work, I was quite impressed by the quality of their discussions and progress. (While I had been disappointed with my earlier attempt at a creativity project, it seemed to have paid some dividends—the students seemed much more comfortable with the process.) It was quite rare for them to ask for help or comments from others. For the most part, the groups had completed their work within six class periods.

In most cases, students started tackling the assignment with a discussion about the mood and meaning of their clips. Upon building consensus, most then began experimenting with sounds. Most chose to use traditional instruments in their traditionally intended ways, but some of the more interesting sounds came from those groups that took the time to experiment with their instruments. Some used different-sized mouthpieces, one used kitchen utensils, and yet another made use of electronic sounds. For nearly every group, the experimentation with sound seemed to take up the most time. It was great fun!

Little by little, the groups slowly developed and organized their aural ideas into a piece that supported their impression of the film. During this stage, the groups often played their pieces over and over with the video clip and made small alterations as a group member offered an idea or suggestion. I was somewhat surprised that the groups worked so well together. While I am sure some students were frustrated with the work of their groups, they did not show it. In the few situations where groups were stuck or in need of some motivation, I found that the creativity steps were helpful prompts. I would try to assess where students were at with the process and offer a suggestion about the next step. There was never an instance where I offered a suggestion about the actual music that they were creating. I only made attempts to help them with the process. It seemed to work well.

The last step for each group was the notation of their scores. I had asked the students to make large scores on poster board or large sheets of paper (from the rolls of paper often used to make signs in the building) so that the rest of the class could see the score when it was time for the performance. As anticipated, most groups elected to do something more like a pictograph or a chart than to use standard notation of their music. In most cases, it worked very well and the students' scores were indeed representative of the sounds that they were creating. Some groups had hand-drawn pictures of the scenes, while others use time durations to synchronize the score and performance of the piece with the film. The groups rehearsed with their scores and then performed them for the class with the film loops rolling. The performances were terrific, and there was little redundancy in the performance.

In addition to their performances, the students were asked to explain their work to the class. Again, we used the basic questions from our earlier study of film music: How does the music support the action in the scene? And how can you describe the musical elements of that supportive music? The class was permitted to ask questions of the groups as well, most pertaining to the score and comments about the interpretation of the action in the films. While there was a great deal of variety in the sounds used by the groups, there was a lot of similarity in the descriptions and explanations. It was clear that the groups had given more attention to their own performances! I had anticipated more depth and musical vocabulary in their explanations, but their terminology and descriptors were rather rudimentary.

Students were assessed (by their peers through the use of a five-point rubric) on their ability to

1. musically describe or express the clip,
2. incorporate as many musical concepts as possible,
3. perform their work for the class,
4. notate their score, and
5. explain their decisions.

The performances were video recorded for further reflection and as an evidential component of their learning. The students' performances, scores, and journals showed a great deal of thought and learning. Many students indicated a very strong desire for more opportunities to work on music-creation activities.

REFLECTION

I certainly felt as if the project provided the entry-level creativity experience that I had desired for the students. The attention that I had given to the stages of creativity coupled with the concept of starting with sound seemed to make the experience work smoothly even with all of the students' disparity of skills. My only disappoint was in the students' ability to explain their choices. But even this improved in later iterations of the project as I emphasized the importance of explaining one's work.

As the students and I gained more experience with teaching creativity, the projects become better and more interesting. I still use this film-scoring project in my current setting, although the final scores are heavily influenced by the technologies that are readily available to students. Using tools like iTunes, iMovie, GarageBand, and other software, students are now writing their own scripts, editing their own movies, and adding music that they compose, arrange, or sample from a variety of sources with a justification for their choices. Students now maintain an electronic portfolio of their files, and we take the time to screen them on a regular basis.

Since my first experience with teaching film music and scoring to students in 1997, several resources have been developed that may be of interest to readers. In particular, *The Enjoyment of Music* by Forney and Machlis (2007) includes a strong section on film music and its role and function. An Internet search will also reveal a wealth of books on the topic, and most are excellent. Several professional orchestras regularly feature film music during their performance seasons. Often, these performances include clips from the actual films. YouTube and other Internet resources have also been an invaluable source for discussing film scores. Readers should also note that a similar composition project to the one described here appears in the *Instructor's Guide* that accompanies *Music: Its Role and Importance in Our Lives* (Fowler, Gerber, and Lawrence 2000, 261). That book, geared toward secondary students, contains other ideas related to the teaching of film music to students.

This project still comes up in conversations and e-mails from former students. In fact, I recently attended a movie premiere that was entirely scored by a student who had been a part of this initial experience. While I can't say that this project was responsible for my student's eventual success, I am certain that my creativity project not only yielded strong results at that time but also piqued my students' interest in further exploring composition. While the project was difficult and frightening, it was worth it in the end.

REFERENCES

Eisenstein, S., et al. directors. 2006; 1938. *Alexander Nevsky*. Mosfilm Studios. Video/DVD. New York: Janus Films.

Forney, K., and J. Machlis. 2007. *The enjoyment of music*. 10th ed. New York: W. W. Norton.

Fowler, C., T. Gerber, and V. Lawrence. 2000. *Instructor's guide to music: Its role and importance in our lives*. New York: Glencoe / McGraw-Hill.

Fretland, D. 2007. Comprehensive musicianship in high school instrumental music: A historical study of the Thomas Jefferson high school band curriculum. Master's thesis, University of St. Thomas.

Orzolek, D. 2004. Absolute musicianship for performers: A model of general music study for high school performing groups. *General Music Today* 17 (Spring): 21–27.

Perpich Center for Arts Education. 1997. *Minnesota frameworks for arts for arts curriculum strategies.* Golden Valley, Minn.: Perpich Center for Arts Education.

Wells, H. G., D. Sutherland, and D. Minor, directors. 1996. *The war of the worlds.* Discovery Channel Video, Discovery Communications and Learning Channel. Video/DVD. Bethesda, Md.: Discovery Communications.

12

Alternatives to Music Education: East Meets West in Music Education

Lisa M. Meyer, Catherine Odom Prowse, and Terese Volk Tuohey

ABSTRACT

This chapter highlights two elementary music teachers working with Arabic student populations in the greater metropolitan area of Detroit, Michigan. Lisa Meyer found innovative ways to incorporate the music and culture of her students into a program that became the district-wide Arabic Oral History project, which had a strong music component and made frequent use of culture bearers both from within and outside of the school building. And after attending an in-service on Ghanaian drumming, Catherine Odom Prowse recognized the power of drumming and, with the help of parents, the community, and fellow staff members, founded the Arabic Drumming Ensemble at her school.

TERESE VOLK TUOHEY: INTRODUCTION

Dearborn, Michigan, is a large city in the metropolitan Detroit area. It is home to the largest population of Arabic-speaking people in the United States. Signage in parts of Dearborn is written in both Arabic and English. There is the Arab-American Museum, a yearly Arab-American festival, and a plethora of Arabic food shops and restaurants.

As a result, in Dearborn schools music education is taught to a population reflecting a predominantly Arabic culture. Lisa M. Meyer is the music resource teacher for Dearborn Public Schools. Catherine Odom Prowse teaches in Dearborn at Maples Elementary School. I met both of them through my position in music education at Wayne State University (WSU). I had the opportunity to bring Mrs. Prowse and the Maples Elementary School Arabic Music Ensemble to WSU several years ago for a performance. This event has in turn brought us into closer collaboration on a number of other projects.

In the following, Lisa Meyer and Catherine Odom Prowse describe music education in the Dearborn Public Schools. Lisa Meyer first offers a broad picture of the situation as she sees it from her office as music resource teacher. And then Catherine Odom Prowse shares about her particular, and very successful, music education program bridging Arabic and Western music cultures.

LISA M. MEYER: THE CASE

Dearborn Public Schools have enjoyed a long tradition of musicianship. As our community embraced a Middle Eastern population, we faced challenges unprecedented in our community. Initially, minimal adjustments were made to instruction, but as schools received a higher percentage of Middle Eastern students, it became clear that the traditional Western approach to music education was not going to be sufficient for our population.

Students who attend the Dearborn schools begin taking music classes in kindergarten, where they receive thirty minutes of general music once a week. Students in grades 1 through 5 attend two thirty-minute general music classes a week. In fifth grade, students also get the chance to begin participating in band or strings, meeting once a week for forty minutes. Each school is equipped with an inventory of instruments that the students can rent at a nominal per-year cost. In middle school, students can opt either to continue with instrumental music or take a choral-based music class. These classes feed into a strong instrumental and vocal high school program. Groups from our middle schools and high schools are routinely recognized at district and state festivals for their superior performance. Many students continue to pursue music after they leave the school system, either as a career or as a hobby.

The Dearborn community is also a strong proponent of the arts. There are many performing opportunities for our students, including an internationally touring community chorus, community theater, the Dearborn Symphony, a professional community orchestra, and the Dearborn Youth Symphony, which consists of students in elementary school through college. The community is encouraged to express itself artistically in one of these many, excellent civic programs.

Dearborn Public Schools (DPS) has a very diverse student population. In the 2008–2009 school year, DPS enrolled 18,035 students, 60.2 percent of whom were part of the free-/reduced-lunch program. Twenty-nine point nine percent of the student body has limited English proficiency. The top five languages spoken in the school system are Arabic, Spanish, Romanian, Albanian, and Urdu, with 95 percent of the Limited English Proficiency students speaking some dialect of Arabic. DPS has twenty-one elementary schools, one intermediate school (grades 4 through 8), six middle schools, and three high schools. Ten of the schools rank as 70 percent or above in Limited English Proficient Students.

Teaching music to Arabic-speaking students has its challenges. A lack of a common language limits the idiom "music is the universal language." And yet communicate we must. Many adaptations have been made by the music staff to include as much nonverbal teaching as possible, but there remains a need to communicate through language. Garnering parental support has also posed a challenge. Parents who do not speak English are often intimidated when meeting with teachers and administrators within the school. It is important that school staff not equate this resulting lack of involvement with a lack of caring. But since family support is paramount in any successful school program, time must be spent educating parents about the curriculum taught and the requirements for success within a program.

As educators, we know that learning needs to be tied to previous experiences and knowledge. As we in DPS began seeing kindergarten classes consisting of 98 percent English Proficient Learners, we realized that the usual nursery rhymes and songs we had been using would not be familiar to these students. It became clear that we had no common musical ground on which to build learning experiences. Some parents and community members would provide teachers with recordings of children's songs, but these recording were in Arabic and had neither English translations nor traditionally notated music that our musicians could play. We discussed our dilemma with Arts Education IDEAS president Dr. Susan Snyder, who suggested that we join with her company to create a resource to meet this need.

And so the Arabic Oral History project was underway. Arabic staff and community members were approached and asked to share stories and songs they had learned as children and that they in turn sang to their children. The songs were performed in Arabic and recorded. The lyrics then were translated into English and the melodies transcribed into Western notation. Lyrics in both Arabic and English, along with background information as described by the person performing the songs and games, were included. The completed resource, *Children's Arabic Songs* (available through www.AEIdeas.com), also included a video of these interviews, allowing the viewer to see and hear the singing games. This served as a beginning point for teaching these early elementary students with songs and games that they already knew. What fun it was to perform a concert for parents and see how pleased and surprised they were when they recognized these songs! It served to remind the music staff that cultural pride has a place in the music classroom.

At times our music staff has experienced resistance to music education. Parents have requested that their children not participate in the general music class during certain religious holidays. Although there is a strong Christian presence in the Dearborn community, the majority of the Arabic community is Islamic, requiring DPS to coordinate events around the Muslim calendar. Some Muslim holiday observances include fasting and mourning. During these times, Muslim students do not participate in singing, listening to music, playing instruments, attending concerts, and so on. During other religious observations, students fast from sunup to sundown, breaking their fast only after dark. We make sure that neither concerts nor any other after-school musical activities are planned during this time. The Muslim calendar is based on the lunar cycle, which changes from year to year, unlike Western traditional holidays, which are date- or season-specific. The dates and seasons of the observance of Muslim holidays change annually. This adds to the already considerable challenge of planning for concerts and other community and school events.

The initial response of the teachers to all of these concerns the parents expressed was reactive, not proactive. Each incident was dealt with on an individual basis. Some teachers validated the concerns by making adjustments to their teaching, while others decided to hold to traditional music instruction. But soon it became clear that as a district we needed to make a more concerted effort to address the parental concerns voiced. In addition, there was a new influx of very conservative Muslim families that viewed music education as a forerunner to MTV, which they considered distastefully secular. Even though our music curriculum was educationally sound, there was still fear from a growing community group that we were going to expose their children to inappropriate material via music education.

Building trust with the community presented a challenge. Each music teacher worked within his or her school community to help educate the community about the curriculum, but the sense of mistrust still pervaded. Many of the parents simply found Western music alienating. This is in part due to the vast differences between the Arabic musical world and traditional Western music. Arabic music uses scalar patterns based on a quartertone system (*maqamat*); harmony is minimal, often only a drone. The melodies are intricately embellished and traditionally are performed over a background of rhythmic patterns (*iqat*) performed on drums.

The music staff attempted to make connections between the two music cultures but found the two worlds very far apart. It was very difficult to find music that could be played on Western instruments with traditional Arabic drumming accompaniments, which are extremely complex, consisting of multimetered patterns that often vary from measure to measure. The idea of a "steady pulse" is not prevalent in Arabic music. So it was an uphill battle for each individual teacher who tried to convince disapproving parents that the Western program had value.

One of the approaches that staff took was to get instruction from musicians from the Arabic culture. This was not successful for a few reasons: The sense of mistrust among the Arabic community proved too pronounced for our staff to overcome. Furthermore, there are Islamic restrictions governing behavior for males and females not related to one another that seriously curtail interactions between genders, and so meetings between strangers was unacceptable.

But one commonality among many musical cultures is the central use of the drum. In an attempt to build on this shared cultural practice, I brought in Margaret Campbelle-Holman, a specialist in Ghanaian drumming, to work with the music staff. One staff member transferred what she'd learned from the lessons back to her school and created the strongest tie between the two cultures that DPS has achieved to date. This is how Catherine Odom Prowse approached her school.

CATHERINE ODOM PROWSE: THE CASE

After attending the in-service on Ghanaian drumming, I realized that there were more similarities than differences between the drumming styles of West Ghana and the Middle East. I isolated those similarities and began using them in my classes. I believed that the drum could be the catalyst to changing the way the Arabic community viewed music education. And so were sown the seeds for the Arabic Music Ensemble.

I asked my students if any of them played drums at home and encouraged them to bring their instruments to class to demonstrate for us. The students' families soon grew excited about what was happening within the music classroom. They and other members of the community began to provide authentic drumming patterns for our class that we could practice and perfect.

One of the musical forms that I used with my students was labeled *free-style playing*. The students first learned a common drum pattern and then, once that was established, alternated it with an improvisational solo by each child. This soon became a favorite practice with the students. Through improvization each student got the opportunity to display their own expertise, rolls, and fancy techniques on their drum. To signal the return to the common pattern, or to signal another student's turn, the soloist finishes the free style with the common pattern. That pattern is then repeated, signaling the next drummer to begin their free-style solo. In essence, this creates a rondo with the common pattern as the A section. The use of this well-known musical form allows students to see and experience a connection between the Arabic musical experience and a musical form used in Western music.

With the high concentration of Arabic students at the school, I started to focus on the Arabic drum (*derbeke*) and then began to reach out to the community to share our success and hopefully continue to improve relations. A performing ensemble of the most talented drummers was established, as well as a large second ensemble for the beginners. Authentic costumes were handcrafted for the members of the Arabic Drumming Ensemble, and before long children, parents, school, staff, and other members of the community became engaged in this creative endeavor. Parents would return from travels to the Middle East with hand-embellished drums, embroidered hats, golden brocade vests, carved finger cymbals, tambourines, and a great variety of elaborate and beautiful crafted embellishments that they gladly gave us for ensemble and classroom use. On one occasion a family brought in a hand-embroidered vest with gold thread, very elegant, which they gave me to wear at all the shows. I am honored to wear it, and the audience remembers that I, too, am a part of the Arabic Ensemble.

As our group has improved and expanded, we have added soprano recorder, voice, Orff instruments, and dance along with the *derbeke* drum. Arabic and Western folk songs performed in Arabic and English have allowed us to continue to bridge the two cultures. And the addition of these musical challenges has taken our students' musical skills to an even higher level. The students create all of the accompaniments for the selections, which continues to hone their compositional skills. Our group is very mobile and can easily perform in concert halls, at festivals, and at outside venues with little equipment transported and minimal setup time required.

Families have begun encouraging their children to participate in the school ensemble and now increasingly support the extra time students spend in rehearsal and at performance. Parents, siblings, grandparents, aunts, uncles—families teach one another the patterns, recorder parts, and dances. Many parents have purchased recorders so that they can play the folk songs along with their children. Several families have had multiple children perform in the ensemble, with their older children returning to the elementary school to play for and teach the younger children. Over the years, many of the first students, now in high school and college, return to perform for me and to view the photos that fill my room. Occasionally we have an after-school drum session where we share our talents with one another, get back in touch, teach the younger children present, and reminisce about the fun times and days now past.

The Arabic Music Ensemble, like all music ensembles, builds self-esteem, creativity, listening habits, concentration, problem solving, motor skills, critical judgment, music appreciation, performance expertise, self-discipline, and social facility. These skills are essential as students face the world of tomorrow. And the music they create also provides a vital outlet for their emotional, intellectual, creative, and social expression.

Looking back, it is clear that the drumming ensemble has positively influenced our students, school, and community. Fostering cultural pride has built a bridge between our two musical communities. Our welcoming elements of the Arabic musical experience into the music classroom has made community members much more open to the instruction their children receive there. A foundation of trust has been established between our communities. Parents are thrilled with the creativity and enthusiasm that brims over as their children carry into the classroom their own ideas, patterns, musical motives and then work to develop them together, adding musical elements of form, dynamics, call-and-response style, introductions, interludes, codas, and more.

As we look back on the relationship our music department has built with the community, we recognize now that the critical step was our recognizing the rich musical heritage within the Arabic culture, working to learn more about Arabic musical expression, and then incorporating elements of that music into our daily instruction. The journey is not over. Our staff has much more to learn, our curriculum must be further adapted, and there is much more to share with the community about the role music education plays in the overall educational experience of our students. We've just begun to pave the paths between our two communities. Now our job is to make sure that they are well traveled and maintained.

13

Steel Drums in a Middle School Setting

Barbara J. Resch

ABSTRACT

Originally conceived as an after-school activity designed to engage at-risk students and develop a unique identity in a struggling urban school, the steel drum band at Kekionga Middle School has evolved over its ten-year history to include standards-based curricular and extracurricular classes for beginning and advanced players. Students are attracted by the distinctive sound of the pans, the repertoire of calypso and pop music, and the energetic playing style, as well as the opportunity to perform and travel with the group. Membership is contingent on maintaining good grades, attendance, and work ethic, in addition to musical skill and achievement. Participation in the ensemble motivates students to meet both musical and extramusical goals.

INTRODUCTION

Kekionga Middle School houses 536 sixth-, seventh-, and eighth-grade students in a single-story brick building constructed in the 1960s. One of eleven middle schools in the Fort Wayne, Indiana, school corporation, KMS is located on the outskirts of this mid-size city, in an area of low- to middle-income housing and industry. In 2008 and 2009, 84 percent of the student body qualified for free and reduced lunch. That same year, 41.7 percent of students passed the English and math portions of the state's standardized test, compared with the state average of 65 percent.

"Kekionga" was the capital of the Miami Indian tribe in this area and was an important trading post in the 1700s. The KMS sports teams are called the Warriors, and their mascot is an Indian chief in full headdress, but no students at Kekionga are classified as Native American. Forty-four percent of the student body is white, 33 percent black, 15 percent Hispanic, 7 percent multiracial, and 1 percent Asian. These demographics parallel the school district as a whole, in which 53 percent of the school population is white, 26 percent African American, and 12 percent Hispanic.

The music room at Kekionga Middle School looks like a typical middle school music room: a large rectangular carpeted room with chairs, music stands, instrument lockers, a row of guitars, posters of instruments and musicians, and a white board with musical notation scrawled on it, along with reminders to students about turning in forms. For much of the day the configuration of the room adapts to the requirements of beginning and advanced bands, choir, and general-music classes. As the last period of the day begins, however, students clear away the chairs and pull out of a storage area more than thirty bright-blue steel drums, plus a traditional drum set and other assorted percussion instruments. These seventeen seventh and eighth graders comprise the Kekionga Steel Drum Band, or, as their T-shirts proclaim in their own appellation, "Kekionga Steel Drumz." Overseeing the setup is their director, Mike Horan, a thirty-year veteran music teacher in his seventh year at the school.

Students quickly line up the steel drums, or *pans*, which is the preferred term for the instruments. Like orchestral instrument families, the steel drum family includes a range of sizes: leads, seconds, cellos, and basses. Kekionga's array of instruments includes five leads or tenors, with one student per pan; three sets of double-seconds, with each player responsible for both pans in the set; two sets of four cellos; and two sets of six basses. Other students are in charge of the "engine room"—the drum set, congas, bongos, and incidental percussion such as claves, brake drums, or shakers.

The location of each pitch is clearly indicated with marker or a vinyl sticker on the shiny surfaces of the pan heads. On some drums the pitches are laid out in an arrangement similar to the circle of fifths, and on others the arrangement necessitates alternating between drums. Most pans or sets of pans have a range of about two and a half octaves, and whether playing a melodic line or the "strumming" of chords that is characteristic of this music, the students' mallets move smoothly and accurately around the surface of the instrument. When a new piece is announced, all of the players move by predetermined assignment to different drums, seemingly at ease with each position in the ensemble.

Some of the music the ensemble plays reflects the instruments' origins on the islands of Trinidad and Tobago: reggae, calypso, and soca, a twentieth-century offshoot of calypso with a prominent percussion part. The group also plays American pop music that seems to have a connection to the Caribbean, such as "Margaritaville" and "Kokomo" (whose lyrics actually mention a steel drum band), and a diverse mix of other tunes, including arrangements of songs by Santana and the Ramones, the '80s hit song "Africa," and the group's professed favorite, "Wipeout." Mr. Horan points out that virtually any kind of music—classical, folk, oldies, hymns—can been arranged for and played on the steel drums effectively, but that this repertoire is one thing that draws students to the program.

The Kekionga steel band program includes two ensembles, named for the school colors of blue and gold. Most of the students in the room began as sixth graders who auditioned and were accepted into the Blue Group, the twenty-one-member beginner band that meets after school twice a week, and a year later were accepted into the Gold Group, which is a curricular offering meeting every day during the school day. Many more students audition than are chosen for the limited number of places in both the beginning and advanced bands.

The ensemble receives many invitations to perform; they did thirty-seven performances over the past school year and summer, including at nursing homes, arts festivals, street fairs, and elementary schools, and they recently played at the state music education conference. When an area high school chose a "tropical night" theme for its fall marching band show, the Kekionga pans played in the pit at all of the marching contests. Concerts often take place during the school day and necessitate loading up the drums and leaving school. The group also performs during the summer. Previous groups have traveled to steel pan conferences in Ohio and Illinois, have heard steel drum ensembles from around the world, and have met Dr. Ellie Mannette, considered by many to be the inventor of the steel drum.

Graduates of Kekionga Middle School go to one of several high schools, none of which has a steel drum program. Some students continue their musical involvement in a traditional ensemble like band or choir, and some play in their high school's drum line, but students have always gravitated back to the Kekionga steel drums. A group of high school students currently meets with Mr. Horan one night a week at the middle school. He arranges music for this group, but they are largely self-directed. A high school senior said, "This was something we all liked doing, and as high school students we have broader horizons and some of us thought we could do different things with the drums now." Some of them form duos or other small groups and play other gigs, using the Kekionga drums or drums they own themselves.

HISTORY

Fifteen years ago, steel drum bands did not exist in Fort Wayne Community Schools. There is no documentation that the corporation included students from the Caribbean islands who knew this music as part of their heritage, and no indication that the school system was searching for an alternative to the usual middle school music offerings of band, choir, strings, and general music. One former administrator called the discovery of steel drums "pure serendipity—a most fortunate accident!"

For a number of years, Fort Wayne had been operating a system of magnet schools on the elementary level. Parents from any part of the district could choose to send their children to one of the magnet schools that specialized in areas such as the arts, math and science, or Spanish. A Montessori magnet program had been implemented at Bunche Elementary School in 1990. The first public school Montessori program in the country to be accredited by the American Montessori Society, Bunche's program was highly respected and sought-after by parents from the entire district.

As children began to graduate from Bunche Montessori and move into traditional middle schools, some of these parents began to advocate for the establishment of a public middle school Montessori program. Discussion with the school corporation administration explored the possibility of housing a multigrade middle school Montessori program as a "school within a school" at Kekionga, which was in the same attendance area as Bunche. Thus during the 1997–1998 school year a group of involved parents, teachers, and administrators from Bunche and Kekionga traveled to Cincinnati to visit an example of the program they envisioned, a struggling public middle school in which a Montessori track existed within a traditional school. It happened that this school also had a highly developed steel drum ensemble that was featured in the welcome program presented for the visitors.

The members of the Fort Wayne group all describe this experience in similar terms. Each one reports being immediately struck by the sight of reportedly at-risk middle school students completely engaged in producing a beautiful sound on these unique instruments, and by the idea that this could be the link that would complete the relationship between Kekionga and a middle school Montessori program. The thought was that Montessori-trained children, who might not appreciate traditional music classes, would enjoy the eclectic and creative nature of this art form. At the same time, Kekionga's constituents saw the steel drum option as something that would bring the school's diverse neighborhood population together in a creative and integrative activity. Everyone agreed that the program would be an identity builder for the school that would set Kekionga apart in this era of school choice.

Transferring this excitement to the other stakeholders who had never seen or heard steel drums was the crucial next step. The Cincinnati steel pan group proved to be a valuable resource by coming to Fort Wayne to demonstrate the instruments to parents, students, and administrators, who were also enthralled by the sound and energy emanating from the band. The Cincinnati teachers also recommended Panyard, Inc., of Akron, Ohio, a young company with a growing reputation for making high-quality pans in the United States, as a good source for the instruments. The Panyard staff gave helpful advice about which drums to purchase, and soon a specific goal emerged: the set of thirty-one steel pans, and additional percussion, at a cost of about $30,000.

A member of the group that visited the Cincinnati school was the area administrator, who supervised nineteen of the Fort Wayne schools. She was able to convince other area principals to release funds for the drums, and money designated for the corporation's magnet programs was also diverted to this project. Kekionga's principal at the time had begun his career as a music teacher and was an enthusiastic proponent of the project from the beginning. The assistant principal enlisted the help of a parent with grant-writing experience and received small grants from area businesses and civic organizations. Other parents held fundraisers in the community. The area administrator describes these efforts as "a great time of bringing people together around a cause, a 'Kumbaya' kind of communal effort, the likes of which I have never seen again."

The steel pans were individually made and tuned at Panyard and were delivered as they were completed; by late October 2000 the full set had arrived. The Kekionga Pans, as they were known then, met twice a week after school. They were directed by the music teacher, who had played mallet percussion in college; he also hired a percussionist to assist with some teaching and to play drum set with the pans when necessary. Interest was high from the start, and soon thirty to fifty students were auditioning each year for the band, including a large number of students from the Montessori program, which had been implemented at Kekionga as originally hoped. The band soon became a well-established extracurricular activity with a beginner and advanced group of enthusiastic players.

IMPLEMENTATION

When Mike Horan was assigned to Kekionga in 2002, he had been a high school band director with no experience playing, teaching, or even listening to steel drums. The school owned very little printed music for the pans, so he began to take songs from the general music textbooks, teaching some students to play the melody and others to strum the chords, while at the same time immersing himself in traditional steel drum music by listening to CDs. Soon it became obvious to him that he would learn the drums best—their ranges and particular timbres and what sounded good on each one—by arranging music for them. The school purchased music-printing software, a scanner, and a keyboard, and he began to expand the groups' repertoire with his own arrangements.

Although an increasing amount of published music for different levels of steel pans is being published, Mike continues to arrange much of the ensembles' music. He buys guitar or piano books and rewrites the music for the steel drums or transcribes something he finds on a CD, an admittedly challenging and arduous process requiring permission from the copyright holder. He likes to be able to arrange specifically for the needs of his groups. After the initial period of learning to use the software program, he finds it a useful tool, especially the capability of playing back his arrangement with the sound of a steel drum ensemble.

A significant milestone for the steel drum program came in 2004 when the advanced group became a curricular instrumental music class with daily rehearsals during the school day. Mike made this request of the school administration because the group was outgrowing its role as an after-school extracurricular activity: it was performing a lot in the community and with limited rehearsal time was struggling to learn enough new music to meet those demands. To have the pans accepted as an official music class Mike had to submit a curriculum based on the state standards that also met criteria established by Fort Wayne Community Schools. The plan was approved, and while the beginners continued to practice after school, the Gold Group became the seventh-period music class, meeting every day for fifty minutes.

The audition for entrance into the program is a month-long process at the start of each school year. It begins with prospective members responding to a questionnaire that asks questions like these: (1) Why do you want to be in the Steel Drum Band? (2) Describe your ability to cooperate, listen, and work hard. (3) When we go out for concerts you are required to complete schoolwork and keep up with all homework. If at any time you fall behind academically, your teacher has the right to pull you from the group. . . . Explain how you will prevent such a problem from occurring.

During the audition period the students learn techniques and information that will be included in their final audition: two musical pieces and five scales played on two different pans, as well as a rhythmic call and response. Determination of acceptance into the beginner group is also based on attendance and a willing attitude toward playing. Persevering through the lengthy audition process is in itself a strong indication of a student's interest and dedication. Acceptance into the advanced group is an honor determined strictly on the basis of the teacher's recommendation, but by the end of a year in the Blue Group, Mike knows the students and their work well. He admits that he gives considerable weight to a student's work ethic and says he would rather have a group of hard-working students who want to play than a group of higher-achieving students who are not invested in the band.

These middle schoolers arrive from different elementary schools with different levels of music training. While acknowledging that it would be easy to teach them to play by rote, Mike is committed to developing the musical literacy of this group. As part of the learning process he lets the students write the note names in their music and has the note names written on the pan heads. The calypso and soca rhythms are difficult to read, but he works with the students on counting and trying to figure them out. He insists that the band members keep their scores out, even when they have learned the music from memory, so they become used to following a conductor's directions regarding the score.

He also makes sure that the players all know the history of the steel drums and how the drums are made, and will use the long bus trips to concerts as an opportunity to "tell the story" of the evolution of steel pans from their beginnings in Trinidad. The students report that they love the moments after a concert when people come up and tell them how good their performance was and ask them about the drums, and they are all ready to talk about the instruments.

Students are quick to point out that Mr. Horan has rules. Members of both the beginner and advanced group are expected to maintain a C average in their classes. At the end of each quarterly grading period they are required to show Mr. Horan their grades, and if the grade point average has fallen below a C the student is not allowed to rehearse or perform with the group. Referrals to the principal's office for disciplinary reasons are also monitored, and students who get more than two referrals during the school year are also dismissed from the group. Both parents and students support these rules. Parents whose child has been removed from the band because of grades have called to say that they understand and appreciate the fact that he holds the children to such a high standard. Students say, "He's strict because he wants to make us the best that we can be."

PRESENT-DAY OUTCOMES

Now, more than ten years after a few parents and administrators had the idea that a steel drum program would be a good thing for Kekionga, it is interesting to compare the original arguments for the program with the outcomes apparent today.

Many of the benefits projected by the initial steering group were what music educators consider extrinsic values. The letter accompanying grant applications stated, "Successful (steel drum bands) help to build student self-esteem, provide a 'hook' and a connection to school for at-risk students, provide opportunities for students to represent their school throughout the community, and provide an excellent arena for students of different ages, cultural backgrounds, and SES [socioeconomic Statue] to blend into a team that works together." And these goals have been met at Kekionga.

Students' conversations and demeanor all indicate their pride in being chosen for the ensemble, with all the benefits that come along with membership. Some say that their peers think the steel band is cool and are jealous that the musicians get out of school sometimes to perform.

There is no doubt that the GPA requirement to participate in the pan group is a powerful motivator. One girl spoke honestly and passionately about her love for the band: "It's seventh period, so from first period on, that's the only thing that's keeping me coming to school. I don't care about the rest of it. I just want to get good grades and I want to make it to that seventh period, so I'm doing my work in my other classes, and I'm thinking, *It's coming,* and I'm watching the clock all sixth period so I can get down here."

The steel drums have become part of the identity of Kekionga Middle School. The brochure distributed at the school corporation's annual School Choice Fair includes the information that Kekionga has the only middle school steel drum band in the state, and the band's many appearances in the community have reinforced that recognition. Performances at elementary schools are especially well received, and several band members remember first seeing and being attracted to the group as elementary students. Now when they go to elementary schools to play they say that they love seeing the reaction of the young students: "The little kids just start clapping and jumping up to see the drums. But you can understand why, because when I first heard it, I went, 'Wow—what's that beautiful noise?'"

It is also true that participating in the steel drum ensembles requires teamwork, both in an ensemble sense and in the reality of moving the drums in and out of the main part of the music room each day. When the program started, the music room was on the second floor, and the process of moving all of the drums down the stairs and into a truck took over an hour. In 2006 the Montessori program left Kekionga to become part of a newly formed Montessori school for grades 1 through 8, and the music program took over the former Montessori classroom, a large, sunny room on the ground floor, with a direct entrance to the parking lot. Even under these circumstances, taking the steel drums out to a concert is an effort requiring the help of every member.

The hoped-for academic and social outcomes identified by the original advocates of the program have not been formally assessed. Anecdotal evidence suggests that at least some of the students are motivated to achieve academically so they can stay in the group, and others recognize the teamwork and cooperation needed to make the group viable. Nearly every student who currently plays in the Gold Group spoke of being connected to this ensemble and its goals and of wanting it to continue for others. One girl said, "Whatever I do in my career, I'll probably start a steel drum group in a school, just be a volunteer after school. I don't know if there are other teachers like Mr. Horan out there, but I would want my kids to do something fun like this."

Kekionga continues to offer the traditional middle school ensembles of beginner band, advanced band, and choir, and some steel drum students also perform in other ensembles. But there are several reasons why the pans may be more attractive than the other ensembles. One explanation is financial: students participate in the steel drum ensembles at almost no cost. Once the drums were purchased, they require only an annual tune-up by a professional tuner. Unlike the traditional band, this ensemble does not require students to purchase or rent an instrument, which is an important consideration in this community. Several students mention this availability as being crucial to their participation in the group.

The area administrator who rallied support for this effort at the outset recalls her own experience as a child in the 1950s whose mother could not afford the $2.75 to purchase a recorder and who was thus barred from recorder class. Since recorder proficiency was considered an indicator of potential success with school band or orchestra instruments, those further possibilities were also eliminated for her. She cites this experience as an important motivator in her efforts to make this ensemble available to all children.

The sound of the instruments themselves is another draw. From the first experimental efforts, the player makes a nice sound—which is not true of a beginning clarinet or trumpet player. The timbre of the instruments is unique, mellow and rich, and varied enough to do justice to the driving energy of "Wipeout" and the peaceful "Africa."

Another incentive to playing steel drums is the repertoire. The students describe the music they play as cool, catchy, and fun. Some say that they like playing songs they have heard before, like Beach Boys songs, which does not happen in band: "In band we play 'band songs.'" They also like learning something new. One said, "I like the difficult songs because it's funner. You're not just playing a pattern—you're playing all these different notes that are flowing together, and it's hard. I love challenges."

While he continues to teach the other ensembles at Kekionga, Mike reflects that the steel drum band has revitalized him as a teacher. He too talks about "band songs." The beginner and advanced bands are not large and have limited instrumentation, so over the years he tends to use the same pieces that work with small instrumentation. He admits that even teachers get bored if they do the same thing year after year. Learning the instruments and arranging the music have been a healthy challenge for him as well as for the students.

One of the parents who first saw the steel drums in Cincinnati observed that the large muscle skills needed to play the drums would be more accessible than the finer motor coordination of traditional band instruments. An administrator agreed, speculating that this kind of movement would be developmentally appropriate for adolescents. It is true that the players move much more than their seated counterparts in the traditional band or orchestra, especially the ones playing the set of four cello or six bass pans, who stand surrounded by a circle of drums and constantly pivot as they play. Factor in the students' natural physical reaction to playing lively and rhythmic music, and some of the players are almost dancing as they play. One described the kinesthetic learning process this way: "The technique is fun. Your muscles learn where the notes are: it's like a routine. One day they just go, Aha! Now I get it."

At the outset, some parents thought that playing the steel pans would be "a fast learn," that the students would not have to read music and would have the satisfaction of presenting a finished product in a short time. Mr. Horan acknowledges that it would be possible, even easier, to teach his students by rote, the way steel drum is learned in its natural environment as a Trinidadian folk instrument. He has chosen to approach this nontraditional ensemble in a fairly traditional way that addresses local, state, and national standards: the students learn to read music as they learn to play the instruments; they listen to, analyze, and describe it; they learn the relationship of this music to history and culture; and the high school students are following Mr. Horan's lead in arranging music for their own purposes.

THE KEKIONGA MODEL

The steel drum program at Kekionga, as successful as its outcomes have been, was not an initiative emerging from the domain of music education. The school was not actively seeking an alternative to its existing music program based on the needs or interests of its students; it stumbled upon this option while looking for support for another curricular model. The idea was put forward by parents and administrators, not music teachers. The original goals for the program were primarily social and focused specifically on the extrinsic values of music education. No training was provided for the music teachers, each of whom found his own way to teach the drums and to provide appropriate music. The positive music education outcomes came after the program was redesigned. Therefore this school's approach to implementation may not be the most efficient model for teachers seeking an alternative approach to music education.

Since the Kekionga project was instigated, MENC: The National Association for Music Education, in collaboration with Rowman and

Littlefield Education, published Chris Tanner's *Steel Band Game Plan: Strategies for Starting, Building, and Maintaining Your Pan Program* (2006). Teachers who are considering introducing pans into their music curriculum will find this book to be an invaluable resource that covers everything the title indicates: buying the instruments, basic playing technique, rehearsals, repertoire, and ideas for further reading and listening—all the aspects that Mike Horan and his predecessors investigated and discovered on their own.

Whether the alternative approach is carefully planned with goals and objectives or evolves in a serendipitous fashion like Kekionga's Steel Drumz, the retooling of the traditionally trained teacher is crucial. Immersing himself in the new musical language and the way the instruments express that language was a significant factor in the evolution of this teacher's professional growth. Although he was trained and licensed in traditional instrumental and choral music K–12, Mike initially spent months listening to pan music, talking to instrument makers, and figuring out how to arrange for the pans in his efforts to understand and teach the instruments, their music, and their culture. Teachers who find themselves in this position should see the MENC Copyright Center (www.menc.org/resources/view/copyrigh-center) for issues relating to arranging, transcribing, and performing copyrighted music.

Mike's professional development continues: he recently applied for and received a Teacher Creativity Fellowship Grant from a major philanthropic foundation that will allow him to go to Trinidad during the summer to study the folk music of the island and to learn how to tune the steel pans himself. Conceived as an extracurricular option for at-risk students, this ensemble is remarkable in the way it has expanded the musical and creative horizons of the teacher as well as the students.

REFERENCE

Tanner, C. 2006. *The steel band game plan: Strategies for starting, building, and maintaining your pan program.* Lanham, Md.: MENC / Rowman & Littlefield Education.

14

Talkin' Turkey: Incorporating Music from Turkey in the Elementary General Music Class

Christopher Roberts

ABSTRACT

This project describes an eight-lesson unit for elementary students on music from Turkey. In selecting repertoire that would provide "hooks" for the fifth-grade children who participated, musical material was chosen from the folk and classical Turkish traditions that had some or all of the following characteristics: repetition, timbral contrast, faster tempi, thinner textures, and minimal words. Lesson plans built on performing skills (e.g., drumming, singing, and xylophone playing) and music literacy skills (solfège, rhythm syllables, and meter) that the students already possessed. Although the repertoire was completely new to the children, the lessons structurally resembled previous experiences in music class, in that the thirty-minute classes contained four to six different musical experiences and included a wide range of objectives. Generally, the students had deeper, active experiences with individual pieces, interacting with them in a variety of ways over multiple classes, but fewer pieces with which to engage. Other cultural experiences, such as folktales, riddles, and visual representations of Turkish culture, were included in the design. Challenges included finding repertoire appropriate for children and concerns surrounding altering instrumentation from Turkish instruments to common classroom instruments such as xylophones.

INTRODUCTION

"The music of Turkey? Are you kidding me?"

That was my first response when I was asked to be part of a team to create and implement an eight-class unit on Turkish music for elementary school children. This unit would be part of a study on the effect of an intensive curriculum on children's musical enculturation. As an elementary music teacher, my experience with music of Turkey was limited to "Five Fat Turkeys" and "Turkey in the Straw"—not exactly what this study had in mind. Clearly, I did not feel I was the best teacher for such a project.

Previously, I had been asked to integrate content with homeroom teachers. For example, sixth graders in my school spent two months studying China and two months studying southern Africa. While I brought in some examples of music from specific cultures when asked, it generally led to what I felt was a surface-level understanding, both for my students and me. Becoming a part of his project would allow me to explore an unfamiliar musical culture a little more deeply, so I decided to give it a go. My experience with the unit, both in planning the lessons and teaching them to my fifth-grade students, raised valuable questions (and some suggestions) concerning the ways to teach novel musics to children successfully.

Four central questions emerged as the project unfolded:

1. As a teacher unfamiliar with the music of Turkey, how could I learn enough about the music and the culture to be able to present it adequately to my fifth graders?
2. Assuming I was able to learn about Turkish music, how could I design and teach the unit in such a way that the students learned some of its characteristics while also continuing with my curricular goals?
3. How much should the students employ non-Turkish instruments when trying to replicate the music they were hearing? Doing so would engage the students in active music making but would sometimes make for a radically different sound.
4. How would the unit-based approach work for my students? My students had a fair amount of experience with music of unfamiliar cultures, but they had never spent two months completely immersed in it. Previously, I had used a "drive-by approach" to world music, with songs from throughout the world sprinkled through lessons that generally focused on folk repertoire of the European American and African American traditions. As fifth

graders heading toward the common preteen "attitude," I felt that it was important that they find the experience enjoyable as well as educational.

THE MUSIC AND ME

What is the music of Turkey? This was problem number one my collaborator and I faced when beginning the planning part of the experience.[1] As a Western-educated musician and music educator, my experience had been primarily in marching bands and wind ensembles, and choirs and children's singing games. I had experience with world music, but generally that had been through broad, survey-type classes as an undergraduate. But Turkish music seemed awfully specific, and learning it appeared daunting, if not altogether frightening. As most teachers know, the best place to start is to simply dive in. Thus I began to attempt to build a basic understanding of the music.

In order to do this, my collaborator and I embarked along a self-designed learning odyssey. We read a few broad surveys about different types of Turkish music, such as *Grove's Dictionary of Music* and other basic resources. By far, though, the most important aspect of our growth was to listen, listen, listen. Our first listening stop was Smithsonian Folkways (www.folkways.si.edu). This website is a treasure trove of music from myriad cultures, and it is easy to sort the music through characteristics like country and culture group. Music found on the website is easily downloadable and is accompanied by renowned liner notes from the original albums, some of which were produced decades ago and are difficult to find in other sources. Being able to sit in my house, coffee at my side, and listen to short samples of music before deciding whether to buy the recordings was instrumental in developing a sense of the types or styles of music that would be appropriate to our project.

However, online resources only provided a limited amount of musical material. Libraries were also key to the learning process. As a student at the University of Washington, I had access to their listening library, and I spent many hours poring over their resources, trying to get these sonic experiences "in my ears." My local public library system also had a surprisingly varied collection of music from Turkey, so I checked out as much as I could. Listening while in the car on longer drives was essential for immersing myself in Turkish music. On my way to work? Pop in a CD. Cooking dinner in the evening? More listening time. Even a slowdown in traffic, a constant issue in the greater

Seattle area where I live, became less of a burden and more of an opportunity. The more I listened, the more the music began to seep into my understanding, becoming a part of my being in a way that never would have happened had I simply downloaded a few lesson plans.

After much listening, it became clear that "Music of Turkey" was a *very* large subject. The idea that trying to teach our children about all the different facets of Turkish music began to feel like an infomercial ("You Too Can Learn *All* about Turkish Music in Eight Easy Lessons! Call Now for This Once-in-a-Lifetime Offer!"). Therefore, we limited ourselves to two genres: Turkish classical music and Turkish folk music. The classical genre was appropriate because the study we were involved in as graduate students used it to assess musical enculturation. Folk music from around the world was a staple of our classes, so it appeared to be a logical choice.

Even though confining ourselves to these genres limited the scope of our project, it still appeared impossible to teach the students all about Turkish classical and folk music in the brief time we had. We began to reconceptualize our unit as Music *from* Turkey, rather then Music *of* Turkey. That is, we needed to own the fact that we couldn't teach our students all about the many facets of Turkish classical and folk music—for that, we would need years and years, which our curricula wouldn't allow. Instead, we needed to choose pieces of music that our students would connect to, as well as identify the ways that this music highlighted specific aspects of the genre.

Gradually, my listening moved from an individual immersive experience into one that incorporated more critical and specific issues, such as, How can we get our students interested in this music in order to learn the most significant information about it? I had spent over forty hours listening, but our immersive curriculum would only have four hours of contact time. What types of music would work for our students?

THE MUSIC AND OUR STUDENTS

Repetition

First, we wanted the music to have recurring elements. Since the overall musical context would be unfamiliar, repetition within each musical excerpt would allow us to focus the children's attention on specific aspects of the music. If the students engaged in four or five minutes of uninterrupted listening with no repetitive elements, it was hard to imagine how they would remain engaged. Recurring melodic motifs, rhythmic patterns, and instrumental splashes of sound were aspects of the musical examples around which we were able to design our lessons.

Faster and Consistent Tempi

As elementary music educators, we have found that our students appear to prefer faster-paced music, and research has supported this view (LeBlanc and Cote 1983). Using music with quicker tempi would be more likely to head off the age-old (and devastating) critique from upper-elementary students: "This is so *boring.*" In addition, we found that much of the Turkish classical music we had identified was metrically free, making some of the basic tasks that we sometimes start a lesson with—such as "show me the beat"—impossible. So we chose examples of Turkish classical music that had more consistent tempi.

Different Timbres

Playing and listening to instruments have been found to be favorite activities of many elementary students (Bowles 1998), and our students were no exception. We definitely wanted our activities to involve instruments, and we searched for recordings that had a variety of instrumental timbres on the same recording. For example, we found a recording of "Ucayak, Halay," a folk song that used a single-headed goblet drum, called a *darabuka*, and a twelve-stringed instrument that resembles a banjo, called a *cŭmbŭs*. The sounds were distinctive enough that the students could clearly identify the differences and then discuss the ways in which the performers might create these sounds.

Thin Textures

In the piece with the darabuka and the cŭmbŭs, not only were the sounds distinctive, but also there were only two instruments. Asking our students to discriminate between different timbres while listening to a large ensemble with five or eight different instruments would have proved much more challenging. A piece with a simpler texture was more likely to produce positive results.

Performability

We knew that listening needed to be the basis of our lessons. However, for my fifth graders, simply listening and describing would lead to "zoned-out students," no matter how well-planned the questions were. So we looked for music in which the students would be able to engage in active music-making experiences, either playing along with a recording or replicating part of it. This proved to be challenging, as the performers on many of the pieces had been studying their instrument for years and had the virtuosity that was difficult to reproduce. Many recordings we considered were rejected due to the high level of skill required, but we found ways to make some recordings more accessible. For example, in "Ucayak, Halay," the students could not learn the part of the cûmbûs but could learn a basic drum pattern of Turkey that accompanied the stringed instrument.

Songs with Minimal Text

For both of us, singing is an essential part of our curricula. Thus, while we wanted to use instrumental pieces, we also wanted our students to continue singing for, at least, part of every class. Learning the words to songs in unfamiliar languages can be very time-intensive, and so to minimize that time, we looked for songs that had as few words as possible. We wanted the students to sing but did not want to spend a significant portion of every class echoing foreign-language words.

Cultural Relevance

We looked for musical examples that had some sort of relevant cultural information that would draw the students in. Ideally, we wanted music from children's culture—children's songs, children's singing games, and so on—but these were surprisingly difficult to find. However, when possible, we found other ways to connect. For example, in "Ucayak, Halay," the performers were a father and his teenage son. We felt that talking about the son would be a way to give our students a nonmusical hook to keep them engaged. This did not work for all the musical examples we chose, but we did it when possible.

THE LESSONS

As we began planning lessons for our fifth graders, we faced an overarching tension between listening and more-active forms of music making. In order to learn an unfamiliar song, we felt that the lessons had to be rooted in the sounds of actual culture-bearers making music as much as possible. If I were to stand in front of the class, teaching the students a Turkish drum pattern while accompanying them on my Appalachian lap dulcimer, it would not immerse them in a foreign musical culture—it would immerse them in my version of it, an interpretation that would necessarily be restricted by my limited skills. Providing the students with numerous opportunities to hear the music from people who lived and breathed the musical culture was essential. However, as we felt that our students learned best by being actively engaged, listening to recordings, uninterrupted, for thirty minutes would lose the students' attention. How could we design lessons that were listening-based while still remaining active?

Ideally, we would have liked for the students to "learn like a local," by being surrounded by the music, experiencing much like we did—in their cars, at their soccer games, while going out to a restaurant with their families. We faced the reality of eight thirty-minute classes, so we felt that we had to carefully prepare each lesson in order to maximize the available learning time.

In order to connect to the students' previous experiences, we decided that the lessons would be as similar in format as possible, so that the only major change would be the repertoire selected for each lesson. The lessons prepared for each thirty-minute class meeting had *short, varied activities*, with typically five to seven lesson segments each. We have found that our students do not typically focus terribly well for more than five to eight minutes at a time, and varying the segments helps maintain that attention span. We also tried to allow movement in the middle of every class, usually in the form of a folk dance. Movement activities are, first and foremost, fun for most students and have the side benefit of giving their brains "rest time" so that they can focus on what might be more mentally challenging activities later in the class period.

The short lesson segments within the larger thirty-minute lesson had a *variety of objectives*, including singing, moving, playing instruments, active listening, and dancing. Not only are these important skills in the music classroom, but the variety of activity goals also allowed us to differentiate instruction. For example, a student who is good at notating rhythms might not be as successful in dancing or playing a xylophone, and vice versa. We wanted to both improve the skills of our students in these different areas while also ensuring that all students felt successful in some portion of every class.

We *related lesson segments to previous knowledge and skills*. In our Kodály-inspired music classrooms, the students had developed performing skills in singing, xylophone playing, and drumming. They also held music literacy skills, using solfège, rhythm syllables, and Western meter markings. It was important to continue our work in these areas, both in order to stay with the curriculum and because we felt it would lead to more effective and efficient learning. For example, we could have chosen to use the guitar to teach elements of playing the cümbüs, the banjo-like instrument mentioned above, but since our classes had not explored plucked string instruments like the guitar, the entire unit might have felt disjointed and separate from the rest of our curriculum. By connecting the classes to skills and knowledge bases the students already held, their understanding of Turkish music would be integrated more seamlessly with their previous knowledge.

We built on students' previous skills and knowledge by focusing on *incremental learning*, breaking down the learning into as many small steps as possible. For example, with "Ucayak, Halay," we first played a recording of the piece of music, with focused questions about the timbral qualities of the two instruments. After viewing pictures of the instruments, the students listened for the different sounds of the drum, identifying them as low and high. The teacher informed them of the names—*dum* and *tek*—and then the students experimented with body percussion, trying to replicate the sounds. After the students approximated the two sounds, we demonstrated a common rhythmic pattern in Turkey, which the students played on their bodies, first without the recording, then while the music was played. Then the students transferred the pattern to hand drums and finally added their own improvisation.

The lessons included *multiple experiences with fewer pieces of music*, rather than fewer experiences with more musical examples. That is, we emphasized depth over breadth. We felt that it was more important for students to actively engage with the music many times, over many days, rather than listen a few times to more musical material. For example, the "Ucayak, Halay" activity above was stretched over four or five classes. While a broader array of selections could have potentially exposed the students to a wider range of musical traditions, we felt that they would have engaged with the material in a much more superficial fashion.

Since we wanted the students to hear the music but did not want them sitting passively for long periods of time, we used *short musical excerpts*. Each segment of the lesson was between five and eight minutes long, so in order for the students to hear the music and actively engage with it (e.g., play a drum while listening, etc.), each example was not more than one- to one-and-a-half minutes long. Carefully choosing and editing our short musical segments was essential.

Finally, we briefly *integrated other cultural experiences*, such as folktales, riddles, and visual representations of culture. Music was definitely the main focus of the unit, but showing the students pictures of children in Turkey and sharing short riddles at the end of class was a way of providing the students with a broader range of cultural experiences.

CONCLUSION

To return to my original questions, there were a number of issues that arose.

1. How would I learn about Turkish music? The constant listening ultimately proved to be essential in my learning process, by far the most important aspect. I thought that reading about music would be important as well, but it did not have as much impact as I expected when I started the process. I do not consider myself an expert on the music of Turkey, but I feel like my knowledge base grew immensely over the course of the project. It is worth noting that this was a very time-intensive process for me. I spent many hours listening, all of which were beneficial. Even listening to music that was ultimately not included in the unit deepened my understanding of the musical culture and was worth the time spent. It is also worth noting that the listening activities were usually fun—immersing myself in a novel music, gradually improving my understanding of it, was deeply satisfying.

2. What would prove to be an effective curriculum design? Given that my students were not used to intensive forays into one musical culture, I think it was important to use the same lesson-plan structure with which they were familiar. The focus on multiple objectives, including performing skills (drumming, singing, and playing xylophones) and music literacy skills (solfège, rhythm syllables, and meter), kept the students actively engaged and generally enthusiastic. Similarly, the musical characteristics we identified (repetition, timbral contrast, faster tempi, thinner textures, and minimal text) seemed to lead to positive attitudes about the curriculum.

3. How out of context should we go? At one point, the students listened to a piece of music played on the Turkish ud, a plucked string instrument, and then transcribed it. The students did not have skills to play it on a stringed instrument but did have enough facility with xylophones to be able to reproduce the notes relatively accurately. Performing the piece on the xylophones produced a much different sonic experience than the ud, one that

sounded decidedly un-Turkish. Was it worth it? Ultimately, we decided that the students' successful and active music-making experience outweighed the significant change in instrumentation, but this decision was not made without reservations.

4. Would the unit-based approach work? An "alternative" approach to music education is only alternative in the eye of the beholder. In my elementary school music classes, I had not included intensive investigations into unfamiliar musics. Indeed, other than a recorder unit in fourth grade, my classes had been distinctly unit-free. For my students, this was definitely a new experience, one not altogether comfortable. Focusing on music from Turkey in such an in-depth fashion allowed for deeper experiences with Turkish music, but student attitudes, while not negative, were perhaps not as enthusiastic as they might have been had the activities been sprinkled in throughout the year. A trade-off was made.

In review, I had to ask myself, Would I do it again? Yes! As a musician and a teacher, I grew immensely through my involvement in this project. Exploring an unfamiliar musical culture, and becoming skillful and knowledgeable enough to teach it to my students, was an immensely satisfying experience. More importantly, I feel that my students learned a great deal through the unit, both about music from Turkey and also about the discipline of music itself. It allowed me to highlight the ways in which basic musical concepts exist across musical cultures, an important message in our rapidly globalizing world.

NOTE

1. Sarah Bartolome, a fellow graduate student and elementary music educator, was instrumental in the creation of this curriculum. Without her, this project would not have occurred.

REFERENCES

Bowles, C. L. 1998. Music activity preferences of elementary students. *Journal of Research in Music Education* 46:193–207.
LeBlanc, A., and R. Cote. 1983. Effects of tempo and performing medium on children's music preference. *Journal of Research in Music Education* 31:57–66.

15

Enhancing the Instrumental Music Program with Creativity

Nancy Beitler and Linda Thornton

ABSTRACT

Creativity is integral in the middle school instrumental classroom of veteran teacher Nancy Beitler. Among the varied activities, from traditional to alternative, this band and strings program incorporates student-centered musical creativity, including arranging, improvisation, and composition. With the goal of developing well-rounded musicians, this program allows students to experience skills and concepts in various creative contexts alongside performance to build deeper musical understandings.

INTRODUCTION

A visitor to Nancy Beitler's middle school instrumental classroom will, over several days, see students making music in a variety of ways. Ensemble rehearsals and small-group lessons are complimented with independent, student-run ensembles, students improvising and composing for their instruments, and traditional chamber groups. From sixth through eighth grade, Nancy's students create the music they play while developing skills in re-creating music written by others.

The creative activities do not drive the instrumental program, but Nancy's instrumental program represents quality traditional bands and orchestras enhanced by well-planned and consistent opportunities for students to be creative and develop a musical voice.

Instrumental programs have long-standing traditions and are often comprised of multiple ensembles. An instrumental teacher needs to conduct the jazz band, the marching band, the concert band, pit ensembles, basketball bands, and often chamber or select groups, such as a flute or percussion ensemble. It can be hard for an instrumental teacher to imagine adding more to his or her program. However, creating well-rounded and thoughtful musicians often involves more than a variety of ensembles. Can graduates of an instrumental program make music alone, or with a few friends? Are they prepared to be independent music makers as well as thoughtful ensemble members? Are they able to express their own ideas through their instrument as well as the ideas of others?

NANCY'S PROGRAM

My instrumental program has a well-defined curriculum that follows a sequential progression through performance techniques and skills based on the National Standards for Arts Education. My students perform traditional concerts and actively participate in state festivals. They read music very well, and meet or exceed performance standards of traditional instrumental programs.

My program is unique for two reasons. First, I not only have but follow a clearly defined curriculum for my students. I carefully sequence their learning of performance skills and interpretation. Second, I believe that every music educator—instrumental, choral, and general—should be meeting every National Standard. Standards 3 and 4 involve composing and improvising; therefore all my students compose and improvise. In addition, my students work independently in chamber groups once a month in lessons. They create their groups and write music or find music they like to play.

I believe this program makes the students better performers. They think like musicians and composers. They are concerned with interpretation. They understand intention in a piece of music. It is not uncommon for a student in my band or orchestra to raise his or her hand in rehearsal and ask to change the way a phrase or section of a piece is marked. Eavesdropping on my students one day, a math teacher commented, "I can't believe how they talk like musicians!" meaning they use appropriate vocabulary and terms.

CONTEXT

There is no reason to think anything unusual would occur in Nancy's school regarding the music program. It is in a smallish, suburban, middle-class, white-collar school district. One would expect there would be active band and orchestra programs. One would expect high achievement and supportive parents in all aspects of the school. The band program consists of small-group lessons for all students, a sixth-grade band, a seventh-through-eighth-grade band, and a jazz band. The orchestra students participate in small-group lessons, string orchestra ensemble, and a fiddle group. The ensembles have always done very well in festivals and competitions.

Despite a successful traditional program, Nancy had an important realization about her role in the musical development of her students.

> The desire to infuse my curriculum with creative activities came from my personal sense of doing right by my students. If I had not started doing this, I would have exploded. Because I suddenly discovered what I was missing out on personally—missing out on half of the piece of being a musician. It almost made me angry when I realized how crippled I was. The whole idea [of improvisation and composition] scared the living daylights out of me. I watched young general music students have such joy creating music, and I realized I couldn't do it. I resolved that I was going to get past this. I felt a piece of me was missing. And then when I got past it enough to realize I could do it, I realized I couldn't teach my students without giving them the same opportunity. (Beitler 2009)

Nancy realized she had been passing on a tradition of teaching how one was taught, but in her case she knew more was needed. She wanted to break the cycle of teacher dependence and fear of mistakes and provide her students with lessons she herself learned much later in her musical life.

NANCY'S JOURNEY

Nancy began a journey toward being a creative musician and also helping her students to be creative musicians. Her first challenge involved dealing with her critical inner-voice regarding two aspects of her classroom: mistakes and control.

Like many collegiate-level trained musicians, Nancy believed mistakes were the enemy. Mistakes were something to be avoided if success was a goal. The point of practice was to eliminate mistakes and never let them occur again. However, through learning how to be a creative musician, Nancy realized mistakes are not always a problem. They are a natural part of experimentation and discovery. She found that allowing herself to make mistakes was eye-opening. She came to terms with making mistakes in her own improvisation and became less fearful of them. "Now I impress upon my students that even the word *mistake* is not a good thing to say" (Beitler 2009). She tells them to just say what you played was not what you *intended*. Sometimes you may label it a mistake—but sometimes it ends up being something you like.

Nancy's biggest challenge was letting go of the control in her classroom to make room for creative activities. Teachers may assume they must have all the control in order for the students to have the best experience and learn the most. Nancy has found exactly the opposite. The more she asks of the students, the more she asks them to contribute their thoughts and ideas, and the more she asks them to be involved in music creation, the more the students grow. With her prior more traditional teaching, she was not serving them; "I was getting in their way" (Beitler 2009).

FIRST STEPS

When I committed to this journey, I struggled with finding resources. I read books (Bailey 1992; Nachmanovitch 1990), took college courses in improvisation—both general and jazz—and attended workshops in using music technology to enhance the students' compositions. I found there was not much available regarding the pedagogy of improvisation and composition. Especially absent were resources for teaching instrumentalists, unless for jazz improvisation. I was influenced by aspects of Edwin E. Gordon's music-learning theory. I was able to speak with Daniel Deutsch, who teaches a full-fledged composition program in New York. I picked up what I could. But it was difficult.

I began to experiment on my own. I struggled with how to describe assignments, how to make an appropriate environment for creative expression, and eventually with assessment. However, as I began to hone my instruction, I saw the benefits for my students increase, and this reinforced my desire to provide these opportunities for my students.

I realized reflection was a very important aspect of the creative process. This allows students to reflect on their own improvisation and compositions and on each others' creative output. I needed to develop that environment. I developed a cycle that was critical to the safe kind of environment I was trying to establish. First the students would perform, and I would ask, "What did you hear?" The responses would have no value judgments, just what the students heard. Then I discovered the performance by the next student would have elements of what we were discussing, and we could continue our discussion—"*Now* what did you hear?" I found a constant cycle between the "audience" (the peers) and the performers. They would not discuss "the noise," or the nonintentional parts of what students played. We focused on the content.

The students seem to accept the creative activities as a normal part of being in band or orchestra. I may have some sixth graders hesitate—but only hesitate. On occasion I have a student who does not wish to improvise or share their compositions in front of other students. In those cases, I arrange for the student to play only for me. Eventually I have them invite a friend. In a short while, they are comfortable in the group with all the other students.

EXAMPLES

Creative activities are part of my regular rehearsal and lesson strategies. I use creative tasks to help teach performance music while also developing the generative skills needed for its performance. These tasks may become part of the everyday occurrences in the ensemble and lesson setting through development of short activities or involve a more extensive, long-term project that may take place over several weeks.

The short activities typically use only five to ten minutes of a period and permit the entire activity to be completed within one or two meetings. An opportunity to complement the skills and concepts being taught on any given day can be as simple as student-created warm-ups for a rehearsal or a closing activity for assessment. In this way you can complement each lesson or rehearsal with a creative element.

Once a year I have students compose a larger work that is set up more as a unit. They are given extended periods of time—several weeks—to produce this piece, culminating in a performance for their peers and sometimes the public. This larger project remains part of the performance and curricular experiences of the student.

STEPS FOR DESIGNING A CREATIVE ACTIVITY

Each planned activity includes some—or preferably all—of the following steps:

1. a simple *structure* containing a clear goal,
2. a *model* from the teacher or a skilled student,
3. time for student *exploration* (at times part of practice at home),
4. an opportunity for student *performance* or sharing,
5. and reflective *self-evaluation* as well as peer and teacher *evaluation* when appropriate.

STRUCTURE

When planning for a short activity, I find it crucial to identify a clear goal for the project. Structure provides comfort for the students and direction for the teacher. Conversely, too much structure can create an environment where the student is simply plugging in notes and subsequently loses a sense of meaning and expressiveness. Jackie Wiggins (1999, 33) encourages teachers to use "engaging parameters" that present one broad idea in order to "allow students to make their own decisions."

An example of an activity with well-defined structure follows:

- Arrange a given phrase (see figure 15.1) from "Shepherd's Hey"—a traditional English folk dance by adding articulation and expression symbols appropriate for the style of the piece.

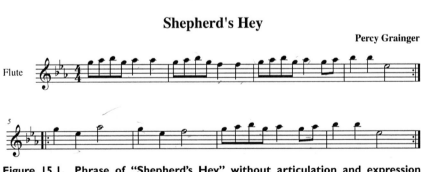

Figure 15.1. Phrase of "Shepherd's Hey" without articulation and expression symbols

- Keep in mind that you will perform the arrangement for your peers, so you must be able to play it.
- "Sheperd's Hey" is a tune John O'Reilly uses in his *Two English Dances* (1992)

MODEL

Teacher modeling helps the student draw a clear sound picture of the skill or concept presented. A model can be sung, chanted, or played on an instrument. No notation or detailed explanation of the patterns is needed. Warren Haston (2007, 27) describes this strategy as first establishing a steady beat and starting pitch, then initiating a "call-and-response session . . . and the students imitates." The imitation or echo at this point should be exact, not an improvised answer to the call.

A good model for the introduction and subsequent practice and application of 6/8 time in 2 follows:

- The teacher plays or sings various triple patterns in 6/8 on a single pitch, such as in figure 15.2.
- The student responds by playing the exact pattern back to the teacher within the established tempo without dropping a beat.
- Repeat the pattern until the student responds with an exact repetition of the original.

A model may also take the form of the analysis of a piece by one of the masters that exemplifies the style, form, or compositional techniques of the assignment, such as in preparation for composing two phrases: the students analyze phrases from various composers and styles, giving attention to tonality, melodic contour, rhythmic continuity, and cadential considerations. This includes discussion about how two phrases may work together to create a feeling of tension and release or question and answer—antecedent and consequent—called a *period*.

Patterns for modeling in 6/8

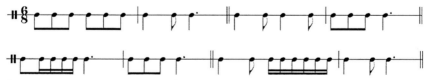

Figure 15.2. Patterns for modeling

EXPLORATION

exploration → start as an echo

The student's exploratory time will start as an echo of the teacher's model. With encouragement, the student will experience freedom to wander through original musical ideas and away from the teacher's modeled patterns. This is an important portion of the process, and students should be encouraged to develop and refine their own ideas. This may take place in school during the planned activity, or they may continue to explore sounds and patterns at home.

Sketch staff paper

For shorter activities, these explorations are generally not written down; however, if a student desires to repeat a created idea in a written composition, a staff-paper sketchbook is very helpful. Students need time to develop their ideas through playing and sketching motives for use in their larger works. Consequently, all my students have a music journal with blank staff paper they keep in their folder. Ongoing teacher feedback throughout the exploratory step is very important—words of encouragement and reassurance as well as refinement and enhancement go a long way in helping the student to identify their best writing.

A wonderful example of exploration for a short project occurred recently when my school received funds for an electric violin. This alternative instrument provided a perfect opportunity for improvised solos in one section of a concert piece. I presented the following pitches as a starting point for the students' improvised solos: G–A–B♭–B–C–D. After all the students played through the pitches, I modeled ideas, which they echoed. The students were given a week to explore their own ideas—applying rhythms and melodic motives from the concert piece. Through their own exploration they developed ideas beyond the

Improv Accompaniment

Figure 15.3. Improvisational accompaniment

presented pitches, working as far as their technique and confidence would take them.

The results were amazing. Each of the thirty string students shared a four-measure improvised phrase with their peers above the accompaniment shown in figure 15.3. This grew into a performance opportunity discussed in the next section.

PERFORMANCE

During the performance step, the students share some of their favorite patterns, ideas, and/or completed pieces with their peers. This is difficult at first. Establishing a criticism-free environment is crucial for students to feel at ease. All students are encouraged to share; however, I never force a student if he or she is not comfortable. I encourage excruciatingly shy students to play their piece for only me and eventually ask them to invite one or two additional friends to their private performances. Generally after a few weeks of repeated opportunities all students will play for their peers.

I also encourage my students to share their pieces in a more formal manner. When a student has worked extensively on revisions and completion of a full piece, the production of a recording to be shared with others or a formal presentation at a public performance is strongly recommended. This opportunity to perform their work not only provides incentive to complete their project, but it also gives the whole process a sense of purpose and meaning.

From the previously mentioned exploration came a wonderful performance opportunity. Some of my string students volunteered to expand their improvisational material to eight measures for presentation at our concert. Four students played their improvised solos on the electric violin. We also had an amplified cello solo and a piano (our student accompanist) solo during the concert selection. This was very well-received by the audience—a highlight of the concert.

EVALUATION

Reflective evaluation of their performance provides the student with the ability to identify the strong points of their piece. These reflections may be written in a journal or simply discussed with the class. By asking nonjudgmental questions such as "What did you hear?" "How did you create this?" or "What were the best portions or features of your piece?" students formulate verification for some or all of their work.

Peer and teacher evaluations need to take the same form. John Ginocchio (2003, 54) suggests that evaluation and discussion should "accentuate the positive. Every idea has merit." It is important for the student to identify the strong features in his or her work so that they can find confirmation for repeating those portions and understanding to revise the others.

Teacher feedback can have lasting influence on a student's growth as a creative musician. Our response needs to be more than an acknowledgment of their effort; it needs to take the role of facilitating the development of musically creative ideas. Sam Reese (2003) lists a continuum of teacher responses and presents examples of various types of responses. I found his article "Responding to Student Compositions" very helpful when providing feedback to my students' creative endeavors.

Also of value is the use of a rubric with written comments by the teacher. It can give the student a clear picture of the expectations for the piece. I caution teachers to include a category for originality and creative expression within their rubrics. Completing the technical and structural elements without attention to the use of imaginative ideas may turn the project into an exercise of fill in the blanks. Table 15.1 is an example of a rubric used for a project based on theme and variations.

CONCLUSION

Adding creative tasks to each day has had a profound effect on my students and their musical performances. Improvising and composing, along with modeling, provide additional opportunities to hone performance skills and musical concepts beyond performance music. By experiencing skills and concepts in various contexts, students are more apt to transfer them to a new musical context with more musical sensitivity.

In addition, as music students interact with their peers in a unique musical setting—the creative environment—they gain confidence not only in their music skills but also their creative-thinking skills. This may give them self-assurance to react creatively in other areas of their lives.

I sometimes question myself because no one else was doing this, it seems, in instrumental programs. Why is it just me? Because I use

Table 15.1. Assessment Rubric for Theme and Variation

Element	1	2	3	4	Score
Theme	less than 8 measures unfamiliar theme no dynamics no tempo marking	less than 8 measures familiar theme few or no dynamics no tempo marking	8 measures familiar theme few dynamics tempo marking	8 measures familiar theme effective dynamics appropriate tempo marking	
Variations	1 variation no recognizable compositional devices	1 variation 1 compositional device	2 variations difficult to distinguish between different compositional devices	2 distinct variations 2 distinct compositional devices	
Creativity	no original ideas no development of elements*	few original ideas no development of elements*	some original ideas explores at least one element*	original ideas explores at least 2 elements*	

(continued)

Table 15.1. (continued)

Element	1	2	3	4	Score
Notation	notation of theme is not accurate does not follow rules of notation difficult to read	notation of theme is fairly accurate bends rules of notation difficult to read	notation of theme is nearly accurate aware of rules of notation fairly easy to read	notation of familiar theme is accurate applies rules of notation easy to read	
Performance	fair performance of notated piece no application of markings	fair performance of notated piece difficulty executing markings	good performance of notated piece applies most of markings	near perfect performance of notated piece applies all markings and nuances	
Promptness	handed in late	handed in on time sloppy	handed in on time	handed in on time completed neatly	
Total					**/24**

*For example, range, timbre, dynamics, tempo, rhythm, or melody
Source: Adapted from M. Hickey. 1999. Assessment rubrics for music composition. *Music Educators Journal* 85 (4): 26–33, 52.

technology in my classroom to assist with the program, the school is supportive. They are supportive of the music program, but they are not very concerned with how I get there, as long as my students are producing great music. Ultimately, I do this because students receive an inimitable joy from creating music of their own, something that is new and original. These opportunities offer a sense of pride and accomplishment in their own creations.

REFERENCES

Bailey, D. 1992. *Improvisation: Its nature and practice in music.* New York: Da Capo.

Beitler, N. 2009. Interview by author. Kempton, Penn. January 28.

Ginocchio, J. 2003. Making composition work in your music program. *Music Educators Journal* 90 (1): 51–55.

Haston, W. 2007. Teacher modeling as an effective teaching tool. *Music Educators Journal* 93 (4): 26–30.

Hickey, M. 1999. Assessment rubrics for music composition. *Music Educators Journal* 85 (4): 26–33, 52.

Nachmanovitch, S. 1990. *Free play: Improvisation in life and art.* New York: J. P. Tarcher / Putnam.

O'Reilly, J. 1992. *Two English dances.* Van Nuys, Calif.: Alfred.

Reese, S. 2003. Responding to student compositions. In *Why and how to teach music composition: A new horizon for music education,* ed. M. Hickey, 211–32. Reston, Va.: MENC.

Wiggins, J. 1999. Teacher control and creativity. *Music Educators Journal* 85 (5): 30–35, 45.

Part 2

SCHOOL TO COMMUNITY AND HIGHER EDUCATION CASE STUDIES

16

O Passo (The Step): A Critical Pedagogy for Music Education from Brazil

Frank Abrahams

ABSTRACT

This chapter presents a music-teaching method from Brazil called *O Passo* (The Step). Developed by Lucas Ciavatta, the method connects to critical pedagogy for music education by providing the tools that empower children to be musicians. Grounded on the precept that musical experiences always engage the body, the method presents students with graphic, oral, and written notations, sight-singing using numbers, and group experiences in music making that include a specific type of movement or *step*. The music studied and performed is situated in the cultural context of the performers. The process bridges a gap between what children listen to and enjoy outside school and the musical content in the general music classroom. It is a catalyst for children to make autonomous musical decisions. American music teachers using *O Passo* in their classrooms report an enthusiasm on the part of their students and note the improvements in their musical skills and attitudes toward the general music class.

THE CONTEXT

The purpose of music education, as I teach my students, is to empower children to be musicians and, in the process, transform both the students and their teacher. By posing and solving problems and dialoguing and making music together, a deep understanding called *conscientization* emerges, where students and their teacher know that they know. This transformative state results in a broader perception of one's own reality and a wider view of one's relationship with the world (Abrahams 2005e). This approach, I call Critical Pedagogy for Music Education (Abrahams 2004).

One may define *critical pedagogy* as a postmodern teaching model that views teaching and learning as a conversation or dialogue among teachers and their students. It advocates a shift in the power structure of classrooms by acknowledging that students come to the class with information gleaned from their own life experiences. A goal of critical pedagogy is to use that knowledge as a bridge to new learning. In music classes informed by critical pedagogy, students learn to connect music they learn inside the classroom to their own unique conception of the world. This results in a change of perception or transformation for both the students and their teacher (Abrahams 2004). .

These ideas are not original. Paulo Freire introduced them in 1970 with the publication of his seminal work, *Pedagogy of the Oppressed*, where he argued against what he called a "banking concept" of education.[1] In this model, the teacher deposits information into the students' knowledge reservoir much like one deposits money into a bank account. Freire's subject domain was literacy. His goal was to teach the poor, oppressed adults in his native Brazil to read their language. To do this, he advocated a pedagogical approach that connected the words on the page to the world of the students. His teaching methods relied on dialogue or critical conversations where he engaged his students in posing and solving problems and connected the solutions they found together to the act of reading and writing Portuguese. His work, banned in Brazil during his own lifetime by an unsupportive dictatorship, has attracted international attention. *Pedagogy of the Oppressed* has been translated into nearly every language and is a text that is often assigned to students studying to be teachers.

McLaren (1998) writes, "Critical pedagogy is a way of thinking about, negotiating, and transforming the relationships among classroom teaching, the production of knowledge, the institutional structures of the school, and the social and material relations of the wider community, society, and nation-state" (45). In *O Passo* the focus is on developing the potential of both student and teacher. It expands possibilities by acknowledging the respective "worlds" of the students and their teachers, building on their strengths, and recognizing and assessing their needs.

In other words, critical pedagogy for music education enables teachers to create a rich and varied music program and encourages learning experiences that are multiple and liberating. Teachers play a key role in fostering such freedom since the choices of what to teach and how to teach it ultimately lie with individual teachers and their own particular students. They come to know each other best and collectively have the expertise to make thoughtful and informed decisions as to what is appropriate for themselves and their individual situations. Huff (1989) explains that teachers' actions and choices grow out of their socialization process and are shaped by interactions with fellow participants within the context of school. As reported by Rose (1990), results of his study showed that teachers are actively constructing their own perspectives.

The notion that Freire's conception of a critical pedagogy might be applied to music education in schools has been a research interest of mine for some time now and motivates this chapter (Abrahams 2007, 2005a, 2005b, 2005c, 2005d, 2005e, 2004; Abrahams and Schmidt 2006). The parallels are many. For example, if an outcome for students studying music education in schools is the ability to read and write notation—a language not familiar to them—then Freire has much to offer. Next, if students come to music classes with a view of music that is shaped by and limited to the popular music they hear outside of class, Freire's interest in broadening that view is applicable. Further, if all students have musical potential and, as a result of formal schooling, that potential remains underdeveloped, students may indeed be classified as oppressed.[2] Such a claim is made regardless of their economic or social status or regardless of the economics or social status of the community where they attend school. In such instances, Freire's pedagogy is applicable.

PURPOSE

In 2004, to further my studies of critical pedagogy and to explore the implications and applications for music education practice, I traveled to Brazil to see what instances of Freirian ideas and ideals were in evidence in music education programs there. My hope was to meet music teachers and other educators who were applying Freirian principles in

180   FRANK ABRAHAMS

their classrooms and to see if what I observed there might be applicable to music education in the United States and particularly to music education in urban settings. This chapter chronicles my introduction to a music teaching method called *O Passo* (The Step) developed by Lucas Ciavatta (2003) that embodies the goals and ideals of critical pedagogy for music education.

THE CASE

What follows is a description of a middle school music program I observed at a private school in a very pleasant neighborhood of Rio de Janeiro called Tijuca. This chapter is not an infomercial for *O Passo*. It does not advocate or promise a panacea for music education in American schools or guarantee its place in the school curriculum. It does not offer a DVD or a package of lesson plans to buy. There are no claims to make students smarter or to improve their scores on standardized tests. Instead, this chapter describes a music education method developed by a music teacher in Brazil to unlock the musician inside each of the students he teaches.

   Those who attended this particular school were sons and daughters of wealthy parents who believed that the school's constructivist mission would be appropriate for their children. The students, like their American counterparts, came to class chewing gum and eating food. While they did not wear uniforms, most wore tee shirts with the school logo, shorts, and sneakers. They all carried book bags that appeared to be quite full. I was told that a typical day for these students was from 7:30 AM to 6:30 PM and that classes were held Monday through Saturday. The music classroom was a rather large room with chairs, an old piano, and a few tables. There was a portable dry-marker board and storage for musical instruments and also for art supplies, as the room was used for visual arts as well. Large windows opened onto the school courtyard. Next to the classroom was the school library. For security, the school complex was gated and guarded.

   The music teacher, Lucas Ciavatta (his real name, used with permission), arrived on his motorcycle about one minute before the first class began. To teach, he wore a white T-shirt, black jeans, and sandals, and he spoke English moderately well. His assistant appeared to be a college student who worked with the groups and assisted with setting up the instruments.

   As in middle school classrooms everywhere, Lucas (teachers are called by their first names) checked notebooks to see that the students had the materials they needed and then led the class in singing a Bach chorale in four parts using scale-degree numbers in place of the German words. Instead of reading the chorale from traditional musical notation, students had sheets with a notational system designed by their teacher that consisted of numbers arranged in blocks. Lucas took his pitch from a tuning fork. The sopranos began, then basses were added, then tenors, then altos. The students sang without accompaniment, and the entire process, until Lucas was satisfied, took about a half hour. Later, Lucas told me that he found the student's rhythm to be better than their singing. I found that to be true as well. Nonetheless, I was impressed that the students were singing in four parts, something one would not see in American middle school general music classes.

Later in the class, students worked in small groups on exercises to drill tonal chordal progressions. The purpose, Lucas explained, was to familiarize the students with an aural vocabulary of Western tonality. Many students had keyboard skills, and in each class a student played chords on the piano to accompany their classmates who played drums and other percussion instruments.

During the middle portion of each lesson, students broke into groups to "study" (Lucas's word). This happened outside in the school yard. Lucas rotated from group to group to assist and to assess. Many worked through packets of worksheets with various rhythm challenges. Others worked on harmonic progressions. When they returned to the classroom Gabriel, the assistant, had several sets of native Brazilian drums arranged in a circle. There were large conga-type drums, surdos (bass drums), caixas (smaller tenor drums made of metal with skins stretched over them), and tamborims (hand drums). There were also pandeiros (tambourines) and agogô bells (two-bell instruments like cow-bells). The caixas were played with traditional drumsticks using both matched and traditional grips. The large surdos were played with wool mallets much like large tam-tam (gong) or tympani mallets. In the center of the circle was a set of orchestral bells that two students played. Students appeared to know what to do and what to play. Always, they played while stepping the pattern with their feet. Such stepping is a foundational component of the method Lucas developed and taught. Later, I learned that the students were drumming traditional Brazilian rhythms. Toward the end of the class Lucas introduced a samba rhythm. He said, "We play patterns that we imported, assimilated then transformed, and play them in complex arrangements. Often they are in five-bar phrases and in several meters" (personal correspondence).

After the classes, Lucas explained that what I had seen was a teaching method he developed called *O Passo* (The Step). It is his original approach to music education that integrates the body, several types of notation, group effort, and culture to affect what Brazilians call *musicalization*, the process by which students are empowered to be musicians. This is consistent with the goals of critical pedagogy for music education. Several principles provide the foundational concepts of *O Passo*. They are presented here as translations that paraphrase the Portuguese writings by Ciavatta.[3]

1. *The body is a means to not only make music but to understand it.* Whenever students make music, their bodies move. Whether they are singing or playing musical instruments their bodies are engaged. Often, the engagement is involuntary. At other times the movements are planned. In either instance, the connection of the body to the music informs the performance. Lucas contends that the body is an autonomous repository for the construction of musical knowledge. He writes that it is the body itself that learns independent of intellectual schema.

2. *The ability to represent musical ideas through notation is a tool toward musical independence.* Teachers of *O Passo* advocate three types of notation. For example, a guitarist shows the chords through a particular hand position on the neck of the instrument. Conductors use patterns to communicate. Students use hand signs to delineate melodic contour. These are examples of *body notation*. Teachers use *oral notation* when they teach music by rote or when they apply solfège syllables to facilitate music reading. *Graphic notation* refers to the writing of a musical score. This is the most sophisticated form of notation, as it is a catalyst for the students to become musically independent and make music without the teacher and on their own.

3. *Constructivist teachers purport that students learn best when they learn from each other in groups* (Fosnot 2005: Wiggins 2007, 2000; Wink 2004; Wink and Putney 2001). In *O Passo* classrooms, students develop skills for listening, as they must interact with their peers to make music. In fact, according to Ciavatta, there has to be equilibrium between the emphasis on the individual and the emphasis on the group. Students learn ensemble skills and acquire a sense of self-worth as they contribute to the musical accomplishments of the group.

4. *Music resides in a context rich in culture.* Culture defines the music students hear and the music they study. It includes the music inside of school and also the music students know, love,

and enjoy outside of school. The *O Passo* approach helps students to connect "their" music with "our" music.

In classrooms where teachers apply *O Passo*, they engage physical movement as students shift their body weight in response to pulse and meter. It provides the "swing" by fostering precision, fluency, and intention. Students in *O Passo* classrooms learn sight-singing using numbers. In middle school, they begin with Bach chorales and move on to music of other genres. In Brazil, students learn to play indigenous rhythms on Brazilian drums. In American classrooms students use classroom drums, marching drums, Orff drums, and other percussion instruments. Drumming is the crosswalk to internalizing meter and pulse.

O PASSO IN AMERICAN MUSIC CLASSROOMS

Thomas Regelski (1981) writes,

> Music education is not the employment of a "method." No single method or strategy is necessarily the best for any teacher, child, or school system. No teaching approach can be transported intact from one place and one teacher and used with equal success in another situation by another teacher. Teaching methods must be in accord with the nature of the students, their readiness, the instructional format of the class or school, and the personality, inclinations, skills, and weaknesses of the teacher. (36)

Enacting the pedagogies of Kodály and Orff approaches in American music classrooms required teachers to make compromises. Kodály's concern for the preservation of culture, or Orff's desire to teach dancers, were not issues in American music education in the 1960s when music teachers began using these curricula (Mark and Gary 1992). Teachers liked the play party games, hand signs, barred instruments, and improvisation that those pedagogues advocated to provide activities for general music students that would build musical literacy and foster musical creativity. Richards (1964), Choksy (1974), Nash (1967, 1974) and others (Orff and Keetman adapted by Murray 1958) wrote materials keyed to the objectives of American music education. Wheeler and Raebeck combined approaches in their text *Orff and Kodály Adapted for the Elementary School*, published in 1972. Landis and Carder (1972) advocated an eclectic curriculum including approaches by Dalcroze, Kodály, and Orff. The translation of *Eurhythmics, Art and Education* by Dalcroze was published in 1972.

Connecting to critical pedagogy for music education, *O Passo* presents options for teachers and students in American music class-rooms. First, it promotes dialogue among students with each other and with their teachers. Teachers of *O Passo* advocate inclusion for all students as creators, performers, and critical listeners of music. Second, teaching *O Passo* promotes experiences that are empowering and "value added." Teachers promote musical autonomy and musical freedom. Third, the *O Passo* approach helps students learn to think as musicians knowing that the possibilities for making musical decisions are spontaneous and infinite. Students who engage in *O Passo* experiences do so in ways that "break down the barriers that separate the music students hear in the classroom from the music they prefer in their world outside. When these barriers disappear, students and their teacher are changed" (Abrahams 2005e). Lessons focus on the music itself and emphasize the body's connection to the rhythm in deep and significant ways. Students learn to view the landscape of rhythm. Challenges are identified and conquered as they appear in the context of the music learning experiences. The content of each lesson comes from the music itself. That is, lessons are not designed to teach a specific musical topic or concept such as 6/8 meter or rondo form. Instead, each lesson integrates experiencing music by moving the body in step, while simultaneously listening, performing, and creating music by composing or improvising. All are authentic tasks that real musicians encounter in the process of being musicians. Teaching *O Passo* requires a teacher who is a musician. The lessons do not teach themselves. Delivery of the curriculum requires a teacher who sings, plays classroom instruments, and listens to, honors, and values music and music makers of all types. The ideal teachers for this program are those who view teaching music to students as a means to constantly renew themselves as musicians.

Teachers in American schools using *O Passo* report that their students are more engaged in class (Young 2008). Muka (2008) studied the application of *O Passo* for students with learning disabilities. She reported that *O Passo* techniques enabled students to acquire musical skills and competencies beyond those previously achieved. Joe Piccirillo, a music teacher in a New York City high school, does *O Passo* with his students. In fact, his students have a saying that "nothing is impossible if it's o-passo-ble" (personal correspondence). James Schnyderite, a music teacher at a middle school in central New Jersey, writes,

> When I examine what music teachers do, it often consists of talking about music, listening to music, writing about music, and thinking about music. If you teach a nonperformance ensemble, there may be

little actual music making. I used *O Passo* in my general music classes for over two years. It was amazing how *O Passo* guided students to engage in music reading, solo and group performance, composition, and, most importantly, improvisation. In my seven years as a music educator, I have found that students find spontaneous creation of music a great challenge. These are all skills that musicians use while they are making music. The *O Passo* method is easily accessible to all students, helps them understand music in an easy way, and provides the opportunities for students to find their musical voice. In the three years that my students have been working with *O Passo*, it is obvious that they have grown through the use of *O Passo*, and it has, without a doubt, changed my life as an educator. (personal correspondence)

Amy Zakar, a preservice graduate student in music education, notes the following after attending a week-long teacher-training workshop in *O Passo* at her college in central New Jersey.

I found that *O Passo* has some similarities with parts of Orff, Kodály, and Dalcroze and also has components that are new and stimulating. I have also found that Lucas Ciavatta's approach is compatible with all nine National Standards and can be adapted to classrooms from early elementary through postgraduate level. It works in an instrumental, choral, or general music classroom. (personal correspondence)

One sixth-grade student in a Philadelphia middle school wrote of *O Passo*,

It changed our class by teaching us to pay attention and to know that we are a good class. When Lucas came and helped us with the *O Passo* step, I think that it really gave this class influence by us knowing what it is and how it is. If it did not teach my class a lesson, then it taught me something. And I think that it taught them something too because we don't act like wild animals or curse and fight. It's like that step actually just went into our minds and said that it is time for a change, and that's what we did. When I said that it taught me something, I mean that it taught me that I don't have to walk around acting like I am crazy. It made me understand that I can be me and nobody else. I can get an A and a B, not C, and D. I can just be me and nobody else. (student journal)

CONCLUSION

Music education is an ideal subject in which individuals can examine their own traditions and practices and in this way become independent, reflective, and critical. Music education, if it is going to be liberating, calls for an analysis of present traditions and practices. Creative experiences and outcomes are boundless when music teachers realize that they are able to analyze and adapt, manipulating the curriculum in an unlimited number of ways. As stated earlier, a goal of critical pedagogy for music education is to use that knowledge as a bridge to new learning. *O Passo* provides the tools that enable students and their teachers to walk across that bridge one step at a time.

NOTES

1. Originally published in 1968 as *Pedagogía del Oprimido*, *Pedagogy of the Oppressed* first appeared in the English translation in 1970, published in New York by Herder and Herder.
2. Edwin Gordon calls musical potential *aptitude* (2003). In delineating his theory of multiple intelligences, Howard Gardner suggests that music is intelligence (1983); he additionally addresses the issue of undeveloped potential (1991, 1999).
3. Ciavatta's writings are in Portuguese and appear on his website at www .opasso.com.br. The texts here are paraphrased from his translations of the Portuguese into English and from discussions with him when he visited the United States during March 2009.

REFERENCES

Abrahams, F. 2004. The application of critical theory to a sixth grade general music class. *Visions of Research in Music Education* 4 (electronic version).
———. 2005a. Applicação de pedagogia crítica ao ensino e aprendizagem de música. *Revista da Associação Brasileira de Educação Musical* 12:65–72.
———. 2005b. The application of critical pedagogy to music teaching and learning. *Visions of Research in Music Education* 6 (electronic version).
———. 2005c. The application of critical pedagogy to music teaching and learning: A literature review. *Update: Applications of Research in Music Education* 23 (2): 12–22.
———. 2005d. Critical pedagogy in the community music education programs of Brazil. *International Journal of Community Music* 3 (electronic version).
———. 2005e. Transforming classroom music instruction with ideas from critical pedagogy. *Music Educators Journal* 92 (1): 62–67.
———. 2007. Musicing Paulo Freire: A critical pedagogy for music education. In *Critical pedagogy: Where are we now?* eds. P. McLaren and J. L. Kincheloe, 223–38. New York: Peter Lang.
Abrahams, F., and P. Schmidt. 2006. A new sound for urban schools: Rethinking how we plan. In *Teaching music in the urban classroom: A guide to*

survival, success, and reform, vol. 1, ed. C. Frierson-Campbell, 153–64. Lanham, Md.: MENC / Rowman & Littlefield Education.

Choksy, L. 1974. *The Kodály method.* Englewood Cliffs, N.J.: Prentice-Hall.

Ciavatta, L. 2003. *O passo: A pusação e o ensino-aprendizagem de ritmos.* Rio de Janeiro: Author.

———. n.d. *O passo.* www.opasso.com.br.

Fosnot, C. T. 2005. *Constructivism: Theory, perspectives and practice.* 2nd ed. New York: Teachers College Press.

Freire, P. 1970. *Pedagogy of the oppressed.* Trans. M. Bergman Ramos. New York: Herder and Herder.

Gardner, H. 1983. *Frames of mind: The theory of multiple intelligences.* New York: Basic Books.

———. 1991. *The unschooled mind: How children think and how schools should teach.* New York: Basic Books.

———. 1999. *The disciplined mind: What all students should understand.* New York: Simon & Schuster.

Gordon, E. E. 2003. *Learning sequences in music: Skill, content, and patterns; a music learning theory.* Chicago: GIA.

Huff, D. 1989. The impact of interactions with students, community, colleagues, and the institution of schooling on the teaching practices of secondary choral music educators: Two case studies. Unpublished Ph.D. diss., University of Wisconsin, Madison. UMI 892337.

Jaques-Dalcroze, E. 1972. *Eurhythmics, art and education.* Trans. F. Rothwell. New York: Beaufort Books.

Landis, B., and P. Carder. 1972. *The eclectic curriculum in American music education: Contributions of Dalcroze, Kodály, and Orff.* Washington, D.C.: MENC.

Mark, M. L., and C. L. Gary. 1992. *A history of American music education.* New York: Schirmer Books.

McLaren, P. 1998. Che: The pedagogy of Che Guevara: Critical pedagogy and globalization thirty years after Che. *Cultural Circles* 3:29–103.

Muka, K. T. 2008. The impact of o passo on students with learning disabilities: A case study. Unpublished master's thesis, Rider University, Lawrenceville, N.J.

Nash, G. C. 1967. *Verses and movement: Music with children, the creative approach to music education.* La Grange, Ill.: Kitching Educational.

———. 1974. *Creative approaches to child development with music, language, and movement.* Ed. J. R. Welsh. New York: Alfred.

Orff, C., and G. Keetman. 1958. *Music for children.* London: Schott. (English version adapted by Margaret Murray.)

Regelski, T. A. 1981. *Teaching general music: Action learning for middle and secondary schools.* New York: Schirmer Books.

Richards, M. H. 1964. *Threshold to music.* Belmont, Calif.: Fearon.

Rose, A. M. 1990. Music education in culture: A critical analysis of reproduction production and hegemony. Ph.D. diss., University of Wisconsin, Madison. Ann Arbor: UMI 9020464.

Wheeler, L., and L. Raebeck. 1972. *Orff and Kodály adapted for the elementary school*. Dubuque, Iowa: William C. Brown.

Wiggins, J. 2000. *Teaching for musical understanding*. New York: McGraw-Hill.

———. 2007. Authentic practice and process in music teacher education. *Music Educators Journal* 93 (3): 36–42.

Wink, J. 2004. *Critical pedagogy: Notes from the real world*. 3rd ed. Boston: Allyn & Bacon.

Wink, J., and L. G. Putney. 2001. *A vision of Vygotsky*. Boston: Allyn & Bacon.

Young, K. 2008. The engagement with o passo (the step) in two sixth grade general music classes: An action research. Unpublished master's thesis, Rider University, Lawrenceville, N.J.

17

Cultural Bearers in the Children's Choral Ensemble

Ruth O. Boshkoff and Brent M. Gault

ABSTRACT

This chapter describes two specific cases in which informants from a specific culture were utilized in a children's choir setting as a way of introducing diverse musical material. The two narratives are organized around questions/statements relating to the choice of informants, the mode of transmitting musical material, the challenges encountered during the rehearsal process, the adaptations made to the musical material during rehearsals and performances, and the benefits singers gained from each experience. Narratives are then compared, and practical suggestions are provided for choral directors interested in utilizing cultural bearers with their ensembles.

INTRODUCTION

Singing is a standard component of music education programs both nationally and internationally. Music educators around the world incorporate singing in a variety of music learning settings due, in part, to the emotions performers can express through singing, the cognitive, psychomotor, and affective processes that are involved in musical performance, and the ability to transmit cultural traditions and beliefs through song (Phillips 1996).

One of the primary vehicles for singing instruction is the choral ensemble. This type of ensemble focuses more energy on the development of vocal technique through repertoire that will ultimately be a part of a given performance. The director of such an ensemble hopes to develop musical and expressive skills through the use of a variety of choral pieces that engage students as they attempt to broaden their musical horizons.

In an effort to transmit the cultural traditions and beliefs that make up the diverse communities found globally, composers of choral music have created numerous settings of traditional pieces that allow students to interact with music from unfamiliar cultural communities. While these kinds of works are valid adaptations and re-creations of music from around the world, they are often approached through a notated score, in the same way as traditional choral music (Goetze 2000). This approach to learning, while valuable, does not necessarily provide a complete picture of how traditional music is learned and utilized in various cultures throughout the world.

Music educators interested in the use of what Goetze (2000) labels as diverse music (music that originates outside the Western art tradition) recommend a number of teaching strategies when introducing this music in instructional settings. Parr (2006) suggests eight guidelines when considering the use of diverse music with a choir. These guidelines include making direct contact with a member of the culture, focusing on one style of music at a time in order to foster a deeper connection with that music, listening to a wide variety of music from the culture being studied, providing students with the meaning of a given piece and its function within a culture, and teaching the music authentically. Goetze also advocates the use of cultural informants in order to create a performance that is both aurally and visually reflective of the culture being studied (Goetze 2000).

Certain challenges arise as choral directors attempt to develop authentic encounters with diverse music. While there are common aspects of music learning that can be seen in the world's musicians, such as the use of imitation and rote-learning strategies (Campbell 2004), there are other elements of given performances that cannot be recreated in an ensemble setting. As Volk explains, "Just as no translation from one language to another is completely accurate, no music can be performed with complete authenticity outside of its culture. The best educators can hope for is a close approximation when performing these musics" (2006, 245). As choral educators seek to present diverse music in meaningful ways, they must strive to find the balance between offering authentic experiences and working within the realities of their given choral situations.

TWO ENCOUNTERS WITH DIVERSE CHORAL MUSIC

The following two narratives provide descriptions of encounters with diverse music in a children's choir setting. Both of these experiences occurred with the Treble Choir of Indiana University Children's Choir (IUCC). IUCC is an organization offering choral experiences for children in the Bloomington, Indiana, community. The Treble Choir is an ensemble of approximately twenty-five fourth-, fifth-, and sixth-grade girls. The members attend afternoon rehearsals once a week and perform in two large concerts in the fall and spring.

The first narrative describes the choir's work with Dr. Erdenechimeg Luvsannorov, a native of Mongolia who taught two traditional pieces to the group during the spring of 2007. The second narrative describes the choir's experience with Dr. Aida Huysenova, a native of Azerbaijan who taught the choir one traditional piece during the spring of 2008. In an effort to compare the two experiences, the narratives were organized around the following questions/statements:

1. How did you select your informants for this process?
2. What was the sequence and mode of presenting material to singers?
3. What challenges did your singers face when working with the informant(s)?
4. In what ways, if any, did you adapt the music or mode of instruction to address the vocal needs or learning styles of the students?
5. Describe the interaction between the choir and the informant, related to both successes and challenges.
6. What do you feel the singers gained from this experience?

Ruth Boshkoff, the conductor of the Treble Choir, addresses each of the questions above. Since these were her personal recollections of the experiences, we chose to use first person for the narrative descriptions.

MONGOLIAN FOLK SONGS: "LULLABY" AND "YOKHOR"

How Did You Select Your Informants for This Process?

My informant, Dr. Erdenechimeg Luvsannorov, was a visiting scholar at Indiana University. Her daughter, Enguunee, was enrolled in my choir. Enguunee was older than most of my choir members so I felt that singing a song from her culture would be a good way to introduce her to the choir and to make her feel comfortable in this new situation. I approached Dr. Erdenechimeg and asked if she had songs she could share with us that would be suitable for performance pieces for our program. Dr. Erdenechimeg was very enthusiastic about the collaboration, as was Enguunee.

What Was the Sequence and Mode of Presenting Material to Singers?

Dr. Erdenechimeg and I met several times to discuss the project. The purpose was for me to learn as much as I could about Mongolia, the country, culture, and language, and to listen to Dr. Erdenechimeg share as many songs as possible with me. This allowed me to choose a song that would fit in with the rest of my program and would be one I knew my choir would like. I subsequently picked two songs that contrasted in style and affect.

The first, "Lullaby," is just sixteen measures long and in a leisurely 3/8 meter. The key is E major, and the song has many repetitions of a perfect fourth—an interval that creates the gentle swinging sound of someone lulling a baby to sleep. The text is limited to one word, *buuvei* (boo-hwey), which is repeated throughout the song. The open vowels lend themselves to a warm vocal timbre, in keeping with a lullaby. This song is beautiful with unaccompanied unison voices over the base-tone sound.

In contrast, "Yokhor" is a boisterous dance, in 2/4 meter and minor mode with two eight-measure verses and a refrain of equal length. Numerous consonants, characteristic of the Mongolian language, give the voices an entirely different timbre than that of the lullaby. "Yokhor" is also unaccompanied but is meant to be sung in two parts, with a second part a fourth lower.

After I picked out the two songs and felt that I knew them sufficiently, Dr. Erdenechimeg came and spent an entire rehearsal with the choir. During this period and over several consecutive rehearsals, she sang the songs, introduced pronunciation, and told us about Mongolia and the circle dance. She related that "Yokhor" is performed in two concentric circles around the ancient Saglagar tree. The song and dance both date from the time of Marco Polo and have their origin in the Buriad Mongolian minority. "Yokhor" is still performed today at joyful events by groups as large as five hundred or more. While the harmony of Western music is based on thirds, Mongolian music, and especially that of the circle dances, is based on fourths and fifths. Strings or other instruments tune not to a single pitch but to the interval of a fourth. This is evident in "Yokhor" when the girls sing a fourth above the boys. Mongolians are known for their horsemanship, and the words of the song speak of a "silver saddle set with stones" and compare the dancing place to "a large horse blanket."

At our first meeting the students were encouraged to ask questions and to attempt the pronunciation of the words. To aid in this task I provided a sheet with the words and phonetics below them. Though we did not spend much time on the melody at this time, during subsequent meetings Dr. Erdenechimeg taught the song aurally.

What Challenges Did Your Singers Face When Working with the Informant(s)?

The melodies were relatively easy, but the words were not. A great deal of repetition was needed to master them. In addition, since "Yokhor" was an ancient song-dance, extra time was needed to learn the dance steps. Though the melody was not difficult for the choristers, harmonizing melodies at the fourth was very challenging.

In What Ways, If Any, Did You Adapt the Music or Mode of Instruction to Address the Vocal Needs or Learning Styles of the Students?

For "Yokhor," I made a few alterations in order to help students feel successful with the experience. Instead of singing in fourths, I added a simple cello part, which created the harmony. I also wrote an introduction for the cello to establish the key of the song and allow the choristers to get information for the dance.

Though the song had two verses, I decided to repeat the first verse and not attempt the second verse. My guest made a tape of both songs so I could burn them to CDs, which I distributed to the choir, and this proved to be very helpful. Dr. Erdenchimeg taught the steps for the dance and explained its history. After this initial teaching session we were able to practice the dance without her help, and it took a relatively short time to perfect it.

For the lullaby, my informant helped us decide appropriate movement for the piece. There was no need to adapt the rather simple
melody, but the choir needed time to arrive at an expressive performance. Dr. Erdenechimeg suggested that her daughter accompany the
lullaby on a jaws harp, an instrument indigenous to Mongolia and
other countries in Central Asia. This made Enguunee a special part of
the performance and helped give the lullaby an authentic sound.

Describe the Interaction between the Choir and the Informant, Related to Both Successes and Challenges.

Dr. Erdenechimeg was generous with her time and talents. She visited
often for short periods of time to reinforce pronunciation of words and
help the choir sing with the proper style for Mongolian folk songs. My
choir respected her as a teacher and enjoyed her visits. Enguunee also
helped us with pronunciation.

What Do You Feel the Singers Gained from This Experience?

Without a doubt, both my choir and I learned a great deal about the
country, customs, and culture of Mongolia. However, because we also
learned two songs from the folk literature of Mongolia, this knowledge
resonated in a special way. Since "Yokhor" is performed in concentric circles around a tree, my choir members had lively discussions
about how we could make this vivid to our audience. We talked about
importing a real tree for the performance, but, in the end, the choir
members decided to show the imagined tree and the joyful words in
their faces, voices, and bodies. The contrasting lullaby became a loving
paean to all babies everywhere.

A SONG FROM AZERBAIJAN: "BERI BAX"

How Did You Select Your Informants for This Process?

I had been to a diverse-music workshop that featured interactive software, intended for oral transmission of music (Goetze and Fern 2005).
I chose a lively song from this collection, partly because I thought the
song had great appeal but also because the informant for this song was
currently living in my vicinity while working on a Fulbright Fellowship. I realized that I had a double blessing and contacted her to ask if
she would help with the project. She immediately agreed.

I selected "Beri Bax" (Look at me!) for my choir because it was infectious and was performed on the DVD by a small choir of older boys and girls who obviously enjoyed it tremendously. The words describe a boy trying to get the attention of a girl by various means and then begging her to "look at me!" In addition, there is a charming dance between verses and a vibrant ending. I thought my choir would enjoy this clever and cheerful song from another culture and appreciate the similarities between our two cultures.

What Was the Sequence and Mode of Presenting Material to Singers?

After I reviewed the song and the cultural material presented on the DVD, I met with my informant, Dr. Aida Huysenova. Dr. Huysenova also served as accompanist for us, so we went over the accompaniment, pronunciation, cultural information, and translation of the Azeri words.

From the very first rehearsal with my choir Dr. Huysenova began to teach and shape the performance of "Beri Bax." We listened to the DVD performance first, and then she began teaching the text and melody. Subsequently, she visited our rehearsals several times. When there, she assumed the role of teacher. She also taught the dance steps and provided the accompaniment so we could practice them. When she was not able to be at a rehearsal, we used the DVD of "Beri Bax" that included a performance, cultural information, and an interactive way to learn the words and pronunciation. In essence, I had the best of both worlds: a guest teacher who was the original informant for the DVD.

What Challenges Did Your Singers Face When Working with These Informants?

As is sometimes the case with songs in other languages, the words were more difficult than the melody. I printed a chart of the words, but we learned the melody by rote from the DVD and from our guest. I sometimes found that singers got so focused on the difficulties with pronunciation that they lost sight of the meaning of the song. In addition, the movement steps and the characteristic Azeri hand movements were difficult for my choristers and needed special attention. On the DVD there was a solo dancer, but girls were hesitant to take this on.

In What Ways, If Any, Did You Adapt the Music or Mode of Instruction to Address the Vocal Needs or Learning Styles of the Students?

Vocally, the song was well within the capabilities of the students. Basically, the form of the song is three verses, each verse being: A refrain ("beri bax, beri bax,"), A refrain, B refrain, B refrain, with a twenty-four-measure piano interlude between verses 2 and 3 for the dance and a coda following verse 3. The first verse has the most repetition of words so was easiest to learn.

Initially, the choir and I thought we would repeat verse 1 in place of verse 3, but the choristers decided they could learn all three verses. However, to recreate the infectious spirit of the song, the students needed to get beyond the words and into the meaning of the words. To remedy this, we came up with a boy-girl storyline and enjoyed some role-playing. This brought the song to life.

I decided to have more than one dancer and asked for volunteers. Dr. Huysenova then took them to another room to work with them. In addition Dr. Huysenova came up with a simplified variation of the dance that would suit the addition of dancers to the performance.

Describe the Interaction between the Choir and the Informant, Related to Both Successes and Challenges.

Dr. Husenova is a fine, experienced teacher and an excellent pianist and musician. My choir and I were quite in awe of her. She was generous with her time, even though she was extremely busy. I was able to introduce her at our concert and express my gratitude to her for all she shared with us. She spoke to the audience about the song and about Azerbaijan.

What Do You Feel the Singers Gained from This Experience?

This was a very successful performance that my choir thoroughly enjoyed. In addition to this, though, I feel that it was important for them in other ways. Most students of this age have a limited knowledge about this part of the world. The song and the interaction with Dr. Huysenova opened my choristers up to a new understanding of Azerbaijan—a small country on the coast of the Caspian Sea with its distinctive language, culture, music, and musicians.

COMPARING NARRATIVES: IDEAS FOR APPLICATION

When viewing the two experiences described above, there are a number of observations that could serve to help choral directors who wish to utilize cultural bearers during their rehearsals. An initial look at the two experiences reveals that in both cases the informant in question provided the one, in-depth immersion experience for the choir in each given semester. This experience was complimented by other choral encounters utilizing more traditional choral music for this type of ensemble. This idea of focusing on one specific culture during a given rehearsal period is a view shared by Parr (2006), who encourages this singular focus as a way of providing a deeper understanding for the given culture being studied.

With regard to the first question related to selecting informants, both cultural bearers were currently residing in the Bloomington community and were therefore readily available to assist with the rehearsal process. In the case of the first experience, the informant came directly from the family of a chorister, and this provided additional meaning to the experience. This illustrates the idea that one very legitimate place to look for possible informants is within a given school or community. Choral directors who are aware of the cultural groups and experiences available around them can use these as a means of not only introducing diverse music but also making singers aware of the many varieties of music available in their own "backyard." Just as the Treble Choir also utilized a DVD recording of an authentic performance to serve as a "teacher" when Dr. Huysenova was not available, music teachers can rely on authentic recordings, Web resources, video conferencing, and other electronic means to provide authentic examples of diverse music.

When looking at the sequence of how the music was presented to singers, in both cases the director made a point to listen to and become familiar with the given music and its cultural importance before the first rehearsal began. The use of aural imitation of singing and language and of kinesthetic imitation of movement was common in both scenarios and illustrates some of the widespread ways musicians around the world transmit musical information (Campbell 2004). In addition, the rehearsals combined these traditional approaches with the use of DVD recordings and rehearsal CDs of the spoken language, illustrating how technology can compliment the learning process.

In both instances, the singers found the text of the pieces more difficult than the melody of the songs. The use of informants, rehearsal CDs, and performance DVDs allowed for multiple opportunities to rehearse the text both conversationally and in the context of the song. In addition, the use of informants relaying not only the translation of the text but describing how the songs functioned within the given cultures allowed students to form a deeper understanding of what they were singing about.

While the informants allowed the Treble Choir to learn and perform this music in as authentic a way as possible, there were elements that needed to be modified during the rehearsal process. Because harmonization at the interval of a fourth was not accessible for the choir in the amount of time provided, an instrument played the second part for "Yokhor." Movements were added to "Lullaby," and the dance for "Beri Bax" was modified to suit this particular ensemble. While these were changes to the way that these performances would have taken place in a traditional setting, each was done with the counsel and approval of the given cultural bearer and did not detract from the overall authenticity of the choir's experience. Teachers who do find it necessary to modify diverse music should consider seeking the advice of a given cultural expert in order to ensure that any modifications still allow for a meaningful experience with the given musical material.

While both informants described in the narratives interacted well with the singers, not all informants may have experience working with children in an ensemble setting. Both informants in the narratives visited the ensemble frequently, and this allowed for them to become better acquainted with the group while also observing how the ensemble approached learning other choral pieces. The more an ensemble director can do to ensure a given informant is familiar with the students in an ensemble and how they typically rehearse, the more effectively that informant will be able to design a learning process that provides a smooth transition to diverse-learning situations.

Finally, in both cases, a holistic approach that focused on both musical and sociocultural elements of the given music was utilized. This in-depth focus on both the music and the way it functions within the culture allowed the students to gain a deeper appreciation for the music being presented. Abril states that this type of sociocultural focus is crucial because "if educators do not engage students in explicit discussion surrounding sociocultural issues, students may react negatively to the unfamiliar musical styles or cultures" (2006, 40).

These narratives provide a snapshot of two possible ways to utilize cultural bearers in a choral ensemble. As educators seek to develop a well-rounded choral curriculum, the use of authentic encounters with diverse music can further enhance quality of an ensemble program.

REFERENCES

Abril, C. 2006. Learning outcomes of two approaches to multicultural music education. *International Journal of Music Education* 24 (1): 30–42.

Campbell, P. 2004. *Teaching music globally: Experiencing music, expressing culture.* New York: Oxford University Press.

Goetze, M. 2000. Challenges of performing diverse cultural music. *Music Educators Journal* 87 (10): 23–25, 48.

Goetze, M., and J. Fern. 2005. "Beri Bax" from *Global Voices, Grade 5 DVD.* Bloomington, Ind.: MJ and Associates.

Parr, C. 2006. Eight simple rules for singing multicultural music. *Music Educators Journal* 93 (1): 34–37.

Phillips, K. 1996. *Teaching kids to sing.* New York: Schirmer Books.

Volk, T. 2006. An application of Thai music for general and instrumental music programs. *International Journal of Music Education* 24 (3): 243–54.

18

A Unique Collaboration: The Fairview Elementary School String Project

Brenda Brenner

ABSTRACT

This chapter describes a unique collaboration between an urban elementary school in need of instrumental music instruction and a university music education and music performance strings program in need of real-life diversity training. The elementary school described within the chapter contains a large population of minority students, has a low socioeconomic standing, and previously had extremely limited instrumental music education opportunities for students due to pressures related to No Child Left Behind. Brenda Brenner and the Indiana University Jacobs School of Music saw the need and potential benefit of this collaboration, which has resulted in bettering both the local community and the undergraduate music and music education majors as they prepare for diverse teaching environments.

INTRODUCTION

The Fairview String Project is a music education collaboration between the Indiana University Jacobs School of Music and the Monroe County Community School Corporation in Bloomington, Indiana. Housed at Fairview Elementary School, a school that has struggled to meet achievement standards under No Child Left Behind (NCLB), this project provides group violin instruction for every first grader. Under the direction of Associate Professor of Music Education Brenda Brenner, music education students from the IU Jacobs School of Music assist in teaching both large- and small-group classes several times a week, providing hands-on teaching experience for teacher trainees with a school population that is otherwise unlikely to have the opportunity to study a stringed instrument.

A vital aspect of this project is the research that is being conducted to examine the impact of violin study on cognitive development, attendance, and parent and student attitudes toward school. Research questions include the following: Do teachers perceive changes in the children in relationship to the ability to concentrate, maintain self-discipline, and attack difficult problems? Are parents more involved and excited about their child's educational experience as a result of this project? What is the effect of the project on emergent reading patterns? Overall the project will serve as a tool, allowing researchers to gauge the statistical significance with respect to student attendance, verbal and math test scores, and reading skills. The aim of this project is to bring instrumental music education to underserved students and to measure the positive effects on students' learning, growth, and development.

A UNIQUE COLLABORATION

One of the most unique aspects of the Fairview Project is that it is a collaboration between a world-renowned music school and a population in the community for whom participation in precollege music programs is rare. The Indiana University Jacobs School of Music is known as one of the most comprehensive and acclaimed institutions for the study of music, playing a key role in educating performers, scholars, composers, dancers, and music educators who influence performance and education around the globe. The 160 full-time faculty members in residence include performers, scholars, composers, and teachers of international renown. More than 1,600 students from all fifty states as well as fifty-six countries study at the Jacobs School and benefit from the intensity and focus of a conservatory setting combined with the broad academic offerings of a major research university.

The Jacobs School offers multiple precollege programs including the String Academy, Young Winds, Children's Choir, Young Pianists, Harp, Guitar, Recorder, and Dance. Children from Indiana as well as several neighboring states participate in these various programs. The typical population enrolled in the precollege String Academy is drawn from the upper-middle class as well as children from the international community of graduate students at Indiana University. While several need-based scholarships are given to children in the String Academy (currently there are thirty-eight partial or full scholarships given out of an enrollment of 152), they are usually given to students who have already reached a high level of development on the instrument and are rarely, if ever, given to a beginner in the program.

The population at Fairview Elementary School presents a stark contrast to the students who typically enroll in IU precollege programs. In the heart of the downtown historical district, which is currently undergoing revitalization, the Fairview attendance area includes a government housing project, trailer courts, apartments, and a protective shelter for abused or homeless families. The majority of students live in government-subsidized housing. Between seventy-five to ninety students, approximately 30 percent of the Fairview student body, attend the school district's Extended Day Program, Fairview's To the Bell and Beyond program, Boys and Girls Club, Banneker Community Center, or Girls, Inc. instead of going home after school (Monroe County Consolidated School Corporation). Currently, 90 percent of students at Fairview qualify for free or reduced lunch. Ethnically diverse, 38 percent of Fairview's current population is non-Caucasian (Indiana Department of Education). In addition, Fairview Elementary is the site of the Hearing-Impaired Program for MCCSC. Students in kindergarten through sixth grade who are deaf or hard-of-hearing attend this program if their needs require concentrated services.

Fairview has struggled to meet federal academic standards for the past six years and is currently in the restructuring phase of No Child Left Behind (Indiana Department of Education). With dwindling enrollment, partially caused by the ability of parents to choose an alternative school for their child due to NCLB sanctions, questions have arisen regarding the possibility of closing the school. Several issues have kept the school open, not the least of which is the desire to keep a "neighborhood" school where students with transportation issues could walk to school. In 2009, a new building will be constructed adjacent to the current school. Both the physical and curricular and administrative restructuring of the school as a result of NCLB have encouraged much community discussion about the future direction of the school and the success of the students.

The Fairview Project brings together first-grade students from Fairview with music education and performance students from the IU

Jacobs School of Music in a curricular program in which they learn violin in two large-group classes and one small-group session each week. The ability to provide service-learning opportunities for the music students in an environment that is very different than their personal experience, as well as the opportunity to observe and assist a master teacher in an actual teaching environment, was a strong motivation for establishing this program. The opportunity to practice the ideas that the university students are learning in an actual classroom has enriched and enlivened their educational experience. In addition, the students at Fairview, who were previously unlikely to receive instruction on a stringed instrument, gain a positive instrumental music experience and develop relationships with the IU Jacob School of Music faculty and students over an extended period of time.

The Fairview Project presents an opportunity for children who traditionally would be unlikely to sign up for string instruction either in the IU precollege programs or within the school system. String instruction in America is less likely to occur in an urban school setting like Fairview, and the vast majority of school string programs are in suburban schools (Doerksen and Delzell 2000, 58). Research also shows that socioeconomic level is a strong predictor of the existence of a string program at the elementary level—the higher the socioeconomic level, the more likely there will be a strong string program in existence (Smith 1997, 37). Historically, students at Fairview are not likely to enroll in precollege programs at the Jacobs School of Music. In the fall of 2006, for example, only two Fairview students were enrolled in a precollege program out of a total of 239 elementary public school students registered. The three elementary schools in the district (out of thirteen schools) that represent the highest socioeconomic levels had a combined total of 199 students enrolled for the same period. While Fairview students travel to IU to one of the series of campus musical performances offered by the Jacobs School of Music for MCCSC students, typically these are not children who would be found on campus for musical or cultural events.

While Jacobs's music education students often do field observation or student teaching in area schools, they are not typically involved in volunteer activities in a single school over a long period of time. One exception, interestingly enough, is at Fairview, where several IU students teach free after-school music lessons once a week for students in the fourth through sixth grades in a program called the Coda Academy.

In addition to building strong town-gown relationships and enriching the educational experience of both the university and first-grade students, the Fairview Project is unique in that it begins instrumental musical instruction in the first grade. According to the research study "Status of Orchestra Programs in the Public Schools," most school string instruction in the United States begins in grades 4, 5, or 6 (Hamann et al. 2002). In the MCCSC school system, string study is traditionally a before-school program beginning in the fifth grade. The Fairview Project begins at a much earlier stage of development and offers classes during the curricular day.

The Fairview Project is also unusual in that there is no choice of instrument: every child in the first grade at Fairview studies the violin. The choice of instrument was made in part because fractional-sized violins are readily available and are easy to store in limited space and also because the faculty member supervising the project specializes in violin. Through establishing a curricular program at a very early age, in a population that is not self-selecting and is unlikely to have the opportunity to study music because of socioeconomic and cultural reasons, the Fairview Project presents a unique set of opportunities and challenges.

FROM IDEA TO ACTION

The idea to create the Fairview Project came originally from a mother of two students who were enrolled in the IU String Academy for many years. This mother was also a first-grade teacher and an emergent reading specialist at a local elementary school. Through years of observing early violin lessons and working with new readers, she became interested in the parallels between the learning processes of students in both endeavors. She believed that the process a child went through in learning the violin—the systematic problem-solving and persistence learned by doing correct repetitions—would be helpful in learning to be successful in the classroom. This teacher was interested in establishing a violin curriculum in her classroom that would support the academic skills she was teaching her students.

Concurrently, the dean of the Jacobs School of Music, Gwyn Richards, became interested in the newly publicized Venezuelan music education phenomenon El Sistema. A program that takes poor children from the slums of Venezuela and trains them to be classical musicians, El Sistema has revolutionized the idea that music education is only for a select group of students and has transformed the lives of countless children for which music education would previously have been impossible.

In a discussion with Dean Richards, I mentioned my desire to establish a violin program in a local school in which every student in the class would study the instrument. I was interested in measuring the effects of such a program on achievement in reading and math. Dean Richards was very enthusiastic about the idea but was interested in establishing the program at a school where the population was unlikely to get lessons outside school, either in the IU precollege division or elsewhere. An analysis of enrollment in the precollege division was done, and it was discovered that there were historically very few, if any, Fairview children enrolled in lessons on campus.

Though the idea had taken form, the reality of establishing such a program presented several challenges. It seemed, on the surface, very presumptuous to go to a school facing highly publicized sanctions for failing to meet federal academic standards and announce that we would like to start a violin program in the very grade that students were learning the skills that would allow them to be successful academically throughout their education. How could we justify taking away valuable curricular time for something that seemed to be on the surface completely unnecessary?

The answer to this question came incrementally through developing relationships with teachers and administrators who ultimately believed that the goal of the violin program would strengthen their academic objectives as well. The general music teacher, Kathy Heise, contacted me to recruit string teachers for her after-school instrumental program, the Coda Academy. We had developed a relationship over the period of a year, during which time I brought students from the IU String Academy to Fairview to present recruitment demonstrations for the Coda Academy. Through supervising the university students who were working in this program, I realized how committed Ms. Heise was to providing musical opportunities to the children of this school.

When Ms. Heise called me to solicit performers for the demonstrations for Coda Academy the second year, she mentioned that there was a large number of string students interested in taking after-school lessons. At this point, I asked her if she would be open to having a curricular program for children who were too young for the Coda Academy (which starts in fourth grade). Ms. Heise was very excited about this possibility.

Soon afterward, I saw Dean Richards and mentioned that Ms. Heise was enthusiastic about a curricular program for the first grade at Fairview. He suggested that a group of teachers, administrators, and school board members visit an established program on this model that was currently in place in Michigan. The chair of the Department of Music

Education at the Jacobs School, Dr. Lissa May, had been the fine-arts supervisor in this school district when the program began. After taking this trip, seeing firsthand how the program was structured, and hearing the effects of the program from the teachers and administrators, the group was ready to move forward with the Fairview Project.

It was instrumental at this point to make sure that there was strong support not only from the music teacher, Kathy Heise, but also from the teachers and administrators at Fairview. I spent time talking with the teachers, listening to their concerns, and discussing the goals of a violin program and how it might affect their academic objectives. Lissa May spoke with the superintendent of Monroe County Consolidated School Corporation (MCCSC) as well as with the director of curriculum, and several school board members were interested and excited about the possibilities of this program. When the IU team was assured that both MCCSC and Fairview backed the establishment of this program, we moved ahead to the planning stages.

THE PLANNING STAGE

It took a group effort to get the Fairview Project off the ground. Lissa May, Kathy Heise, Kasia Bugaj (the graduate assistant in the program), and I met on a weekly basis throughout the spring prior to the beginning of the project. Dr. May was in charge of the research portion of the project. She wrote and got approval for the research proposal through IU and MCCSC and communicated between the administrations at MCCSC, Fairview, and IU. Ms. Heise acted as the liaison from Fairview, answering scheduling and curricular questions. I wrote the curriculum, cross-referencing the goals and objectives with the music, math, and language-arts standards for grade 1 in the state of Indiana. I also purchased the equipment necessary to begin the project, which was funded from private donations through the Jacobs School of Music.

Through these initial discussions, the Fairview Project began to take shape. Two thirty-minute group classes per week would take the place of the traditional general music classes. The general music teacher, Kathy Heise, would participate in the violin program, learning alongside the students. The curriculum was developed to integrate not only violin-playing skills but general music standards, which include singing, pitch, interval identification, and some written theory. A small-group class once a week during recess was added to give individual attention to the children. In order to make losing a recess easier, all the children from one class stay in from recess and are divided into small groups at the same time. A practice pod from IU was installed in the music classroom to allow these small groups to take place while other music classes were going on in the larger classroom. Classroom teachers allow small groups to practice in the academic classroom during recess when they are in the room.

On a typical school day, there are two or three small-group lessons going on in the building. Each group class is lead by a lead teacher who is assisted by a minimum of one helper teacher. For the larger-group classes, there is a lead teacher, two to five assistant teachers, Ms. Heise, and a pianist. The assistant teachers all move around the classroom, working silently to correct instrument placement or focus individual children. This ensures that each child gets the individual attention that is necessary to make improvement.

Once the structure of the weekly lessons was in place, the priority became establishing how to physically house sixty-five violins and most efficiently get them to the children during the classes. Because the students were not taking the violins home, a cabinet was built where the instruments were hung in rows of four. Each child was assigned a violin, which was outfitted with a colored dot indicating the class the child was in and the name of the child who uses that particular instrument. It was important that each child has their own violin so that they could take pride and ownership over it. Shortly before each class, the IU student assistants moved the appropriate violins to a table in the music room and tuned them. When the children entered the room, each child was presented with his or her instrument. This system saved storage space at the school and made giving the appropriately sized instrument to each child easy and efficient.

IMPLEMENTATION AND THE EFFECTS

The intention of the Fairview Project was twofold: to provide instruction on the violin to a group of first graders who would otherwise not have had this opportunity, and to measure the cognitive, academic, and social effects and attendance rates as a result of this program. One benefit that has been enormous, and for which the researchers were totally unprepared, was the impact this program has had on the IU students. A particularly poignant moment occurred during the first visit to the school to size the violins. Two graduate students went with me to help, and when the first class came in, a little girl looked up at one of the IU students and asked, "Are you going to teach me violin?"

When the student said, "Yes," the little girl gave her a huge bear hug and said, "Thank you!" The student looked completely stunned and had tears in her eyes (this was a doctoral performance major who had little experience in schools). Ultimately the effect this program has had in helping university students understand the power of teaching, no matter what level, has been profound.

The goals and objectives for each class were very systematic. The curriculum began with learning classroom procedure and the parts of the violin, and the children worked for several weeks on how to hold the instrument correctly with no bow. Simple left-hand pizzicato pieces were introduced that allowed the children to learn the names of the strings and basic group rhythmic pulse. Often, counting games were played while the instrument was held in a muscle-strengthening position for a specific sequence of numbers (counting by twos, fives, tens, backward counting). Songs that matched the beginning sounds of words to the open strings were sung, transferring written language into verbal and musical sounds. In the beginning classes, students were at first perplexed about why we were only working with the violin and not the bow. There were lots of comments like, "Where is the stick? This isn't playing the violin!" Once the students realized that they needed to achieve mastery over a particular portion of technique before an additional step was added, they became more patient. Several students observed that in each class we reviewed what we had learned before but always added one new challenging element.

When the class finally got to use the bow, their violins were taken away. It was frustrating for a few of them that specific benchmarks were insisted on before they were allowed to move to the next step. The result, however, was that when the violin and bow were finally put together, the students were physically more coordinated and prepared for that step. The curriculum was designed for the students to practice old skills and build on them incrementally. By the end of the year they would be able to play simple folk songs like "Twinkle, Twinkle, Little Star" with a variety of rhythms and bowings with a good physical setup and free and open motions. A portion of each class was devoted to singing, often using the solfège syllables with the "Sunflower Song"—a series of motions corresponding to body parts ranging from the toes to above the head. By the end of the year, students were be able to identify and sing a variety of intervals including the octave, minor second, perfect fifth, and major and minor thirds.

One obstacle faced at the beginning of the program was behavior. The Fairview students seemed accustomed to failure in school. When difficulties were encountered, many of the students would misbehave, quit, or melt down in the classroom. It was important to move in incremental steps in the curriculum so that the majority of the students were successful. Positive behavioral reinforcement was essential: when a student was doing something right, whether it was on the violin or in the classroom, that student received a compliment. Often that led to other students emulating the positive behavior. A comment from the teacher such as "Susie, your violin position is terrific!" would often be followed by other children making a flurry of corrections and then shouting, "What about my violin position?!" Sometimes rewards were used in the small groups—stickers, hand stamps, small candy, or other prizes—to reward good behavior and effort.

The biggest reward, however, was in doing the given task correctly. One student, named Hannah, was often uncooperative and even defiant in the classroom. The teachers at the school had a negative attitude about Hannah, who was difficult to work with and had experienced little success in the school environment. In the initial violin classes, Hannah more often than not had her violin taken away from her due to lack of cooperation. She often cried or whined during class and selectively chose to participate (often only when candy or some other reward was involved). One particular small-group class saw a true breakthrough in behavior that completely changed Hannah's attitude. When asked by the teacher to try a piece on her own, Hannah declined, saying "I ain't good at nuttin'." Her peers in the group started encouraging her, saying that her statement wasn't true—that she was in fact good at math. Hannah decided to try the piece with everyone in the group rooting for her. When she made it through the piece the first time alone, she was shocked and immediately wanted to do it again without any help. Her attitude toward trying new things completely changed: she believed she could do something that before had seemed impossible.

In addition to changing children's attitudes about what they viewed as previously unachievable, the Fairview Project has also changed the parent's attitudes toward school and the opportunities it provides for their children. Because Fairview is a unique program within the school district (and nationwide), the parents appreciate the opportunities this provides for their children. Several parents and grandparents attended the first concert from out of state and were visibly moved by the music their children were making. When the principal of Fairview, Karen Adams, was asked her opinion of the biggest impact this program had made after the first concert, she stated that she felt that the parent behavior at the concert was in stark contrast to what she had seen in previous school programs. The parents stayed seated throughout the concert and were supportive and respectful throughout the program. Several parents have visited the classroom to observe their children in the learning process and have commented on the interest in music these classes have sparked as well as changes they have observed in their children. *Ryder Magazine* published an article featuring parent reaction to the Fairview Project: "These violin classes really help him focus" and "The lessons have really helped . . . with patience. It helps his social skills, being in a group with friends; and it helps him mentally. And he really loves it and talks about it all the time, and I think this is amazing. . . . The teacher said that he would rather go to practice violin than play on the playground" (Sturm 2008, 19–25).

The long-term goal of this project is not only to change the perspective and experience of the children but also to open the avenue of possibilities that parents view as available to their children. As Kathy Heise so aptly said,

> I think the biggest thing is that the children don't realize in themselves what their possibilities are, or what the probabilities could be for them, just because of the way things are. . . . If we start changing that idea and get them connected with some people outside of their own community, maybe it'll start changing their ideas about what they can do, help them get out of the circle of generational poverty that starts when you don't see any other lifestyle for yourself. And so for them to have the opportunity to try out things that so many kids do that they don't get to—and the fact that maybe they start to, and their parents too, they start to see some different things, some new possibilities for them and their children—that for me is probably the most important benefit. (Sturm 2008, 19)

CONCLUSION

The Fairview Violin Project has many unique qualities. The interaction of a world-renowned music school with a "failing" urban public school in a collaboration that is opportune for both parties has been a winning combination. The fact that both schools were open to alternative ways of approaching education and combining musical and academic goals is instrumental in the success of this program. Building relationships and common objectives among the many people involved, all with the best interests of the children of Fairview in mind, was the first step in creating this program.

The intersection of research and practice adds another important quality to this project. Not only are all children in the first grade gaining practical, positive instrumental music experience (which is unusual at this early age), but the research data gathered from this program over a period of years will answer some important questions regarding the cognitive, academic, and social effects of instrumental music study on a nonselective population. Ideally the research will lead to more children gaining experience in instrumental music at an early age within a school setting.

The structure of the classes themselves is also unique. Multiple assistants within the class present a distinctive model for teaching large-group classes. In addition, offering both large- and small-group settings each week ensures that every child gets individual attention and is able to improve. The musical success that the children achieve within this program will hopefully transfer into the classroom in the form of increased academic and cognitive skills, will provide incentive for children to look forward to attending school, and ultimately will allow children to view themselves as musicians and cultural enthusiasts throughout life.

REFERENCES

Doerksen, P. F., and J. K. Delzell. 2000. Beginning band and orchestra programs in the United States. *American String Teacher* 50:58–63.

Hamann, D. L., R. Gillespie, and L. Bergonzi. 2002. Status of orchestra programs in the public school. *Journal of String Research* 2 (2002). www.arts.arizona.edu/jsr/jsrhome/index.html.

Monroe County Consolidated School Corporation. http://mccsc.edu.

Indiana Department of Education. 2006. *School Snapshot, Fairview Elementary School, 6197.* Indianapolis: Indiana Accountability System for Academic Progress. http://mustang.doe.state.in.us/SEARCH/snapshot.cfm?schl=6197.

Smith, C. 1997. String education: The stepchild of American music education. *American String Teacher* 47:37–42.

Sturm, P. 2008. String 'em up: The Fairview Elementary string program. *The Ryder Magazine* (Dec.).

19

New Wine in Old Skins: Making Music with Older Adults

Don D. Coffman

ABSTRACT

This chapter presents the importance of developing opportunities that support lifelong music making. Music educators generally assert that music is a lifelong activity, yet our efforts are heavily focused on youth, and opportunities for adults to make music are limited in comparison. This case study describes the Iowa City, Iowa, New Horizons Band, which is part of a growing association of musical organizations dedicated to providing musical instruction and performance opportunities for older adults.

INTRODUCTION

> No one puts new wine into old wineskins; otherwise, the wine will burst the skins, and the wine is lost, and so are the skins; but one puts new wine into fresh wineskins.
>
> —Mark 2:22

I chose the title of this chapter to emphasize a point: just because people are old in age doesn't mean that they cannot learn new things. It may be that old wineskins cannot manage new wine, but older adults can thrive in new situations. The core issue of this chapter is the importance of developing opportunities that support lifelong music making. For decades music educators rallied around the motto "Music for every child, every child for music" to such an extent that one might believe that the music education profession has ignored music making outside of the school classroom. Nonetheless, there have been advocates throughout the history of MENC: The National Association for Music Education and throughout its previous incarnations as the Music Educators National Conference and the Music Supervisors National Conference.

The first issue of the *Music Supervisors Bulletin* in 1914 reflected the importance of community music by reporting on an address of Peter W. Dykema to the National Education Association meeting of that year, where he advocated that the director of music in the public schools was the logical leader for the musical life of a community (Music Discussions at the N.E.A. 1914, 26–28). That first issue also announced a series of eight community performances in Winfield, Kansas, under the leadership of Edgar B. Gordon, involving various school choruses and the Winfield Orchestral Club from December 1914 through May 1915 (Music Discussions at the N.E.A. 1914, 28–30).

The world's current economic crisis has caused many people to reflect on the 1930s Great Depression years, and music educators' writings during that era sound familiar because they discussed the relevance of school music to life outside the school. Edgar B. Gordon wrote,

> We face a crisis in our national musical life. The contrast between the world of school music and actual musical conditions in the world outside is startling. . . . No longer do we dare encourage young people to look forward to musical careers, for we know that the future of professional music is an uncertain one; and yet we are faced with the imperative necessity of directing the musical energies of these young people so that they may be utilized and preserved.
>
> The way out lies clear before us. We must cultivate the amateur spirit, the will to sing or play well for the love and joy of it. Our boys and girls must somehow come to prize good singing and playing not only as a classroom and concert-hall activity but mainly as an everyday means of recreation and of enhancement of social life. (Gordon, Zanzig, and Tilton 1933, 17)

Peter Dykema advocated that music teaching "must now be conceived more than ever before in terms of developing such a love that the student will wish to continue with it after he is beyond the period of compulsory study. Eventually, I believe, one valuable measure of the success of all teaching will be the voluntary continuing of it by the student" (1934, 35).

Mary E. Ireland, in her 1935 *Music Educators Journal* article "Does Adult Education Mean Us?" issued a call to action that could have been written today, citing "incredibly rapid changes in the world in which we live," "increased leisure," and "conclusive evidence that men and women of mature years can still learn quickly and effectively" as reasons for promoting music education for adults. She asserted that "education must be a continuous process through adult life" (1935, 11).

Writings on community music, amateur music, music with adults, and so forth have appeared in the *Music Educators Journal* in every decade of the past century (for example, Christmann 1965; Forrester 1975; Haas 1954; Leonhard 1981; Manor 1945; Myers 1992), with increasing frequency since the 1980s. Jumping forward in time to the end of the twentieth century, passages from Judith Jellison's (2000) chapter on lifelong learning in MENC's *Vision 2020: The Housewright Symposium on the Future of Music Education* echoed the concerns of Gordon, Dykema, and Ireland. She cited the low rates of participation by adults in the classical music genres typically taught in school music programs as well as the low music-achievement scores by school children on the 1997 *National Assessment of Educational Progress*.

Jellison urged music educators to consider how to teach music in ways that will foster continued involvement throughout life. Specifically, she advocated the principle of transition, which she defined as the "movement of individuals across a variety of school and nonschool environments through life" and asserted, "Planning for transition requires music experiences in school that are directly referenced to contexts for music experiences valued for adulthood" (2000, 121). One of her strategies for facilitating the transition from school music experiences to adult music making was to have students interact with adult community music organizations, performing with adults in both school and community settings.

MENC's current mission statement "is to advance music education by encouraging the study and making of music by all" (2008). The MENC book that codifies the National Standards for music instruction declares that "while the opportunity-to-learn standards focus on the learning environment necessary to teach music, it is important to note that the ultimate objective of all standards, all school curriculums, and all school personnel is to help students to gain the broad skills and knowledge that will enable them to function effectively as adults and to contribute to society in today's world and tomorrow's" (2008, v).

So, despite repeated calls during the past century for educating youth in music with a view toward adulthood, the music education profession does not appear to have advanced much towards that goal. I view this chapter as describing an alternative *population* (older adults) more than describing an alternative *approach* in music education, because it describes a band program that functions much like a school band, except that the participants vary in age between fifty-five and ninety-three. I view older adult bands as one approach to support lifelong learning, and I believe that until we create more postschooling opportunities for music making, we are failing to educate children for the "real world" situations. This case study begins with a short overview of adult development, is followed by a description of the band program, and ends with an analysis of the outcomes.

AGING AND ABILITIES

America's baby boomers, the generation born between 1946 and 1964, are redefining conceptions of retirement and old age (Cohen 2000; Cohen 2005; Sadler 2000; Vaillant 2002; Warshofsky 1999). Book titles such as *Declining to Decline* (Gullette 1997) and *The Creative Age: Awakening Human Potential in the Second Half of Life* (Cohen 2000) aptly describe contemporary views of aging that are more positive than they used to be. Thirty years ago, our society often ignored senior citizens; now, society is finally embracing the notion that older adults have much to contribute.

Physiologically, the body reaches its maximum physical maturity by the mid-twenties and then begins to experience some gradual deterioration of the senses, cardiovascular and neuromuscular systems, the brain, and internal organs. We know that older adults require more time to cognitively process information, sustain attention, and divide attention between tasks (Cavanaugh 1997). The primary mental abilities (e.g., word fluency, vocabulary, inductive reasoning, spatial orientation) decline with age, usually affecting functioning after age sixty, and more noticeably after the mid-seventies (Schaie 1996).

However, higher-order secondary mental abilities, such as fluid intelligence and crystallized intelligence (Horn 1980), do not exhibit uniform declines. Fluid intelligence (flexible, analytic, reasoning that is relatively independent of experience and education) is theorized to develop earlier in life and decline with age, while crystallized intelligence (culturally based knowledge and reasoning acquired through life experience and education) is thought to increase with age. The increased reliance on crystallized intelligence may explain how older adults are able to compensate for decreases in cognitive speed (Coffman 2009).

Crystallized intelligence might be part of Cohen's (2000) modification of Einstein's famous formula that illustrates the importance of human experience. In Cohen's formula $C = me^2$, "Creativity" requires a "mass" of accumulated knowledge multiplied by "experiences" (internal and external) that interact to produce new insights (2000, 35). It is therefore reasonable to assert that adults experience some deterioration of general cognitive ability with age but may maintain or even increase mental abilities in areas of expertise (Pieters 1996). In short, one can "teach an old dog new tricks" because older adults can rely on learning mechanisms developed over time.

THE PROGRAM

When I was a high school band director I frequently wished that I could reach more students, because 90 percent of the student body was not involved in the school's music programs, which is common in many U.S. high schools. Furthermore, I sadly acknowledged that most of my students would stop playing their instruments after high school graduation, and I wished for ways to increase music-making opportunities for amateur adult players, especially for those who had missed the opportunity in their youth (Coffman 2009).

In 1995 I established the Iowa City/Johnson County Senior Center New Horizons Band (NHB). This concert band is designed to provide instruction in instrumental music to "chronologically gifted" senior citizens. No prior musical expertise is required, and the band attracts both novice and experienced players. To start, I worked with the senior center staff over a six-month period to prepare a number of video promotions and press releases. I held one organizational meeting for interested players in December 1994 that was similar to the typical meetings that band instructors hold for parents and children to see the instruments and discuss purchasing or renting instruments. Rehearsals began on January 17, 1995, and for the first six weeks, the players met in small groups of similar instruments (led by my music education students) and worked on learning, or relearning, to play their instruments using a beginning band-method book. By mid-March we added rehearsal times for meeting all together in a band. Our first concert was to a standing-room-only crowd at the senior center in early May 1995.

The Iowa City NHB is part of a growing association of musical organizations that began in Rochester, New York, in 1991, under the leadership of Roy Ernst (Ernst and Emmons 1992, 30–34). My band was one of the first of what has become an international movement of over 120 bands, choirs, and orchestras across the United States and Canada called the New Horizons International Music Association (NHIMA). NHIMA is an affiliation of musical organizations that share a newsletter, Internet website (www.newhorizonsmusic.org), and national institutes (i.e., "band camps"—gatherings of players for a few days of intensive music making). Most groups rehearse once or twice a week in music stores, schools, or churches. Each NHIMA group usually works with a local music merchant, who offers support that could include rehearsal space, administrative oversight, discounts on purchases, underwriting, and so forth.

NHIMA groups usually are led by one or more retired school-ensemble directors or by college music education professors. My program is not typical, because I rely on a teaching staff of six to eight assistant instructors who are either undergraduate music education students or graduate students with teaching experience. As a teacher of future teachers, I am pleased to note that over one hundred undergraduate music students have gained practical teaching experience in "real-life" teaching situations prior to their student-teaching semesters. Teaching adults has been a supportive, low-stress field experience for my students.

While the typical amateur community musical group focuses on preparing for an imminent performance, most New Horizons groups focus on teaching participants how to play better. For many players, the band is an opportunity to improve skills they acquired years ago in school. For others, the band is an invitation to an experience what they thought was not possible for them.

The Iowa City NHB concert band, which is the centerpiece of the program, has nearly tripled in size from twenty-six players to seventy-seven, and the program has expanded from one band to many ensembles. We meet at the senior center on Tuesday and Thursday mornings for forty-five minutes of small-group instruction or chamber-ensemble coaching, followed by a sixty-minute band rehearsal. The center is a multifloor former post office from the early 1900s, routinely renovated to house a ceramics room, two exercise rooms, assembly room/cafeteria, computer lab, television production studio, library, consignment shop, and various multipurpose classrooms. On New Horizons mornings, music emanates from rooms on all three levels of the building.

The small groups spend a semester preparing for two hour-long chamber concerts (one for woodwinds, one for brass and percussion) every December and May. During these coaching sessions, my student instructors teach about playing the instruments. I am amused that players ask the student instructors for additional opportunities to practice scales and arpeggios, and I am thrilled that this chamber program has spawned other self-directed groups of musicians who rehearse weekly on their own. We all concur that the concert band's technique, tone, and intonation are much better because of the instruction that occurs in these smaller groups.

The groups that formed through members' initiatives have included the Polka Dots, Dixie Kids, Tempered Brass (a low brass quartet), Second Wind (a woodwind quintet), the Latecomers (clarinets), the Post Horns, and the Old Post Office Brass (quintet). In 1998, I added the Silver Swing, which plays big-band swing music from the 1930s and 1940s, and this group has been led by a series of student instructors. As the concert band matured in musicianship I recognized the need for a new entry-level band, so in 2004 I added a Monday evening band for novice players called the Linn Street band. Because this band of thirty individuals meets after the typical workday, adults who have not yet retired from work can participate. Some members of the Linn Street band have "matriculated" to the more advanced New Horizons band.

We rehearse year-round, pausing for four weeks over the winter holidays and during August. Nominal member fees and donations sustain the program expenses for student instructor stipends, music, and equipment. The concert band averages eleven concerts annually, most typically in local venues such as the senior center, concert halls on the university campus, the historic Englert Theatre in downtown Iowa City, pedestrian malls, shopping centers, parks, churches, schools, and area adult-care centers, but we also have traveled a couple of dozen times to other Iowa towns and to two state music teacher conventions. The number of engagements by the small groups exceeds ninety performances annually.

My interest in lifelong involvement in music making led to promoting local intergenerational band concerts with players of different ages, from elementary bands through university bands. A highlight of these concerts has been combining the bands for massed band performances, allowing players of varying ages to literally "rub shoulders"—musically and socially. It takes some planning, but I design seating arrangements that intersperse my players in the sections of the school bands. Then we briefly rehearse some music and allow time for players to visit within the sections. When we rehearse with youngsters, my adults take the lead in talking to the children. However, when we rehearse with college students, the adults often defer to the students. The respect is mutual, because the youth are often surprised at the abilities of the older musicians and remark that music is really something they can participate in throughout their lives.

OUTCOMES

The best way to describe the New Horizons experience is through the players' words and stories, which I have categorized into seven themes.

1. *Dedication:* Band members display phenomenal dedication. For instance, one woman plays clarinet, French horn, trumpet, and euphonium in more groups than I can keep track of and recently completed her three hundredth performance in thirteen years with the Polka Dots.
2. *Humor:* It takes a sense of humor to put oneself in a situation where there is a risk of making noticeable mistakes. Everyone does their best, so I work to tease them gently about playing problems. We try to balance "playing our best" with "not taking ourselves too seriously." If someone plays at the wrong place, misses a pitch or rhythm, there is never any embarrassing awkwardness—someone is bound to come up with a gently witty remark about it. For instance, one player wryly remarked during a rehearsal, "At our age, everyday is sight-reading!"
3. *Socialization:* The band functions very much like an extended family. Band participants can be seen going to lunch together, rehearsing at a member's home, and going to concerts together in the community. Some single women have paired up for vacations abroad. Two marriages have resulted from friendships formed in the band. The socializing is certainly a mixture of making new friends and often renewing old friendships.
4. *Health:* Members' health is an issue. While generally their health is good, it is not unusual for members to suffer sudden setbacks (heart attacks, strokes, broken bones, cardiac bypass surgery) or long-term ailments (Alzheimer's, Parkinson's, cancer). Many times ailing members make remarkable recoveries so that they can return to the band. The importance of the band in forming a genuine community is evident during these tough times. When

one person copes with illness, the other members help with visits, meals, and transportation. We have experienced loss through death, and band members have taught me and one another much about facing mortality with courage and composure.

5. *Mentoring:* My university students and I are the teachers in the program, yet we learn a great deal from our elders. Most student instructors come to the program with understandable nervousness about how to present themselves. They also lack experience in detecting performance errors, expressing how they want the players to sound, how to pace the rehearsal, what music is suitable, and so forth. These older learners graciously guide my student instructors. Sometimes they simply tell the instructors what they are having trouble playing or understanding. Sometimes they ask for a clearer conducting pattern. On rare occasions, they have private conversations with me to let me know about an instructor who seems disorganized or unsure.

6. *Creativity:* Gene Cohen (2000) asserts that one of the keys to living life well is to make use of our creative potential, even in small ways. I have seen this exemplified in band members in small things, both practical and musical. For example, I see an amazing variety of foldable shopping carts, wheeled luggage, and retractable handcarts that are used to haul instruments. There have been big examples of creativity, too. Two clarinet players, one with training in music composition and another who is self-trained, regularly compose and arrange music for their clarinet quintet. One woman became a self-taught video-production expert to develop a ten-year documentary DVD of the band's history.

7. *Sense of Mastery:* Wayne C. Booth, retired English professor and amateur cellist, wrote an autobiographical book on amateur music making, *For the Love of It: Amateuring and Its Rivals* (1999), that asked a fundamental question—Why pursue an endeavor when some version of failure is certain? Booth argues, and I agree, that amateur musicians enjoy the pursuit of mastery far more than needing to attain perfection. Abilities vary dramatically within my band, yet even the best players apologize about playing imperfectly. What continuously emerges from members' comments is the value they feel in contributing to the total sound of the band.

What does making music mean to these older adults? These seven themes have multiple links between them, and discussing one factor inevitably brings in the other factors. The first four themes (dedication, humor, socialization, health) speak to the pursuit of music making, and the final three themes (mentoring, creativity, sense of mastery) reflect outcomes of music making. These amateur musicians *work* hard at *play*, something that Robert Stebbins calls "serious leisure" (1992). They have company along the way—reciprocal relationships with people (peers, student instructors, and a director) who encourage them, support them, and teach them. They acknowledge that "we may not get good, but we get better," yet they do find pleasure in their creative accomplishments and experience benefits to that energize and satisfy them.

TEACHING AND LEARNING ISSUES

Fluid and Crystallized Intelligence

I have visited with dozens of NHIMA directors over the years, and some observe that youthful minds are quicker, grasping the subject matter faster than adults, and indicate that adults are more change resistant and less flexible about changing previous learning (e.g., counting systems). According to one director, "Adults need more time than youth to receive instruction, find and absorb rehearsal focal points, respond to instruction/direction, etc." These observations appear to reinforce the theory that fluid intelligence declines with age.

On the other hand, some directors report that adults learn faster (some adults are actually relearning their instruments), are more able to apply and remember analogies, are more easily led to expressive playing, and more easily grasp the concepts of finesses, ebb and flow, and nuance. Perhaps these adults are relying on their crystallized intelligence. Another director put it this way: "Possibly because of their enormous storehouse of experiences, adults seem to grasp basic concepts more readily. Ideas of tone and phrasing come far more quickly, even though the mechanics may lag a bit. These folks have been exposed to decades of music and know when it sounds good and are eager to sound better themselves" (Coffman 2009).

Reflective Learning

Many of the directors suggest that adults are more reflective about their learning. They reported that adults ask more questions, have longer attention spans, are more cognizant of improvement, and are more patient with the process. Comments include: "Adults ask insightful questions [that] often lead to real learning discussions," and "My adult students are more analytical and at times would rather spend more time analyzing so that when they do play a note they hope it will be perfect. It seems as if younger students just want to play and learn through trial and error. . . . They don't think much at all about the process but sometimes relentlessly play note after note in an effort to improve" (Coffman 2009).

Physical Limitations

Perhaps the most visible aspects of older adult learners are the signs of physical age. Directors comment on both chronic and acute limitations due to vision, hearing, arthritis, heart disease, respiratory problems, cancer, and so forth. They also felt that there was a limit to how far novice adult musicians could progress.

In order to mitigate these problems directors recommend applying simple corrective measures such as eyeglasses, hearing aids, sound-amplification systems, speaking louder and enunciating carefully, and convenient parking for cars. They also suggest allowing more time, "lengthy advance notice before changing dates, times, or even what piece we're doing next." One director remarked that older adults can require "chaperoning, like elementary kids, taking care with going up and down steps, etc."

Teaching Style

Directors uniformly remark that the process of teaching music instruments and music notation differs little between adult and youth learners. This is logical. The skills needed to produce sounds are fundamental, no matter what the age of the learner, and so the sequence of steps needed to acquire the skills is the same. However, directors indicate differences in their teaching *style* between teaching youth and adults. Directors tell me: "The thing I enjoy most is I can be myself. If I want to crack a joke or do something stupid the band laughs with me." "Adults are big kids who understand jokes, say 'Oops—sorry' when they mess up, and go on and try again. It's a director's joy to work with them." "Adult community bands are the ultimate reward to a long teaching career" (Coffman 2009).

I have two reactions to these remarks. How wonderful! How sad! I hasten to say that directors who compared teaching youth and adults remarked that they enjoyed both kinds of learners, and no one specifically indicated enjoying adults more. However, if teaching adults is an "ultimate reward," I wonder whether there are aspects of teaching adults that we fail to consider for our youth, because adults can "vote with their feet" if they don't enjoy the experience while youth can be more of a "captive audience." The culture of formal schooling seems to maintain the notion that schooling is preparation for a future life, so it is accepted that youth should simply "do what's good for them," learn things that they do not feel are relevant, and view learning as work, largely devoid of fun. How might school-ensemble rehearsals differ if school music directors felt that they could be more relaxed and have more fun?

Music educators generally assert that music is a lifelong activity, yet our efforts are heavily focused on youth, and opportunities for adults to make music are limited in comparison. This adult band is an excellent example of what is possible, and I find the members' love of music making inspirational. I hope that readers are inspired as well.

REFERENCES

Booth, W. C. 1999. *For the love of it: Amateuring and its rivals.* Chicago: University of Chicago Press.

Cavanaugh, J. C. 1997. *Adult development and aging.* 3rd ed. Pacific Grove, Calif.: Brooks / Cole.

Christmann, A. E. 1965. Programming for the community orchestra. *Music Educators Journal* 51 (3): 45–46.

Coffman, D. D. 2009. Learning from our elders: Survey of New Horizons International Music Association band and orchestra directors. *International Journal of Community Music* 2 (2–3): 227–40.

Cohen, G. D. 2000. *The creative age: Awakening human potential in the second half of life.* 1st ed. New York: Avon Books.

———. 2005. *The mature mind: The positive power of the aging brain.* New York: Basic Books.

Community music. 1914. *Music Supervisors' Bulletin* 1 (1) (Sept.): 28–30.

Dykema, P. W. 1934. Music in community life. *Music Supervisors' Journal* 20 (4) (Mar.): 34–74.

Ernst, R. E., and S. Emmons. 1992. New horizons for senior adults. *Music Educators Journal* 79 (4): 30–34.

Forrester, D. W. 1975. Adult beginners: Music education's new frontier. *Music Educators Journal* 62 (4) (Dec.): 56–58.

Gordon, E. B., A. D. Zanzig, and E. R. Tilton. 1933. Amateur music. *Music Supervisors' Journal* 19 (3) (Feb.): 17–18.

Gullette, M. M. 1997. *Declining to decline: Cultural combat and the politics of the midlife.* Charlottesville, Va.: University Press of Virginia.

Haas, A. 1954. Correlating school and community music. *Music Educators Journal* 40 (5) (April–May): 71–72.

Horn, J. L. 1980. Concepts of intellect in relation to learning and adult development. *Intelligence* 4 (4): 285–317.

Ireland, M. E. 1935. Does adult education mean us? *Music Educators Journal* 21 (4) (Feb.): 11.

Jellison, J. A. 2000. How can all people continue to be involved in meaningful music participation? In *Vision 2020: The Housewright Symposium on the future of music education*, ed. C. K. Madsen, 111–36. Reston, Va.: MENC.

Leonhard, C. 1981. Expand your classroom. *Music Educators Journal* 68 (3): 54, 61–62.

Manor, H. C. 1945. Community music program. *Music Educators Journal* 32 (1) (Sept.–Oct.): 40.

MENC: The National Association for Music Education. 2008. *MENC mission statement.* Reston, Va.: MENC. www.menc.org/about/view/mission-statement (accessed February 12, 2009).

Music discussions at the N.E.A. 1914. *Music Supervisors' Bulletin* 1 (1) (Sept.): 26–28.

Myers, D. E. 1992. Teaching learners of all ages. *Music Educators Journal* 79 (4) (Dec.): 23–26.

Pieters, J. M. 1996. Psychology of adult education. In *International encyclopedia of adult education and training*, 2nd ed., ed. A. C. Tuijnman, 150–58. New York: Elsevier Science.

Sadler, W. A. 2000. *The third age: Six principles of growth and renewal after forty.* Cambridge, Mass: Perseus Books.

Schaie, K. W. 1996. Intellectual functioning in adulthood. In *Handbook of the psychology of aging*, 4th ed., ed. J. E. Birren, K. W. Schaie, 266–86. San Diego, Calif.: Academic Press.

Stebbins, R. A. 1992. *Amateurs, professionals, and serious leisure.* Montreal and Kingston, Calif.: Magill-Queen's University Press.

Vaillant, G. E. 2002. *Aging well: Surprising guideposts to a happier life from the landmark Harvard study of adult development.* 1st ed. Boston: Little, Brown.

Warshofsky, F. 1999. *Stealing time: The new science of aging.* New York: TV Books.

⑳

Compose Yourself: Older People and GarageBand

Jonathan D. Harnum

ABSTRACT

If music for lifelong learning is a goal in music education, then we should also focus music teaching and learning on those who have lived a long life. Teaching composition to older people fulfills the need to offer music education to a traditionally underserved population. In addition, such a course addresses issues of content diversity, which we see throughout music education. In the winter of 2008, a course in computer-mediated composition was offered to a small group of older people. The construction and implementation of this course addressed issues of aging, the arts (and music specifically) and their relation to aging, and computer use in older people. The translation of the research literature into use in a real class highlighted some of the difficulties found in putting theory into practice. In addition to a summary of some of the relevant literature, this chapter will describe the class and provide recommendations for both the next iteration of the class and for people who may consider teaching such a class.

INTRODUCTION

Playing trumpet saved George's life. Literally. The stateside military base he reported to for duty in World War II needed a bugler, and because George had played trumpet in high school he got the job, a job that meant he could perform an important duty for his country and yet remain out of harm's way. It's a story he delights in telling and is just one example of the rich, unique experiences that older students bring to the music classroom.

Teachers are most often older than students, whether we look in kindergarten or college classrooms. What might it be like to turn that maxim on its head and teach a class of students who were *all* older than you? One of the many differences you might notice is the type of stories your students tell. While it might seem at first glance that great stories may not be the most compelling argument for including older adults when we discuss the total music curriculum; but as it happens, it turns out to be one of the *most* convincing arguments.

Telling stories, according to developmental psychology, is a skill that contributes to the integration and meaning making that is a primary goal in later stages of life (Perlstein 2008; Newman and Newman 2007). Among many other things, teachers can provide instruction that will enable older students to tell their stories through music. Of course, there are many other good reasons for making older students and composition central to our conception of music education, which we will address in the following.

Our discussion is divided into three parts: The first presents a rationale for including both older people and computer-based composition in the practice of music education and introduces some of the literature used to inform this reasoning. While there is no research literature specifically addressing the narrowly focused issue of older-student, computer-mediated composition in music education, there is a large body of literature that addresses older people in general (Perlstein 2008; Butler 1975; Gazzaley et al. 2007), the arts and its relationship with aging (Boyer 2007), older people in other musical settings (Gibbons 1982; Gilbert and Beal 1982; Hays, Bright, and Minichiello 2002; Prickett 2003; Hays and Minichiello 2005; Boyer 2007; American Music Conference 2008), and computer use in an older population (Hendrix 2000; Porter 2000; Poynton 2005). Research from these domains will inform this section.

The second part of our discussion covers the specifics of a six-week course in computer-mediated composition using Apple's popular GarageBand software, taught to a small group of older students in the winter of 2008. Here I offer real-world examples that illuminate how some of this research plays out in practice. And the final section of our discussion, part 3, addresses concerns, strategies, and rationales for offering a similar program elsewhere, in addition to a critique of the successes and failures experienced within this particular class.

PART 1: OLDER PEOPLE AND THE ARTS, COMPUTERS, AND COMPOSITION

General Information on Aging

Adults over sixty years of age comprise one of the most rapidly grow-ing demographics in the United States, and this population is projected to increase over 45 percent by 2020 (U.S. Census Bureau 2004). With the exception of such programs as New Horizons community bands, few music-making opportunities exist for this population, tradition-ally underserved by music educators and music education researchers. This neglect is not purposeful, of course; it is hard to imagine a music teacher who would not agree that older people would benefit from greater musical activity and increased musical awareness. In addition to providing an interesting experience for both teacher and student, research within this population would also be fruitful.

A strong argument can be made for considering educational op-portunity and research within this population both because of the population's dramatic increase and the reality that many older people in developed countries will have more leisure time than at any other stage of life. Filling that leisure time with meaningful, appropriately challenging pursuits may help older people avoid the pitfalls of empty leisure by providing an outlet for "serious leisure" (Coffman 2006, 3). Although the primary focus of music education research has been on younger age groups, much research *has* been done to help us better understand the aging process.

In a broad historical overview of the history of the philosophy of aging, Susan Perlstein—who created the Elders Share the Arts pro-gram in 1979—cites Freudian psychologist Erik Erikson as the first to suggest "that the key psychological task of old age was integration, whereby we reflect on our lives' histories, confront our failures, and celebrate our successes and integrate both into our present. Those of us who succeed in this task achieve wisdom; those of us who are un-able to do so find their last years plagued by despair" (quoted in Perl-stein 2008, 1). It is difficult to think of a better reason for seeking to integrate and understand one's life. Using the arts in general and music in particular as a means of reflection has the potential for deepening and extending the ways in which we come to terms with our life at any age but has a particular resonance when it is our chief undertaking as Erikson's developmental theory implies.

Gerontologist Robert Butler continued to challenge our thoughts on aging with his 1975 publication, *Why Survive? On Being Old in America*, a work that called into question the then-accepted notion that reminiscence was unhealthy. Butler argued convincingly that reminiscing was in fact the very means by which older people strove for the integration spoken of by Erikson.

There are many ways that retrospection and integration might occur, such as the telling of one's stories, like George's story that opened this chapter. Though verbal story telling may well be the most common way we remember, artistic processing of one's life history may be equally valid and beneficial. If reminiscence is important to achieving the integration Butler and Erikson encourage, one might argue that in order to achieve fuller integration the more means of interpretation one has at one's disposal, the more likely integration is to occur on multiple levels, and the more comprehensive it will be. My goal for the course I taught in software-based composition to a group of older folks was to achieve this type of musical integration. In the second section we will see whether this goal was achieved.

The Arts and Aging

The fine arts—music, dance, or visual art—offer distinctive means of telling a story, of communicating, both recursive and transformative in nature:

> Another cognitive function of the arts is that in the process of creation they stabilize what would otherwise be evanescent. Ideas and images are very difficult to hold onto unless they are inscribed in a material that gives them at least a kind of semipermanence. The arts, as vehicles through which such inscriptions occur, enable us to inspect more carefully our own ideas, whether those ideas emerge in the form of language, music, or vision. The works we create speak back to us, and we become in their presence a part of a conversation that enables us to "see what we have said." (Eisner 2002, 11)

But communication, either with the self or with others, is just one benefit of using the arts—and music specifically—to enhance our understanding of the world and ourselves. Creating art shapes us, affecting the ways we grapple with the inexpressible. Again, Eisner illuminates this aspect of the arts with typical eloquence:

> They refine our senses so that our ability to experience the world is made more complex and subtle; they promote the use of our imaginative capacities so that we can envision what we cannot actually see, taste, touch, hear, and smell; they provide models through which we can experience the world in new ways; and they provide the materials and occasions for learning to grapple with problems that depend on arts-related forms of thinking. They also celebrate the consummatory, noninstrumental aspects of human experience and provide the means through which meanings that are ineffable, but feelingful, can be expressed. (Eisner 2002, 19)

Given the context of this chapter, perhaps the most relevant word in the previous quote is *consummatory*, but there are other important elements to Eisner's ideas. The language implies that the benefits provided by the arts are not relegated to a specific age or demographic; rather, the life of any person of any age can be enriched by the arts. As a community of researchers and teachers, we in music have in the past focused narrowly on students of school age, including college students; yet our focus is narrower still, for within this demographic we concentrate our curricula and research mostly on band, choir, orchestra and—for grades K–5—general music. This is said in a spirit of celebration of the work that has been done, without any blame for what has been thus far overlooked. We know that other populations and other musical behaviors, such as composition, improvisation, and the more neglected standards, are equally valid and deserving of pedagogical and research attention. Knowing of the disparity is one thing; doing something about the oversight, however, is more difficult.

In order to address alternative practices in music education, we must consider not only the many forms of musical behavior that exist in the world but, most crucially, the people who would like to engage in them, such as older people.

Music behavior is not limited to people who are youthful, and, in fact, music education's commitment to lifelong learning can be enhanced by stretching the parameters of the populations and research questions included in our research. The stereotype that music educators are only interested in, and only qualified to discuss, school or college bands, choruses, or general music needs to be put to rest, and research might open all our minds a bit (Prickett 2003, 58).

But the arts' contribution to positive aging is beginning to receive greater attention. The term *positive aging* is used in reference to older people, but it compels us to ask, Who in the world is *not* aging? The benefits of music in the lives of older people—and I submit *all* people—are not abstract notions relating to the somewhat fuzzy concept of *quality of life*; they are much more concrete than that. Particular benefits have been shown empirically in rigorous studies with surprising results.

Perhaps the first strictly scientific study of the benefits of the arts in an elderly population (Boyer 2007) was *The Impact of Professionally Conducted Cultural Programs on Older Adults*, a study published in 2001, conducted by Dr. Gene Cohen, director of the Center on Aging, Health and Humanities at George Washington University, and funded by the National Endowment for the Arts. The study (Boyer 2007, 21) found that participants in the arts groups on average

- used fewer medications,
- had fewer visits to the doctor,
- experienced elevated mood,
- showed an increase in the level of independent functioning, where normally decline would have been expected,
- did better on scales for depression, loneliness, and morale, and
- exhibited an increase in the number of activities, while the control group members experienced a decrease.

If we were to look at a study of music's role in positive aging, it would be difficult to find one better than that done by a multidisciplinary research team led by a University of Michigan investigator. The researchers examined the health of sixty-one older adults taking group piano lessons over two ten-week semesters (American Music Conference 2008). The participants showed a dramatic increase in human growth hormone (hGH) levels. Low levels of hGH are partially responsible for aging phenomena such as osteoporosis, low energy level, wrinkling, sexual dysfunction, muscle mass, and aches and pains. While controlling for differences in life events and social support, the study found that participants in music classes also showed a decrease in anxiety, depression, and perception of loneliness (Boyer 2007, 21–22).

It is unwise and philosophically unsound to claim secondary benefits of musical participation as the sole justification for the inclusion of music in one's education. A rich musical life is its own reward in many ways. However, it is equally unwise to ignore any benefits (or harmful effects, for that matter) that might exist. Given the above information, it is not unreasonable to assume that music education for older people is important, desirable, and something to work toward.

Music and Older Populations

Continuing music activity among older adults is perhaps most widely seen in the New Horizons movement, with wind ensembles comprised of older people who perform in communities worldwide. Of course New Horizons does not represent the only adults interested in music. In a 1991 survey (Bowles 1991), out of 275 adults, 67 percent indicated positive response to music participation. It is important to note that a significant correlation was found between course preference and prior experience with similar musical activities. The preponderance of community band as a means of musical activity for older people may well be a reflection of this correlation as well; most older people's experience with music in school has been in a band, choir, or orchestra. The correlation Bowles mentions further argues for the inclusion of alternative practices of music education (namely, all nine Standards) in school music for even young students, because this will in turn mean more diverse musical interests as the population ages. Of course this does not mean we should ignore those who are already older and haven't yet experienced alternative musical engagements like composition.

While many music teachers are making efforts to diversify school music offerings and research agendas (MENC 2008), we should simultaneously diversify music teaching and research for populations outside school. Though efforts to include other forms of music making have made only slight headway in our schools, there is no reason to wait to bring greater pedagogical diversity to an older population of learners as well by offering a class in composing on the computer using GarageBand software.

Computer Use and Older People

In order to address something like computer-based musical composition, it is prudent if not crucial to look at what research has to say about how older people deal with computer technology. While there is little information on older adults and music-specific computer-composition use, there is a wide variety of research into general computer use in this population. For example, only 5 percent of people over sixty-five use computers, compared to around 45 percent of middle-aged and younger adults (Hendrix 2000). One of the overarching, serious issues that arises concerns information poverty.

> Older adults, for whom computers and the Internet were not a part of childhood and early-adult development, are at a disadvantage in terms of access to electronic communication and online information and have even higher risks of developing information poverty than children. (Poynton 2005, 867)

Most studies attempt to classify positive benefits of computer use as well as identify attitudes and abilities that might make learning these new skills a challenge. In addition to a finding that computer use meets older people's need for fun and mental stimulation, Hendrix (2000, 62–63) cites other benefits, including increases in:

- self-esteem,
- education,
- sense of productivity and accomplishment, and
- social interaction.

Two kinds of barriers to computer usage noted by Hendrix are physical and cognitive limitations. Physical limitations include losses in acuity of vision and hearing as well as physical mobility, and all of these potential decrements should be considered when designing a course for the elderly. Additional important considerations are the findings in cognitive limitations related to memory use. Some studies indicate that retrieval is where the deficit lies (Hendrix 2000), while others have found that when working memory is taxed and many distracters are present (as is true with the GarageBand program), there is interference in the encoding of information. Specifically, older adults have been found to be less able to ignore irrelevant information in such settings (Gazzaley et al. 2007). Much of the literature also indicates that older people frequently experience anxiety in relation to computers, including fear, aversion, apprehension, physiological symptoms, and negative internal dialogue (Poynton 2005).

Despite what the research had to say, however, my own experience with these particular students indicated that every person's relationship to technology is different, sometimes profoundly so. While I was teaching this class, science-fiction author Arthur C. Clarke passed away; author of the adage that "sufficiently advanced technology is indistinguishable from magic" (Clarke 1972, 1). For some students in this class, Clarke's statement had the ring of truth; others had a different story to tell.

Bill had been in college at the University of Illinois, Chicago, and was peripherally involved in ARPANET, the precursor to the Internet. In the mid-1970s Bill remembers being excited about successfully sending an e-mail from one room to the next. Bill's background made his experience of the class very different than that of others who were not as technologically savvy. The implications of these differences will be addressed in the final part of this chapter.

Whatever the underlying cause might be, and despite outliers like Bill, the literature makes it clear that it is more difficult for older students to learn this technology. As Ben, one of the students with low computer literacy, said during a tutorial, "It's not that I don't get it. I do. I understand everything you're saying. It's just that a week later, I can't remember anything about what you said, and I have to go through it all over again." All of these findings, in addition to practical classroom experience, implicate specific classroom strategies, which will be covered in both of the next sections.

PART 2: THE COMPOSITION CLASS

The selection of students to participate in a class on computer composition was carefully made. Because the research literature indicated that computer use among older people could be a substantial barrier to learning, enrollment was limited to students who indicated they had at least a rudimentary level of computer literacy. In addition, anticipating difficulties with using unfamiliar technology, I decided to limit students to those who had prior knowledge of the basic elements of music. I correctly anticipated that there would be enough challenge learning how to use the software and that previous experience with music would be beneficial.

To find willing students who met these criteria, I visited a local New Horizons band two times in order to make myself known and to convey information about the class. Three men and two women, ranging in age from fifty-five to seventy-six, decided to take the course. Classes were held over six weeks in the winter of 2008 in the library computer lab at a Midwestern university every Wednesday afternoon from 3:00 until 4:30, with an additional hour of lab time scheduled in case participants wanted or needed extra time to work on their projects. In the end, class often extended a little beyond the 4:30 mark, and participants often stayed later to continue working.

The university's Macintosh lab is well equipped with over forty Macintosh computers, four to a row, each with twenty-inch screens, and all with a MIDI keyboard attached as well as headphones, an important component, given the musical nature of our activities. At the front of the room was a podium with another Macintosh, a high-quality projector, and a large motorized video screen on which lessons and examples were projected. Technology staff were on duty during library hours, an important consideration for any teacher lacking technological trouble-shooting skills.

At the beginning of each class, students received a handout containing detailed step-by-step instructions for the tasks of the day. These included graphic pictures of the GarageBand interface labeled in large print, with arrows indicating relevant locations and actions. These handouts were used both so that students could have multiple representations of what they were learning, and also so the students could quickly reconstruct the steps necessary to completing a particular task when it was time to work independently. During the introduction of a new technique, the class could go through the lesson together with all students creating highly similar recordings. Students who immediately grasped the task at hand would often move to help those nearby who were having a bit of trouble. This social interaction was something I had hoped for in designing the course, because social interaction has been cited as a primary reason for participation in music activities in an older population (Coffman 2006). I was glad to see that social interactions arose spontaneously.

After the introduction of the new material, students would then take time to work on the new concepts and skills on their own, using their own ideas while I helped to trouble-shoot, answer questions, or review material. After this, if time allowed, another technique would be introduced and practiced in the same manner. In addition to the handouts, students had access to online video tutorials that I had created, which showed step-by-step examples (with voiceover) of how to use the program. These were to be combined with the handouts and served both as primary instructional material and as review material as the course moved forward.

Assessment was simple and immediate. Each skill was associated with a small project that could be easily completed during class time. A student was either able to understand how to use the software to get the desired result or not, and if not, then a fellow student, an undergraduate helper, or I would work with the student until he or she was able to complete the assignment.

The greatest challenge of the class was attempting to address varied levels of computer literacy. This was difficult because the range of literacy was so wide. As mentioned earlier, Bill had been in on the early version of the Internet and was something of a gearhead, so he had no difficulty whatsoever with the technological demands of the class. Another student, Anne, was also computer literate, and she was able to teach me things about GarageBand that I hadn't known before. Conversely, two other students truly struggled to understand the technology. One never did seem to grasp the concept of Internet navigation or the concept of *tracks*, an essential component of the software. I would often check in on him to find him happily poking through the deep recesses of the machine's file system, quite unsure of how he got there. Another student had great difficulty understanding how to use the video tutorials I had created for the class; he was confused by the fact that the video looked identical to the program, and his attempts to interact with the video were unsuccessful and frustrating for him.

Early on I realized that even with only five students in the class, it was going to be difficult to keep up with the demands of individualized attention. I arranged for undergraduate music education majors to visit the class on several occasions to help with the teaching duties. Their observations squared with mine—namely, that it was uniformly difficult to anticipate the struggles students would have when foundational knowledge is taken for granted.

I have built several websites, have owned many computers, began learning computer code in 1983, and am comfortable working with software, hardware, and peripherals such as the MIDI piano keyboards used in class. I found my experience to be both boon and hindrance: Trouble-shooting and diagnostic skill that comes from experience is priceless in a class of this type where things are apt to go wrong, most often because those who are most unfamiliar with computers seem to be those who most readily push the boundaries of what the technologies are able to deal with before crashing. However, familiarity breeds not contempt but blindness. It is hard to anticipate difficulties that an older student might have that arise from skills that seem so simplistic to those of us more familiar with technology, including issues we don't even consider to be challenging, such as watching a video tutorial.

The goal of the course was for each student to have composed at least one piece by the end of the course, and while we managed to do this, we weren't as successful as I had hoped we would be. The greater goal of creating a composition that depicted a life story was almost completely unrealized, mostly due to the lack of time necessary to building the required skills. Everyone, however, did produce at least one short and complete composition, and most students produced many more than one.

Perhaps most gratifying for me as a teacher was a composition made for me by Jan, a woman who has played multiple instruments throughout her life including steel drum, marimba, piano, and clarinet. She has studied most of these instruments formally, in some cases with master musicians, and she regularly participates in percussion workshops and attends concerts. In her composition she depicted, through music, my boyhood home in Alaska, complete with a calving glacier, bird song, the dripping water of a temperate rainforest, and pitched percussion. Despite the fact that Jan firmly believes she is not musically creative, I found her compositions to be the most interesting and compositionally sound of all five members of the group. This creativity came in spite of her limited computer literacy. This is interesting because some members who were vastly superior in their computer literacy did not produce compositions that were as sophisticated as Jan's.

In general, I considered the class to be a success, both for myself as a teacher and for the students. Two students were so enamored of what they learned that they purchased new Macintosh computers in order to continue working with GarageBand on their own. There is always room for improvement in even the most successful courses, and in the final section I address issues that arose in the class and the ways in which future iterations of this course might benefit from different approaches. The class will be taught again in the spring of 2009.

PART 3: RECOMMENDATIONS FOR FUTURE
COMPOSITION CLASSES WITH OLDER PEOPLE

The literature cited, in addition to many other studies not cited, was an essential component in my preparation for this class. But as the saying goes, "in theory, there is no difference between theory and practice, but in practice, there is." The reason theories don't translate to the practical is that theories deal with generalizations while practice deals with the wonderfully messy world of individuals. Still, there was a benefit to learning about generalizations within this population. I've divided up this final section as a reporter might, addressing the who, where, when, what, and how of teaching older students music composition using GarageBand. We'll address *why* in the conclusion.

Who should be in these classes rests on the idea of homogeneity, especially the homogeneity of computer-literacy skills, something I considered more important than prior musical knowledge. Knowledge of simple computer terms (*mouse, address bar, click, drag,* etc.), the ability to use a mouse, and an understanding of Internet navigation is a must. In future courses, I will use a simple checklist or questionnaire to assess each prospective student's computer-literacy level. Many community centers and organizations offer introductory courses for novice computer users who might be interested in taking the class.

The other important *who* is the teacher or teachers. While comprehensive expertise isn't necessary, the teacher should have a sound understanding of computers, software use, and at least a working knowledge of the GarageBand program. A dozen hours or less playing with the program would give an interested educator more than enough experience to provide instruction to novices. The ability to troubleshoot problems with either software or hardware is a plus but is not essential, especially if the course is offered in a setting where technology staff are on duty. Often the problems encountered in such a class are easily solvable by someone who possesses both a basic understanding of computers and patience.

As to *where*, the ideal setting is in a staffed computer lab. Access to the lab is an important consideration for this population. The lab we used for the class initially caused some concern as it was not easily accessible by car, and students were required to walk five to ten minutes in frigid winter temperatures. Fortunately these students were veterans of many Midwestern winters, and this proved to be no obstacle for them. Future class facilitators must consider in advance any barriers to access, even stairways.

Speaking of frigid winter temperatures, we raise the question of *when*. Perhaps more important than season is the question of how often the class meets. Students of any age often have difficulty remembering what happened in a class that meets only once a week, and for older people who may have even greater constraints on their memory, more frequent reinforcement of the new knowledge is preferable. The next time I teach this class we will meet two times a week for this reason. Time of day is often not as much of an issue for people who are retired, but like anyone, they often have other commitments. A time in the afternoon before 5:00 usually works best. Class length is also an important consideration. I have found half an hour to forty-five minutes of instruction with an equal amount of time in self-directed work to be the ideal class length.

What is to be taught should be considered closely. In my first attempt, I was overly ambitious in expecting all of my students to compose a piece that depicted some aspect of their life story. Although I will maintain this goal for anyone who decides to repeat the class, it may be too lofty a goal for a class that meets for only a short time. Future classes will instead focus on helping students develop the skills necessary to using all that the program has to offer, as this would then allow the student to continue composing outside of class. For example, toward the end of this class, we experimented with using GarageBand to record sound, and this excited many of the students more than anything they had learned thus far, especially those who were struggling somewhat with their compositions.

The question of *how* to teach this class could very well take up an entire textbook. The most important recommendations for teaching this class echo much of what the literature has said is important— namely pace, repetition, patience, and presenting and practicing skills and knowledge in as isolated a way as possible (Hendrix 2000; Poynton 2005; Gazzaley et al. 2007). It is one thing to read this and understand and quite another to put it into practice in a classroom.

In closing this section, I must reiterate the importance of computer literacy: A relatively high level of literacy allowed Bill to progress at a much faster rate than the rest of the class, and he often completed multiple compositions while other participants struggled to complete even one. It is interesting that although Bill was by far the most prolific composer in the class, the quality of his compositions, in my opinion, were less than other members of the class who had lesser computer literacy. As we all know, quality and quantity are only loosely related. This suggests that although computer literacy is an important skill, there are other skills that may be more influential on the quality of a composition. That being said, computer literacy undeniably contributes to the quality of the experience if not the quality of the composition. Greater literacy means less confusion, anxiety, or frustration in the process of composing in this setting.

CONCLUSION

The *why* of computer composition has already been well covered in the first part of this chapter, but the rationale is worth summarizing: The arts in general, and music in particular, offer singular ways of thinking about the world and about one's life in it. They also offer unique means of shaping our perspective of what it means to be human and "provide the means through which meanings that are ineffable, but feelingful, can be expressed" (Eisner 2002, 19). The expression of what we know—either verbally, musically, or by some other means—is the only way to achieve the integration and understanding that are so important for wisdom in any stage of life.

Computer composition is just one small, somewhat dim, point of light in the constellation that makes up adult music education, which resides in the galaxy of community music, which in turn resides in the universe of all music learning. This does not mean that it is unimportant, however. From a certain perspective, our own sun and our own planet are also simple dim points of light in the vast universe, but they are certainly not unimportant dim lights! As the title of the 1995 album by Soul Asylum says, "Let your dim light shine."

REFERENCES

American Music Conference. 2008. *Scientific findings show that music making increases human growth hormone among active older Americans.* www .amc-music.com/musicmaking/wellness/hormone.htm (accessed March 18, 2008).

Bowles, C. L. 1991. Self-expressed adult music education interests and music experiences. *Journal of Research in Music Education* 39 (3): 191–205.

Boyer, J. M. 2007. *Creativity matters: The arts and aging toolkit.* New York: National Guild of Community Schools of the Arts.

Butler, R. 1975. *Why survive? Being old in America.* New York: Harper & Row.

Clarke, A. C. 1972. *Profiles of the future: An inquiry into the limits of the possible.* New York: Bantam. http://en.wikipedia.org/wiki/Clarke%27s_three _laws (accessed March 15, 2009).

Coffman, D. D. 2006. Voices of experience: Interviews of adult community band members in Launceston, Tasmania, Australia. Paper presented at the Music and Lifelong Learning Symposium, University of Wisconsin, Madison. *International Journal of Community Music* D (2006). www.intljcm .com/articles/Volume%204/Coffman/Coffman.pdf.

Eisner, E. W. 2002. *Arts and the creation of mind.* New Haven, Conn.: Yale University Press.

Gazzaley, A., M. A. Sheridan, J. W. Cooney, and M. D'Esposito. 2007. Age-related deficits in component processes of working memory. *Neuropsychology* 21 (5): 532–39.

Gibbons, A. C. 1982. Music Aptitude Profile scores in a non-institutionalized, elderly population. *Journal of Research in Music Education* 30 (1): 23–29.

Gilbert, J. P., and M. R. Beal. 1982. Preferences of elderly individuals for selected music education experiences. *Journal of Research in Music Education* 30 (4): 247–53.

Glesne, C. 2006. *Becoming qualitative researchers: An introduction.* 3rd ed. Boston: Pearson / Allyn & Bacon.

Hays, T., R. Bright, and V. Minichiello. 2002. The contribution of music to positive aging: A review. *Journal of Aging and Identity* 7 (3): 165–75.

Hays, T., and V. Minichiello. 2005. The meaning of music in the lives of older people: A qualitative study. *Psychology of Music* 33 (4): 437–51.

Hendrix, C. C. 2000. Computer use among elderly people. *Computers in Nursing* 18 (2): 62–68.

MENC: The National Association for Music Education. 2008. *A research agenda for music education: Thinking ahead.* www.menc.org/resources/view/a-research-agenda-for-music-education-thinking-ahead (accessed January 15, 2009).

Newman, B. M., and P. R. Newman. 2007. *Theories of human development.* London: Lawrence Erlbaum Associates.

Perlstein, S. 2008. *Arts and creative aging across America.* www.communityarts.net/readingroom/archivefiles/2002/10/arts_and_creati.php (accessed March 17, 2008).

Porter, K. J. 2000. Terror and emancipation: The disciplinarity and mythology of computers. *Cultural Critique* 44:43–48.

Poynton, T. A. 2005. Computer literacy across the lifespan: A review with implications for educators. *Computers in Human Behavior* 21:861–72.

Prickett, C. A. 2003. Is there musical life after graduation? Mining the resources of an understudied population. *Research Studies in Music Education* 21:58–71.

U.S. Census Bureau. 2004. *US interim projections by age, sex, race, and Hispanic origin.* Washington, D.C.: U.S. Census Bureau.

Democratic Jazz: Two Perspectives on a Collaborative Improvisation Jazz Workshop

Victor Lin and Joshua S. Renick

ABSTRACT

The following chapter describes the circumstances leading up to and surrounding the creation of the Teachers College Jazz Workshop, an experimental and collective graduate student–led weekly session dedicated to the pedagogy of beginning jazz improvisation, which ran from October 2006 to April 2007. It describes a possible model for how not only beginning jazz improvisers but also intermediate and advanced jazz players can learn cooperatively in a democratic and alternative classroom environment given the right circumstance and the right framework and also lays the groundwork for further explorations of effective methods of improvisation pedagogy. The following offers the individual perspectives of each of the authors, respectively.

VICTOR LIN: MY PERSPECTIVE OF THE TEACHERS COLLEGE JAZZ WORKSHOP

Introduction

The Jazz Performance Program at Columbia University has grown steadily over the last decade. In the fall of 2000, Columbia's jazz program consisted of a single class in jazz improvisation and a student-run club, which ran two combo rehearsals that met in the student center. By 2005, the number of participants and the amount of interest in jazz at Columbia had grown considerably: steadily mounting student interest and an active program director had managed to make jazz combos an official class for credit instead of just a student club, and the number of jazz performances on campus was becoming apparent as well. Campus-wide awareness of jazz was becoming more widespread as more concerts were promoted, and a handful of adjunct faculty was hired to teach private lessons and combos.

As a result of the increase in size of the jazz program, Columbia University started to hold open auditions for private lessons and spots in the jazz ensembles. Although the number of students participating in Columbia's jazz program was increasing, so too was the number of students being denied participation due to a lack of skill and experience. It was difficult to see where the beginners and novice jazz musicians could fit into a program that was primarily geared toward students who already had a basic grasp and understanding of jazz performance. A need was becoming clear—How do we address the needs of beginning jazz improvisers with little or no experience?

Subsequently, I began to brainstorm ideas for best including the students who weren't placed in the ensembles and somehow providing them with a foundational experience and a solid background in jazz improvisation. From a philosophical standpoint, it seemed absurd to think that those who were turned down would somehow be able to improve enough to the point that the next year they would be accepted into the jazz program; how would you get better if you couldn't get lessons? How would you know what to do if you couldn't qualify for lessons or you couldn't get placed in an ensemble to learn how to play? Then again, if you had no ensemble experience, would you even know what kind of things you need to play in a jazz combo?

That fall I pitched an idea to the head of the jazz program: was there room to add a beginner-level combo class for introductory-level players? Columbia's jazz-performance program course offerings consisted at this point of an improvisation course, several small jazz combos, and a big band. Beginner-level combos are a large part of the program at the Stanford Jazz Workshop (www.stanfordjazz.org), whose materials and teaching supplements are used all over the world, and where I've been an instructor for the last decade. My thought was that if jazz education could be provided on that sort of level in a week-long summer camp, it could be done in a college setting over a longer period of time. Though the head of the Columbia jazz program lauded my enthusiasm and supported my idea, I was informed that there was no space to hold such a class and no money in the budget to pay someone to do that at this point. Consequently, if I were to create such a program, I would have to do so on my own, independent of Columbia and without any pay. He was happy, however, to give me a list of all of the students who had auditioned for the jazz program and not been placed in a combo or lesson slot of any sort.

With the help of fellow graduate student and tenor saxophonist Joshua Renick, I was able to contact the list of jazz students who had been rejected and offered all of them the opportunity to be part of our experimental beginning improvisation "class" that we were going to put together. After a week, we had responses from a dozen students whom we split up into two groups, one that would meet on Wednesdays and one that met on Fridays.

The Basis for the Teachers College Jazz Workshop

In my opinion, the single most important thing that a jazz improviser needs to experience in order to improve is simply to play as much as possible with a strong rhythm section—particularly a good bass player. That is the premise behind Jamey Aebersold's immensely popular play-along records, which are CDs of strong rhythm sections (piano, bass, drums) playing chorus after chorus of selected songs without any soloist. However, play-along records are a weak substitute for the real thing—a beginner who wants to learn by playing with an Aebersold record receives no feedback and no real interaction with the CD that is playing the accompaniment track, and the unfortunate reality of today's situation is that most beginner jazz musicians simply have very little opportunity to play with excellent rhythm sections. Even in established jazz programs, beginner horn players are usually placed together with beginner rhythm section players, since the majority of advanced rhythm section players are more interested in playing with other advanced players than they are in playing with or for beginners. In effect, the play-along record is something of a last resort.

I often wondered how things would turn out if we were able to match up an experienced bassist with novice musicians and make them play together for extended periods of time. In my own experiences as a jazz piano teacher, I grew so frustrated with the fact that I could never get good bassists to come play for my piano students that I decided to learn how to play the bass myself. After several years of practice, I began playing bass for my jazz piano students and was startled to discover over time that they were improving much faster than I ever did when I was a student. This was in part due to the fact that I could actually give direction to the student and play with him at the same time he was playing piano, an experience that essentially amounted to a guided practice performance. This approach of coaching the student while playing with him at the same time yielded similarly remarkable results with all of my jazz piano students both at the Stanford Jazz Workshop as well as at Columbia.

If consistent playing with a solid bass player/coach was enough to cause my piano students to improve at an remarkably fast rate, what would happen if I did the same thing but this time for a larger number of students on different instruments? Thus, my idea for the class sessions hinged on the premise that I would play bass and be the anchor of the sessions, supplying the harmonic and rhythmic core foundation for the soloists and giving direction as well as holding down the form of the song if the students got lost in it. What all of the students lacked was the experience of playing along with a strong bassist and being given direction and critique while doing it. Joshua and I were determined to give that experience to them all and extremely interested in seeing what resulted from it.

The Class Sessions

We were lucky to have enough participants in each of the classes on Wednesday and Friday to assemble close to a full band each time. Our instrumentation was nearly always that of a typical jazz combo—Joshua played saxophone, I played bass, and to that we added the drums, piano, and an assortment of other instruments—guitar, trumpet, saxophone, and violin. After one or two classes, the sessions started to take on a pretty consistent format: We would begin by clearly stating a theme on which that class would center. I would talk about a basic jazz playing concept (such as improvisation over one chord, or the twelve-bar blues form), discuss and clarify any initial questions the participants had, and then start everyone playing. The fact that Joshua played saxophone while I played bass was fortunate in that we could actually play and model the concept we were teaching (soloist/rhythm section) just by ourselves, something we preferred to do rather than to talk about the concept; more often than not, we would address questions that came up as we played through whatever it was we had decided to work on, an example of reflection-in-action. Joshua and I would often begin by playing through a form several times until eventually all the musicians had joined in.

In a typical small jazz ensemble rehearsal, the players assemble, are given "charts" or "lead sheets" with melodies and chords on them, and then play through the tune, taking solos. The emphasis is primarily on rehearsing and polishing material to get it to a performance-ready level. By contrast, in our jazz-workshop sessions we rarely looked at charts or music, opting instead to focus on very simple song structures and forms that we could either teach by ear or write out quickly on a chalkboard. Often, after beginning the sessions by playing something like a basic twelve-bar blues, instead of merely playing through the blues and giving everyone a short solo and then moving on to something else as most combo rehearsals I experienced might do, we zeroed in and focused on multiple aspects of the music in a number of unusual and experimental ways.

To begin with, we assumed absolutely nothing on behalf of the participants—since the primary goal of our workshop was to give beginners the experience of improvising in a jazz ensemble, we allowed room for every question imaginable, all the way down to the most basic things. We explained terms like *scale, note, time, swing, phrase,* and *form* and, more importantly, demonstrated sonically and physically what each thing meant in relation to the larger picture. We pushed the students to explore the concepts and ideas behind improvisation and allowed them to be tested out, almost as if we were in some sort of jazz laboratory. We encouraged, in fact challenged, the soloists to improvise for unusually large amounts of time—ten choruses, twelve choruses, play until you literally run out of ideas—and then asked them immediately to reflect verbally on what they had just done. We asked the other participants to describe what it was like, or what their opinions were. In a sense, we were providing the students with an environment in which they could feel safe to improvise, safe to explore and stretch out, and safe to speak freely about what they thought and how they felt—not just about other people's playing but, more importantly, about their own.

In many ways the classroom environment was experimental and did not follow a preset order of activities. In later sessions the class would sometimes begin with one student mentioning a musical idea or asking a question that they had been wanting to know an answer to: examples included how a certain scale is used over a certain chord, how to play a certain kind of tune, the challenge of faster tempos and odd meters, and trying different keys. Subsequently, the interaction and learning that occurred was akin to collective discovery, exploration, and a building off of the previous event or events that had just happened. Many times the learning extended beyond just their own instrument—during one class session I had everyone sit down at the drum set and understand at core what it was like to play the drums and to be able to identify each element of the basic drum kit. We then did the same thing for the piano and for the bass so that every student had a very basic understanding of at the very least the mechanical principles behind the instruments of the rhythm section. Out of this collective learning style emerged the creation of a more democratic educational environment that was inclusive of every participant's opinion and observation, not just those of the instructor.

Above all, the most important part of the workshop was that it provided an environment in which its participants were able to receive a significant amount of real-time playing experience in an authentic jazz setting, something that is nearly impossible for beginners to do without a good deal of external assistance. The key element of the workshop was being able to provide a backdrop on which students could practice improvising. Although improvisation itself does not require other people, guided improvisation seemed to yield results that I had never seen before in other classes that I had experienced.

The End Results

For those who participated in the workshop initially, the results varied widely. Several of the participants were seniors or graduate students who would go on to further education in other departments. Others merely thanked us for the opportunity to play and went on to other things. But a small number of students, notably one of the drummers and one of the saxophone players, went on to be placed in Columbia ensembles that same semester. The amount of improvement they showed made such an impression on the Columbia jazz department that I was called on and asked to create the same sort of class at Columbia but to teach it officially as an adjunct faculty member the following academic year. In the fall of 2007, I started teaching my first two classes of beginning jazz improvisation and have been teaching the classes at Columbia every semester since. Joshua was so impacted by the experiences of working with the students that it formed the basis for the doctoral dissertation he is currently working on, a study of the democratic process of learning within a jazz context.

Conclusion

There were three major differences between the workshop and any previous experiences that I had had as a student musician: The first difference was the idea that all participants would receive playing experience and training. The second was that all of the students' opinions and questions would be taken into account and actively solicited, as opposed to my merely telling them what to do. The third difference was the allowance of time for all soloists to explore and discover on their own during real-time playing—there is a tremendous difference between the individual practice session and the performance environment. Most jazz improvisation/combo classes are already close to the performance environment in that it's the complete band and it runs through songs and rehearses them. In the TCJW we were concerned with one objective—the real-time experience of engaging in jazz improvisation, and doing that as much as possible.

The idea was to create an environment in which people could *practice* improvising—and then receive real-time coaching simultaneously. The process of improvising requires a combination of thought, creativity, action, reaction, and, most importantly, *real time*; the difference between improvisation and composition is that one occurs in the moment of execution while the other is independent of it. As mentioned previously, the most popular educational aid to most players who wish to practice with a rhythm section is the Aebersold play-along CD. While the Aebersold play-along CDs and Band-in-a-Box software programs allow for the individual improviser to practice with a rhythm section, they do not allow for discussion, coaching, dialogue, or any sort of interaction. The jazz workshop in effect provided everything that a play-along CD could not.

Beginning improvisers are often not encouraged to take solos, let alone long ones. By questioning and revisiting what had been natural assumptions about beginning improvisation classes, both Joshua and I found that our own assumptions about what musicians do and don't know were being challenged as well. In my experience, classes for beginners were almost always led by one individual who possessed all the knowledge as well as the evaluative power to tell us whether or not our solos sounded "good" or "fit" the requirements. By contrast, Joshua and I made sure that every participant in the workshop had a say in what they felt and thought about how things sounded—from critiquing each other to assessing themselves to making suggestions on how to improve from situation to situation. Our thought was that beginner improvisers had much more musical thought and judgment than had previously been thought or experienced. This was not without basis, as in my own experiences I clearly recall a number of disagreements that I'd had with my teachers as an undergraduate, but I'd yielded to their views and assessments, assuming they were correct, because of my relative inexperience by comparison.

Perhaps more valuable for Joshua and me as teachers here was the discovery of the presence and value of dialogue between musicians, both verbal and musical—collective discussion about what worked and what didn't along with a generous amount of playing time. In my experiences as a jazz educator and as a jazz student, I couldn't recall any group with such a wide gap in the levels of playing ability, nor could I ever recall so much weight being given to each voice in the band. The requisite skill necessary to facilitate discussion, dialogue, interaction, and learning is extremely difficult; it is hard enough to facilitate the same sort of action musically, and yet the consistent result that we came to discover was that as we allowed students to voice their concerns and interact with one another musically, they would do the same things verbally, with fascinating results.

The Teachers College Jazz Workshop initially began with one premise in mind: to give its participants the playing experience necessary to improve as jazz improvisers and subsequently raise their playing level sufficiently so that they would be good enough to play in one of the Columbia University jazz ensembles. Although that goal was ultimately fulfilled, it was the unintended consequences and outcomes of the workshop sessions that were of more lasting interest. By placing beginner musicians with more experienced ones and encouraging dialogue and interaction among all of us, the workshop caused us to critically reflect on not only our own experiences as musicians but on all of us as cooperative learners as well.

JOSHUA S. RENICK: A SECOND PERSPECTIVE OF THE TEACHERS COLLEGE JAZZ WORKSHOP

Working from the theory of John Dewey, David Hansen (2001) writes that concerning the world of the classroom, "the subject matter of teaching and learning describes an *interactive, transactive process.* Subject matter can constitute what teachers and students do. The term describes aspects of activity to cultivate learning and growth" (76). Using Hansen's words as a point of departure, I will speak to the interactive and transactive process of teaching and learning I encountered and observed as a collaborative member of the Teachers College Jazz Workshop between all of its members, both teachers and students alike, and how the activity in which we engaged cultivated our learning and growth as novice jazz musicians and jazz educators respectively. In order to establish a context for my involvement with the workshop, I begin with a brief description of two contrasting perspectives of jazz education from my life as music student.

Two Contrasting Examples from My Jazz Education

In the spring of 2005, after several years away from the world of collegiate jazz education, while studying at Columbia University, I auditioned and was placed in one of the advanced small jazz ensembles. However, during my participation in several different ensembles over the course of the next three consecutive semesters, I began to recognize in the instructors of these ensembles the same style of teaching that had been prevalent throughout my previous participation in similar undergraduate jazz performance ensemble settings—a style in which the instructors appeared to approach the teaching of their ensembles by enacting the role of bandleader.

During a typical rehearsal at Columbia, instructors did little more than provide music to students, which we were then expected to learn to play accurately and were also to then effectively improvise two or three choruses over each piece of music. It appeared that the pedagogical philosophy governing these ensembles was based on an assumption that participating students already knew how to improvise. The instructor's objective was simply to produce a musical product worthy of live performance rather than to focus on the development of the students' understanding of jazz improvisation. As a result of this hierarchical approach to teaching, students were afforded little or no voice as ensemble members.[1]

Standing in stark contrast to my jazz ensemble experiences in higher education were those I had experienced in high school. The learning environment I encountered in high school was unlike any I subsequently experienced until my participation in the Teachers College Jazz Workshop, an environment that would serve as a model of democratic education in the development of my own education.

During my freshman year in high school the band director, Mr. Wood, had decided to experiment with a new pedagogical philosophy to reshape the direction of the ensemble, one centered on the democratic principle of inclusion. Participation in the ensemble would no longer be exclusively reserved for only the best upperclassmen. All incoming freshman who demonstrated an interest in playing jazz and also participated in the wind ensemble would be given a place in the big band. While this decision was widely unpopular with the upperclassmen, it had been carefully conceived by Mr. Wood. No

longer would beginners be separated from the more advanced players—all of the students would now play and learn together, with
the aim of rapidly developing the musical abilities of the freshman
through interaction and peer mentorship with the more advanced
upperclassmen.

By playing with the more-experienced upperclassmen, we freshman not only heard what it meant to be a better player but through
musical interaction actively observed and assimilated a musical model
far more advanced than our own. Over the course of that academic
year, all of us freshman experienced exponential musical growth that
would never have been possible if we had been placed in an ensemble
of novices, isolated from the upperclassmen.[2]

The assimilation and interaction of the freshman and underclass-
men was not the only model of democratic pedagogy I experienced
in high school. Mr. Wood's approach and model of teaching were
far removed from concepts that imposed pedagogical hierarchy. The
band was completely student-run. Section leaders were responsible
for rehearsals, and Mr. Wood never conducted from atop a podium or
from behind a music stand but rather participated musically as the
fifth chair of the trumpet section. Rarely speaking during rehearsals,
he would often interject his musical opinion only if he felt it was absolutely necessary, instead providing space for students to engage in
dialogue regarding the musical direction of the band. The big band was
the most formative experience and model of democratic music education during my time as a young music student. Those experiences
have never left me and in retrospect have become my standard for jazz
education in a classroom setting.

The Teachers College Jazz Workshop

It was not until my colleague at Teachers College, Victor Lin, approached me regarding an idea he had for creating a jazz improvisation
workshop for novice undergraduate musicians at Columbia University
that I would have an opportunity to actually teach jazz improvisation
in a classroom setting. Prior to the workshop, my only experience
teaching jazz in a classroom had been directing a junior high school
big band, in which the teaching of improvisation bordered on trivial.
Aware of my desire to teach jazz improvisation, Victor asked if I would
help form and coteach the workshop.

For well over a month Victor and I shared with each other our personal histories and experiences as jazz musicians, students, and music
educators, which culminated in our conception of the environment

in which the Columbia undergrads would have the opportunity to actively explore and develop as jazz improvisers. In creating the environment for the workshop, Victor and I focused on two clear pedagogical concepts concerning our teaching practice, which would guide the development of the students to ensure that their experiences were not, to use the Deweyian term, *miseducative* (Dewey 1997, 51).

First, we were more than just teachers in the workshop; we were also active musical participants. Victor and I did not direct the workshop from behind music stands but rather guided it from behind our instruments—Victor playing bass and I playing saxophone. In doing so, we deliberately placed ourselves in positions to interact musically with all of the participants. Our playing provided a strong musical model for the students to observe and emulate. Just as I had experienced in high school while playing with the upperclassmen, our musical participation provided our students in the ensemble an opportunity to develop musically by playing with more-experienced musicians, rather than simply being told how to play by them.

The second concept that Victor and I were conscious of in our teaching practice was to never take advantage of our position as more-advanced musicians but rather to position ourselves as musical collaborators, carefully avoiding the creation of a musical hierarchy. By presenting ourselves as "friendly copartners" and working "together on a common enterprise," we established an environment in which all of the students felt safe to engage in musical exploration and verbal dialogue regardless of ability or lack of experience (Dewey 1974, 10). Doing so allowed for the creation of honest musical and verbal dialogue between all of the participants.

As the workshop progressed, I began to realize that Victor and I were also modeling an alternative to the traditional hierarchical, bandleader/teaching model that had been so prevalent in my own experience as a music student in higher education. In taking this particular outlook on teaching and shaping the environment of the workshop, we were obliged to regard ourselves as a critical element in that environment. We did not stand apart from the process of the workshop, as if we ran it from a superior source of knowledge and insight. We were simultaneously not only more-advanced improvisers and teachers but also participants in the workshop who continually learned from the students and our interactions with subject matter and each other (Hansen 2001, 72).

The students were not the only participants actively engaged in learning more about jazz improvisation. As I've mentioned, the workshop was the first time I had ever attempted to teach in a classroom setting with novice musicians learning how to improvise. While the students explored jazz improvisation from the perspective of the novice musician, I was simultaneously exploring and developing an understanding of the subject from the perspective of the novice teacher of improvisation. As a jazz saxophonist with over fifteen years of playing experience, I came to the workshop with a solid understanding of how to improvise but little to no understanding of how to teach it to someone else.

From the beginning of the workshop Victor and I had agreed that he would take the lead teaching role in the first few sessions; since I had far less experience teaching improvisation, I would participate at first but also observe how he guided a session and, over time, would slowly begin to share the teaching. Essential to my growing understanding of teaching improvisation were the private dialogues Victor and I shared after each session.

Independent of the students, Victor and I would retreat to my office and, in a manner that best resembled a debriefing session, critique each session from our perspective as teachers. For often more than an hour, we would discuss the events of each session, challenging each other to improve on pedagogical successes, which in turn provoked "questions and thought, not complacency" related to our understanding of the subject (Hansen 2001, 76). Working with Victor on the development of my ability to teach jazz improvisation was, much like the experiences of the novice musicians, an opportunity for me to practice with a more-experienced teacher. I was, as David Hansen describes, losing myself in the classroom environment as much as the students were, partaking in a process that promoted an environment that drew out similar responses in students and teachers alike (Hansen 2001, 72).

NOTES

1. For a detailed conversation regarding hierarchical pedagogy, see Freire 2005. For conversations regarding hierarchical pedagogy in music and higher education, see Kingsbury 1984 and Nettl 1995.

2. In many ways what I experienced that year resembled a more historical model of jazz education in which less-experienced musicians studied and developed through both peer interaction and through mentorships with older, more-experienced professionals. For detailed conversations regarding these historical models of jazz education, see Berliner 1994, Monson 1996, and Fraser 1983.

REFERENCES

Berliner, P. 1994. *Thinking in jazz: The infinite art of improvisation.* Chicago: University of Chicago Press.

Dewey, J. 1974. *John Dewey on education.* Ed. Reginald D. Archambualt. Chicago: University of Chicago Press.

———. 1997. *Education and experience.* New York: Touchstone. (Originally published in 1938.)

Fraser, W. 1983. Jazzology: A study of the tradition in which jazz musicians have learned to improvise. Ph.D. diss., University of Pennsylvania.

Freire, P. 2005. *Pedagogy of the oppressed.* New York: Continuum International.

Hansen, D. 2001. *Exploring the moral heart of teaching: Towards a teacher's creed.* New York: Teachers College Press.

Kingsbury, H. O. 1984. Music as a cultural system: Structure and process in an American conservatory. Ph.D. diss., Indiana University.

Monson, I. 1996. *Saying something: Jazz improvisation and interaction.* Chicago: University of Chicago Press.

Nettl, B. 1995. *Heartland excursions: Ethnomusicological reflections on schools of music.* Urbana: University of Illinois Press.

If the Shoe Fits: Tapping into the Potential of an Undergraduate Peer-Teaching Experience to Promote Music Teacher and Music Teacher Educator Socialization and Identity

Alison M. Reynolds

ABSTRACT

In this chapter, I share my initial perceptions about an undergraduate peer-teaching program at Temple University. In essence, inquisitive students compete to relive undergraduate course content within their major from a now-dual perspective: On one hand, a respectful "Been there; done that" (and "wanna do it some more") and, on the other, "What's it like to teach this course?" The unique opportunity to solidify elements of preservice music teacher preparation for inservice teaching—while trying on elements of a music teacher educator identity—poses questions: What are the challenges and benefits of fostering an undergraduate-faculty peer-teaching relationship? While my first experience leaves me with more questions than answers, I suggest that further inquiry with the voices of the peer teacher and undergraduates is warranted.

INTRODUCTION

What attracts undergraduates to a major in music education? Researchers have studied preservice teachers' reasons for pursuing music education as a major, persons and events that have inspired them to make that choice, and ways they experience socialization and form identities as music teachers during their undergraduate years (Isbell 2008). Researchers offer evidence to suggest that even though preservice teachers select music education for their major, many identify themselves as *performers* more strongly than as *teachers,* which the researchers attribute to the teachers' numerous and positive experiences with performance, as compared with the number of positive teaching experiences. Also, researchers suggest preservice music teachers' longitudinal, firsthand experiences with schooling, music classes, and music ensembles combine to promote their preconceived notions about teaching practices (Isbell 2008; Woodford 2002).

The two constructs—(1) strong identities tied to performance and (2) strong preconceptions about music teaching practices—no doubt oversimplify and underlie challenges preservice music teachers face as they progress through their undergraduate major. Simultaneously, it is likely those two constructs underlie challenges music teacher educators face as they guide preservice music teachers' progress to inservice careers.

How can music teacher educators best support socialization and identity-formation processes? Researchers and practitioners have only just begun to investigate answers to this question. Woodford writes, "The conscious construction of music teacher identity evidently requires sustained intellectual prompting from university instructors if novices are to question and challenge the currently prevailing educational system" (2002, 687). Preservice teachers who think critically about the educational system are poised to "become teacher-leaders" (Beynon 1998, 101). Poignantly, Isbell concludes, "Nothing that students encounter before attending college . . . appears to affect the strength of occupational identity to the extent that experiences during the undergraduate training years do" (2008, 176).

Understanding factors that contribute to preservice teachers' *teacher* or *teacher-leader* identity balanced with a *performer* identity might help parents and teachers (private studio, preK–12, college/ university) counsel and prepare future music teachers. Given Isbell's findings, however, music teacher educators seem to be in the most advantageous position to positively influence preservice music teachers' emerging socialization and identity as teachers.

MUSIC TEACHER EDUCATORS PROMOTING THE SOCIALIZATION AND IDENTITY OF PRESERVICE MUSIC TEACHERS

Music teacher educators' teaching or directing, supervisory, academic-advising, and student-chapter-advising responsibilities traditionally frame undergraduates' encounters with music teacher educators. More recently, additional opportunities have emerged. Universities have increased emphases on professional-development schools (Henry and Conkling 2002), service-learning (Burton and Reynolds 2009), school-community partnerships, learning communities or communities of practice (Seifert and Mandzuk 2006), and teacher study groups (Carroll 2007), all of which have inspired teaching, scholarship, and service interactions among music teacher educators and preservice music teachers. Music teacher educators have conducted qualitative inquiries that include preservice teachers' voices regarding their development and have even engaged them as co-researchers.

Conway (Conway and Hodgman 2009) teaches instrumental preservice teachers for four consecutive semesters. Each semester, students are required to peer or extern teach. Conway finds that subsequent-semester encounters allow her and her students to successfully share course content with one another. She describes students as feeling both committed to course objectives and self-motivated to achieve them (87). Repeated encounters with preservice teachers may be difficult for a single music teacher educator to replicate, but perhaps a united front within a department would achieve similar goals. Shifting to shared course content may contribute to preservice teachers' socialization and identity formation; foster matured skills, attitudes, content, and knowledge; offer undergraduates alternative notions about classrooms in higher education; and promote preservice teachers' chances to try on elements of music teacher education.

As final examples of more recent opportunities and as examples most relevant to our discussion here, music teacher educators have accessed their university's organized efforts to engage undergraduates in research or peer teaching (the ideas for which are often initiated by the undergraduate, and for which music teacher educators can serve as mentors). Co-constructed experiences that feature preservice music teachers' voices—particularly about transformative experiences—and traditional frames for their interactions with music-teacher educators need not be mutually exclusive. Recent strategies in higher education explicitly feature roles between expert and novice as ever-shifting (Rogoff 1990). The dynamic nature of the relationships may support positive and balanced identities and foster socialization among preservice teachers.

MUSIC TEACHER EDUCATORS MENTORING POTENTIAL MUSIC TEACHER EDUCATORS

Regardless of whether we are considering traditional or contemporary frames in which music teacher educators interact with preservice teachers, it is not clear the ways in which graduate students' *undergraduate* music teacher educators' models directly affect their decisions to pursue graduate studies and, ultimately, music teacher education. How does one prepare for music teacher education? A possible answer to that question would be, again, framed by tradition: one must have lived a somewhat sequential and overlapping trajectory as music student, musician, undergraduate music education student, preservice music teacher, student teacher, inservice music teacher, and graduate music education student. With the evolution of contemporary frames, it seems researchers can begin to investigate whether those frames inspire preservice and inservice teachers' pursuit of graduate music teacher education degrees.

Living the traditional trajectory prior to entering graduate music teacher education may not be enough. Like learning to teach for an inservice career, learning to teach in higher education cannot be learned completely through course content alone (Woodford 2002). Music teacher educators now (more than ever) are structuring graduate students' apprenticeships and independent projects in teaching, research, and service to prepare habits required by most universities for their eventual navigation through tenure and promotion processes. Many music education departments expand traditional course offerings by offering doctoral seminars in teaching in higher education, awarding credit for supervised teaching in higher education, conducting predissertation research, and referring graduate students to university centers for teaching and learning.

I suggest undergraduate peer-teaching as a potential addition to contemporary frames. In contrast to the most traditional image of *peer teacher* (preservice music teacher teaching peers an activity or lesson truly intended for a specific preK–12 music-learning group), for the purposes of our discussion *peer teacher* refers to an undergraduate teaching assistant assigned to a faculty member and specific course. I am imagining this model as offering inquisitive preservice music teachers the opportunity to try on elements of music teacher education.

RESEARCH ON UNDERGRADUATE PEER TEACHING

Studies of undergraduate peer teachers—or undergraduate teaching assistants—in music teacher education seem to be nonexistent. In teacher education, the literature seems sparse as well. In the early 1970s, faculty at Illinois State University wrote about the perceived successes of their undergraduate-teacher assistant program (Jabker and Rives 1976). Researchers began to report conflicting evidence about the value of peer teaching, describing the peer teachers' roles most often as *tutor*. In some studies, researchers found that peers' positive attitudes and increased "academic achievement and motivation," (Mohan 1971) and that peer teachers "[learn] the material better and [retain] the subject matter longer" (Edwards 1972). In others, only female peer teachers increased students' achievement (Benz 1970).

More recently, references to peer teaching have increased, although references appear with many different names: "peer tutoring, writing consultants . . . peer-learning assistance" (Smith 2008). Undergraduate peer teacher (or undergraduate teaching assistant) and faculty partnerships have been more comprehensively defined and different approaches described (Falchikov and Blythman 2001; Miller, Groccia, and Miller 2001). The partnerships cut across higher-education disciplines, and numerous variations on the relationship and responsibilities exist.

THE CASE

This chapter is my initial response to the model of accepting an undergraduate peer teacher into a required general music methods course I typically teach. To provide a context for my experience, I offer the following information about the university setting, the music education department, and the course I identified for my initial experience with an undergraduate peer teacher.

TEMPLE UNIVERSITY

I teach in the Boyer College of Music and Dance at Temple University, a public, state-related, comprehensive public-research university (www.temple.edu). In October 2008, Temple reported an undergraduate enrollment of 26,194. Of those, approximately 160 had declared music education as their undergraduate major.

Students enroll in an average of seventeen hours of credit per semester and typically can complete their 128 hours of credit in four years. Their Pennsylvania K–12 music certification requires a 3.0 overall GPA and passing scores on three Praxis tests. Preservice music teachers enter with a concentration (voice, piano, guitar, or instrumental) and select a teaching specialization (choral or instrumental). However, they take essentially the same courses, regardless of their specialization. With the breadth of courses required for graduation, there is a continual tension between (1) the time necessary to focusing on developing musical-content knowledge and skills and (2) a collective integration of pedagogy, curriculum design, psychology, and philosophy applicable to a wide age range of future students. Historically, our department has offered most music education methods classes each semester, capping enrollment at fifteen students. It was within this context that I first learned about the Diamond Peer-Teacher Program in the spring of 2008.

DIAMOND PEER-TEACHER PROGRAM

In 2006, Temple University's Office of the Senior Vice Provost for Undergraduate Studies established an undergraduate peer-teaching program. Their primary goal was to provide "the opportunity to experience the challenges and rewards of college-level teaching, work with faculty mentors to develop their own pedagogical skills, and provide supplemental instruction in lower-level courses" (Temple University 2006).

Students applying for the program have to meet several requirements. Students with a GPA of at least 3.25 and sixty credit hours by the end of the application semester choose a class within or very closely related to their major in which they achieved an A– or higher. They solicit a professor's recommendation—ideally the professor with whom the applicant hopes to work. Applications are due approximately six weeks into each semester, and announcements are made in time for the next semester's registration period.

Each semester, the undergraduate peer-teaching program accepts up to twenty-five students, attempting to distribute the awards across the schools and colleges. Once selected, Diamond Peer Teachers (DPTs) receive a stipend of $2,250, and mentors receive a stipend of

$500. DPTs attend a two-day seminar at the beginning of the semester and are required to submit midterm and final papers about their experiences. The program pays for one hour of independent study, typically with their mentor teacher. The program director suggests that, at a minimum, peer teachers attend each class period, hold an office hour, and meet separately with the professor to prepare for assigned tasks. Peer teachers are encouraged to assist the professor in as many ways as fit the situation but are advised to avoid assigning grades to their peers.

TEACHING GENERAL MUSIC TO INCLUSIVE POPULATIONS

I immediately considered the description well suited for my general music methods course: Teaching General Music to Inclusive Populations (TGMIP). TGMIP meets three times weekly for fifty minutes each session. Historically, TGMIP has contained the only authentic teaching experience for preservice teachers prior to student teaching. Students complete four observations, followed by four lessons they coteach with peers. TGMIP also fulfills the university's writing-intensive requirement within the major. Preservice teachers hone their skills writing observation papers, detailed lesson plans, narrative reflections, a portrait paper, and a cover letter to accompany a budget request. Finally, the designation *inclusive populations* represents a shift for our methods courses under our new curriculum: to make explicit ways in which course content infuses attention to students' diverse, special, and English-language-learning needs.

Several undergraduates immediately came to mind as potential candidates. But as certain as I was that the Diamond Peer Teaching program was an excellent match for music education courses, I was as certain that a Diamond Peer Teacher match for a music education major could be impossible for one chief reason: which music education major would have time in the schedule and credit-hour allotment to add this to his or her slate?

Even so, in the spring of 2008, I was thrilled to shepherd the first DPT applicant in music education through the process. Upon her acceptance to the program, we began making plans for the fall semester of TGMIP. I knew I could use help with administrative tasks but did not wish to limit her responsibilities to those only. She agreed to review skills and assignments and be prepared to present rote song, pattern, movement, and recorder instruction. She knew she would prepare and present activities for extern teaching assignments. She also would coach peers for their extern teaching assignments. She agreed to provide initial feedback about students' writing. In our first meeting, we talked about the potential for research and practical application; she expressed enthusiasm for reporting beyond giving the feedback that the Diamond Peer Teacher program administrators required.

During fall 2008, we navigated our way through the experience. In the following I offer my perspective of the challenges and benefits associated with the undertaking. After my first experience as a mentor for a Diamond Peer Teacher, I identified four challenges categories:

1. recruiting,
2. structuring a cycle of thought and action with the DPT,
3. constructing meaningful experiences for the DPT, and
4. relying on the DPT program to be a continual source for undergraduates.

I identified five categories of benefits:

1. having an extra pair of hands (eyes, ears, and feet!),
2. relying on the DPT as liaison between course content and peers,
3. creating an intergenerational teaching and learning setting,
4. reexamining course with a students' perspective, and
5. learning about and from the DPT as she tried on the responsibilities.

CHALLENGES

Recruiting a DPT for my TGMIP class under pressure for meeting a fast-approaching deadline gave me little to no time to reflect on the total population who would have met the DPT application requirements. Those who immediately popped into mind as having excellent potential for success were those who had met my expectations for professionalism, organization, and musicality. In some ways, undergraduates I considered were logical choices for stepping into the DPT role: they seemed more socialized into a balanced teacher-performer identity than their peers already. I wonder now whether the DPT might help those who achieve the requirements on paper but personally are struggling with those issues.

Structuring a reasonable schedule to ensure adequate time for a shared cycle of planning, preparing, revising, presenting, and reflecting within an already busy course schedule proved a challenge to both of us. We did make a weekly appointment time with each other, which often one of us would have to abandon in the midst of rapidly changing demands on our schedules (sometimes to do with TGMIP demands!). E-mail exchanges and cell-phone messages peppered our weeks. Toward the end of the semester, face-to-face time seemed to elude us. I frequently wondered whether I was serving as an appropriate mentor and whether the load I carry necessitated a decision to decline recommending a DPT to TGMIP in the future.

Constructing meaningful experiences for the DPT challenged my assumptions about the course structure and the DPT. I relied on my previous experiences with graduate teaching assistants to create an agenda for the DPT. She and I realized quickly that featuring her peer teaching during class seemed the most obvious way to promote her DPT skills to the students. I noticed that her peers readily accepted her relative expertise with course content and incorporated her feedback; yet they clearly were unaccustomed to seeking a peer teacher's help outside of class. When she requested a coaching meeting with an undergraduate outside of class, the student cheerfully accepted her help; otherwise, students sought the help of TAs more frequently. Clearly, if I accept another DPT, I need to be mindful of ways to foster the DPT's engagement with peers outside of class.

Relying on the DPT program to assist with undergraduates' movement toward socialization and balanced teacher-performer identities is precarious. First, the nature of the program is such that interested preservice music teachers must compete with undergraduates across the university, in the College of Music and Dance, and—should the program catch on within our department—within music education. Second, it is unclear whether the university will continue to afford the stipends and tuition remission for independent-study credits. Currently, a limited number of music education majors stand to benefit from the program.

BENEFITS

Having an extra person to organize the people, materials, and space for class is of enormous assistance, especially if the person proactively engages in the tasks. Taking attendance, making copies, rearranging the chairs in the classroom, and organizing recording equipment, props, and music instruments alone would not be particularly rewarding for the DPT. But these menial tasks represent the realities of in-service teaching and music teacher educator jobs. Having the DPT's critical ears and eyes as she floated among pairs or small groups collaborating on traditional peer-teaching assignments was a boon; hearing her offering astute and specific compliments and essential questions to them or constructive suggestions about musical, technical, and pedagogical matters seemed to positively shape undergraduates' improvement. Throughout the semester, she coached students outside of class. I noted priceless, positive reactions students had to her oft-used phrase, "I found _____ helpful when I was practicing (or teaching) this assignment." Finally, having her prepare course assignments such as the notebook and budget presentations allowed her to practice more lecture-oriented or procedure-based interactions.

Having a liaison who spoke comfortably and respectfully during (and outside) class—offering her experiences and additional directions, expressing concerns she anticipated from her peers, and complimenting their teaching and progress—provided an unexpectedly healthy dimension. I think her peers realized her comments—sometimes positive, sometimes constructive critique—were genuine.

She became a professional pipeline for her peers' overall feelings of success or progress. She could offer me advice about when to extend a deadline or when to hold fast. Once she shared about a visit to a peer's Facebook page. Her friend had posted a message about having "cried real TGMIP tears" of disappointment over her teaching assignment (peer teaching in its traditional meaning). The DPT offered electronic empathetic statements about the steep learning curve for the assignment. She assured the friend of her potential for improvement with practice. Was that interaction beneficial? Further inquiry into the effects of Facebook interactions on students' perceptions of coursework may be warranted!

For me, having an intergenerational music education space fueled newfound energies: undergraduates, undergraduate peer teacher, master's graduate teaching assistant, doctoral teaching assistants, and a music teacher educator. I found the dialogues and interactions from "across the ages" thrilling from the mere standpoint that they were occurring at any time during any class! In this particular semester we even had nontraditional-aged postbaccalaureate students in the class. Aside from conference workshops, rehearsals, or research settings (which are limited to short-term interactions), I can think of no other occasion in which I luxuriously learned from such a span of music educators! Occasionally, we had prospective undergraduate students visit the class, inservice teachers present workshops to our class, or prospective masters or doctoral students visiting, making the complement even fuller!

As we prepared for her work as a DPT, I had to reexamine the course content with her perspective. What a valuable opportunity! I had used informal means of hearing from undergraduates (temperature taking, midstream course or instructor evaluations, or general polling) and found them useful. The DPT and I combed through the entire semester ahead of us. As we did so, I gained priceless insights from her perspective, responses, and suggestions.

Finally, throughout the entire semester, I found that I assessed the DPT in relation to the course content. I learned ways in which she improved her teaching and matured in her interactions. I had not anticipated that and consider it an avenue of potential further inquiry. I observed the formation of her identity as a DPT and ways in which she and her peers navigated her socialization within that role. From my perspective, the DPT shoe fit!

CONCLUSION

First, my overall response is that I have committed to repeating the Diamond Peer Teacher (DPT) experience. Second, I have considered broadening the courses within which I will advertise and recruit students to apply for the program. Third, I realize better which administrative tasks will be most helpful to me (another music teacher educator might choose differently) and suggest that while taking attendance and making copies is always helpful, each DPT will bring different strengths and require mentoring for different tasks. Having one undergraduate peer-teaching relationship under my belt, I understand better that the logistics of working to plan, practice, revise, and reflect can be successful without face-to-face contact and am better prepared to work on that cycle at the outset. I can envision ways to modify the assignments so that throughout the semester the undergraduates can interact with the DPT outside of class on a staggered schedule.

I think possibilities exist for socialization and identity formation within the dual roles as preservice music teacher and music teacher may exist for the Diamond Peer Teacher. I think having a DPT reminds me to promote contemporary collaborative educational frames. As Bruffee (1993) alerts, traditional frames in which teachers present front-and-center for the class are less effective. I encourage readers to consider my initial perceptions in light of the references to those topics and to pursue a similar experience if at all compelled by the possible benefits.

I consider mentoring the DPT a new dimension of my professional development. It seems to have much in common with preparing a student teacher and some elements in common with preparing graduate teaching assistants. Systematically studying undergraduate peer teaching will likely yield interesting insights, possibly contributing to the activities currently under consideration by the Society for Music Teacher Education (www.smte.us). For example, having a peer teacher offers opportunities to systematically study peer teachers' and peers' outcomes. We might learn new ways for recruiting music teacher educators and supporting current music teacher educators. Currently, university administrators expect music teacher educators to engage in the scholarship of teaching, research and creative activities, and service. I can envision ways in which mentoring a DPT could meet each expectation.

Clearly, this reflective chapter is incomplete without the voice of the DPT. In fact, it may be incomplete until we can document the voices of all stakeholders within the intergenerational family—undergraduates, undergraduate peer teacher, graduate teaching assistants, and music teacher educator. Such documentation would surely provide insights about previously unimagined challenges or benefits.

I close this chapter having learned that in the fall of 2009 the Diamond Peer Teacher program selected a new applicant for Teaching General Music to Inclusive Populations. I embrace the opportunity to continue extending my understanding about how to nurture this partnership best and to further develop my music teacher educator identity. As the next Diamond Peer Teacher revisits course content, tries on elements of music teacher education, and—possibly—learns more about her identity and socialization as a preservice teacher, I hope she will challenge herself in ways that extend her preparation for student and inservice teaching. Time and further inquiry will be telling of the merits of pairing a Diamond Peer Teacher within a music education methods course. For now, it seems the pairing is an excellent fit.

REFERENCES

Benz, D. A. 1970. *Observations of academic performance by low achieving college freshmen following instruction by academically successful students trained to teach reading and study skill techniques.* Washington, D.C.: Office of Education Bureau of Research. As cited in McNall 1975.

Beynon, C. 1998. From music student to music teacher: Negotiating an identity. In *Critical thinking in music: Theory and practice*, ed. P. Woodford, 83–105. Conference proceedings, University of Western Ontario.

Bruffee, K. 1993. *Collaborative learning: Higher education, interdependence, and the authority of knowledge.* Baltimore: Johns Hopkins University Press.

Burton, S. L., and A. M. Reynolds. 2009. Transforming music teacher education through service-learning. *Journal of Music Teacher Education* 18 (2): 18–33.

Carroll, D. 2007. Helping teachers become teacher educators. In *Transforming teacher education: Reflections from the field,* ed. D. Carroll, H. Featherstone, J. Featherstone, S. Feiman-Nemser, and R. Dirck, 181–201. Cambridge, Mass.: Harvard Education Press.

Conway, C. M., and T. M. Hodgman. 2009. *Teaching music in higher education.* New York: Oxford University Press.

Edwards, K. A. 1972. The student as a teacher. Presented at the annual meeting of the Rocky Mountain Psychological Association. Albuquerque, N.M. As cited in McNall 1975.

Falchikov, N., and M. Blythman. 2001. *Learning together: Peer tutoring in higher education.* London: Routledge Falmer.

Henry, W., and S. W. Conkling. 2002. The impact of professional development partnerships: Our part of the story. *Journal of Music Teacher Education* 11:7–13.

Isbell, D. S. 2008. Musicians and teachers: The socialization and occupational identity of preservice music teachers. *Journal of Research in Music Education* 56:162–78.

Jabker, E. H., and S. G. Rives. 1976. Institution-wide use of undergraduate teaching assistants. *Alternative Higher Education* 1 (1): 68–80.

McNall, S. G. 1975. Peer teaching: A description and evaluation. *Teaching Sociology* 2 (2): 3.

Miller, J. E., J. E. Groccia, and M. S. Miller. 2001. *Student-assisted teaching: A guide to faculty-student teamwork.* Boston: Anker.

Mohan, M. 1971. *Peer tutoring as a technique for teaching the unmotivated.* Fredonia, N.Y.: State University of New York, Teacher Education Research Center. As cited in McNall 1975.

Rogoff, B. 1990. *Apprenticeship in thinking: Cognitive development in social context.* Oxford: Oxford University Press.

Seifert, K., and D. Mandzuk. 2006. Student cohorts in teacher education: Support groups or intellectual communities? *Teachers College Record* 108:1296–1320.

Smith, T. 2008. *Curricular peer mentoring programs.* University of Calgary. Victoria, British Columbia, Canada: Trafford Publishing. (Print version 2009.) http://people.ucalgary.ca/~smit/PeerMentoring/Handbook.htm.

Temple University. 2006. *Honors program: Other Temple opportunities; diamond peer teachers.* Philadelphia: Temple University. www.temple.edu/honors/programs/TUOpportunities.htm.

Woodford, P. G. 2002. Social construction of music teacher identity in undergraduate music education majors. In *The new handbook of research on music teaching and learning,* ed. R. Colwell and C. Richardson, 675–94. New York: Oxford University Press.

Crossing Borders: Building Bridges for an International Exchange in Music Teacher Education

Janet Robbins

ABSTRACT

For preservice teachers, cultural exchange and a semester-long study abroad program in music can lead to more culturally responsive teaching. The formation of an international consortium—Music Alive!—embraced the idea that study abroad has the potential to effect change, not only in students' lives but also in music teacher education. This chapter takes the reader into a study-abroad experience, which takes place between partner institutions in the United States and Brazil. Students' journals and blogs provide a window into the challenges and rewards of studying abroad, and we gain an understanding of the ways study-abroad experiences can lead to new perspectives on music, teaching, and life.

AN INVITATION

Never once in my life did I imagine I would be given an opportunity as amazing as the one I was given within the last four months. In this short period of time I have learned so much about myself through a different culture and music. I will never be able to explain to anyone what this trip has done for me; it is a feeling I have every time I think about leaving Recife when I realize how the people, the food, the culture, and, most importantly, the music have all taken part in changing my life.

—Music Alive! exchange student

Imagine an opportunity to study for a semester in Brazil, travel and living expenses included. Would you go? When considering the choice, one might ask, Why study abroad? No doubt there are several plausible reasons: the chance to travel and see the world, to learn about music and culture, to discover how it feels to live in another country, or to simply escape one's current situation. Like the fish who didn't know it was a fish until it was out of the water, students who leave their familiar classrooms and corridors and open themselves to being the Other are more likely to return with an expanded view of themselves and their world.

CROSSING BORDERS: CREATING A BRIDGE TO BRAZIL

When the idea to submit a proposal for federal funding to support music students' semester-long study in Brazil began to surface, several interested music faculty joined the efforts of our Office of International Program to develop a project, Music Alive! We began to imagine the possibilities for students' professional growth and shared the hope that students' semester-long immersion would expand their perspectives on music and culture in ways that would be transformative for their musicianship and teaching. Ultimately, we embraced the idea that the Music Alive! exchange program had the potential to effect change in music curricula and serve as a model for music teacher education.

The formation of an international consortium involving a multilateral partnership between four universities (two in the United States and two in Brazil) has become a bridge for students and faculty to study, teach, and perform in Brazil.[1] Goals that define the work of the consortium include linking faculty and curriculum in ways that support music students' study abroad. From the outset of the project, core faculty have participated in an ongoing dialogue about mobility issues that included (1) identification of a common cluster of courses that would satisfy program requirements at all institutions, (2) development of cultural-immersion opportunities and independent-study options unique to each institutions' program and regional culture, and (3) the incorporation of language training.

The concept of study abroad is enriched and sustained by the work of faculty who regularly travel to perform, teach, and study at each other's institutions. The result is an emerging international community of faculty performers and scholars who are working together on shared performances, pedagogies, and curriculum initiatives that promote and celebrate the cultural richness and diversity of musical traditions in the United States and Brazil. Because language training and cultural immersion were critical factors in students' academic success, music faculty have also collaborated with foreign-language departments to develop intensive presemester language-immersion courses for students. Project faculty play a critical role not only in helping their own students prepare for the semester-long study abroad, they also work closely with students who arrive to study on exchange.

At the heart of the project is the semester-long exchange of music students who study music in combination with intensive language-culture classes. Stipends to support travel and living expenses in Brazil are an incentive for students and are awarded to four American students each year. Students submit a short application, transcript, and narrative essay articulating their rationale for wanting to study in Brazil, which is then reviewed by a team of music faculty, advisors, and Office of International Programs staff. Awards are based on students' academic progress, readiness to study abroad, and faculty recommendations.

To date, eight American students have received Music Alive! stipends to study in Brazil, and ten students from the Brazil partners have traveled to study in the United States. The cycle of exchange makes it possible for students to connect at each partner institution, with Brazil students studying in the United States in the fall semester and American students studying in Brazil in the spring semester. As the cohort of former, current, and future students participating in the U.S.-Brazil Music Alive! exchange continues to grow, students are uniquely positioned to support each other as they travel across borders and hemispheres.

From the outset of the project, students who were selected knew that they would participate in an intensive Portuguese-language and Portuguese-culture class prior to the semester of study in Brazil. During the second year of the exchange, a conversational Portuguese "table" was formed that brought together Brazilian students who had just arrived in the United States with American students preparing for their semester in Brazil. This semester-long effort was only the beginning, however. Once students arrived in Brazil they had to endure a period of swimming upstream in a sea of Portuguese.

Without a doubt, the first priority when I arrived was to learn the language. Not knowing Portuguese was an enormous barrier for me, so at least for the first month and a half, Portuguese was the focus. Without speaking the language, classes were difficult, it was hard to make friends, and overall I felt bad about myself, because I was disrespecting the Brazilian culture. Everywhere I went I always had my dictionary, looking at road signs, writing things down. After some time I told everyone, "*O meu diccionario é o meu melhor amigo*" (My dictionary is my best friend), and those I told always laughed; but it was the truth. Portuguese remains a priority for me.

—John

One change in the second year involved easing students into their study-abroad experience more gradually. Students now arrive in Brazil one month prior to their semester-long study for intensive language classes. At one site, a special Portuguese class was arranged for the two American music students. The intensity of a four-hour class that met daily made an enormous difference in students' language competence and confidence. Not only did the presemester experience give students time to immerse themselves in Portuguese, but it also gave them time to learn how to navigate through the large, bustling Brazilian cities of Rio and Recife.

First Days

The long journey to Brazil begins with disorientation and excitement as American students arrive in January at the height of Brazil's summer season and pre-*Carnaval* preparation.

It hasn't even been a week since I left, but so much has happened already. Between going to D.C. to get my Visa, a ten-hour international flight, getting accustomed to a city with over ten million people, and starting intensive Portuguese classes, life has been moving fast. I did not know the meaning of *crowded* before this week. Having never lived in a large city before, I still have a hard time conceiving where all these people come from.

—Corey

A view of students' experiences comes through in their e-mail exchanges, blog and Facebook postings, and reflective narratives written throughout the semester. One student who was selected to participate in the university's Blogging from Abroad project enabled everyone to follow his path at regular intervals through photos, video, and short narratives that he posted. His fresh, wide-eyed view of Rio's *Carnaval* was palpable:

> For the second day in a row, I was surprised by a street parade passing directly below my window. My neighborhood has been generally very calm and quiet, but *Carnaval* rolled around, and suddenly thousands of people appeared on my street. For several days, it seemed like everyone in the city was on the streets dancing and enjoying life. I decided to wade in and march with the masses; the best way I can describe it is "suffocatingly close." I didn't move by my own accord; rather I was carried along by the throng of revelers.
>
> —Corey

The sights and sounds of Brazilian music were accompanied by the first tastings of fruits, juices (*sucos*), and fresh fish (*peixe*) that rarely, if ever, reach American shores. Food, like music, is a marker of Brazilian pride. Naturally, students arrived in Brazil to soak up new experiences, but eventually their attention turned to the study of music. Students registered for a cluster of courses that was determined in consultation with WVU and Brazil faculty advisors. Most students enrolled in small ensembles (*conjuntas*), private or small-group lessons, music education methods courses, and the study of traditional Brazilian music. One jazz studies major studying in Rio was thrilled to learn about Brazil's classic choro style of music.

> The choro ensemble class was great, since this style was one of my main projects this semester. The class introduced me to repertoire, stylistic aspects, and techniques for composing and arranging choro.
>
> —Corey

In Recife, all students joined one of the university choirs, which they discovered was an excellent way to improve their language, meet people, and travel throughout the region to give concerts. "The choir, Contracantos, has been a great class. I have met so many amazing people and have created so many amazing friendships that will last my lifetime." One percussion student not only sang in the choir but also learned various types of Brazilian percussion that were used to accompany the group.

It wasn't long before students began to realize that much of the traditional Brazilian music they were hungry for "just happens" in the community, on the streets, and in homes. As a result, faculty began developing new independent-study options that linked students' work at the university to musicians in the community. For one student studying in Rio, this blend of experiences was particularly important:

> In addition to lessons, I also took part in Escola Portatil, a school for choro on Saturdays, where I took a general choro history/listening class and saxophone workshop. Escola Portatil was a very nice addition to my studies. The school is one way to meet students outside of the university, learn more songs and musicians, and meet professors who are some of the greats of choro.
>
> —Corey

Three percussionists studying at the partner university in northeast Brazil, where Afro-Brazilian traditions are so prominent, embraced every opportunity to study the region's diverse range of Brazilian rhythms. Connections seemed to snowball throughout the semester as students heard about local musicians and venues where music was taking place.

> Our first class outside of the school was with Nacão Porto Rico, an ensemble of Maracatu, which is a style of music unique to the state of Pernambuco and Recife. This was an amazing couple of classes, but after a month, we met another American in Recife who was very well educated on Maracatu. . . . Through Aaron we meet Jorge Martins who owns a music school in Recife Antigo. Since March we have been having two-hour classes with Jorge covering Maracatu, Samba, and Ilu drumming. It is a beautiful situation.
>
> —Dan

One musician led to the next, and before long students found themselves not only observing and studying, but actually performing with local groups. This was a turning point for one student who became aware of ways his "formal training" was different from the technique now required.

> I think that technically I can play all the music here in Pernambuco, but the problem is that being technical and using proper techniques does not matter in the least. The people of Recife achieve some of the most grooving sounds I have ever heard in my entire life by playing in some of the most obscure ways I've every seen; for them technique is pointless. The reason they play with such a swing is because for the people of Recife music is far more than academic: it is their way of life.
>
> —John

Students were experiencing the intersection of music and life in Brazil with each passing month, and this led to deliberate efforts to make more connections to the vital musical life taking place beyond the university walls. One professor remarked on the importance of students' experiences in the community: "This is a tried and true method and makes students realize the actual role of informal music education. This is the way most musicians actually learn about music."

For music students studying abroad in the Music Alive! exchange experiences that became the most meaningful were those that they could "fill with their own energy" (Ayers 1995, 323), whether it was finding a way to communicate in Portuguese, join in a *Carnaval* parade, or make music alongside other students and local musicians.

> I got to know the band Trombonada. This is a band of five trombones with a rhythm section playing a mixture of northeastern music and some jazz/rock influences. I was actually invited to go play two gigs with them, one in the city of Santa Cruz do Capibaribe in the interior of Pernambuco and the other in Recife Antigo. I made some great connections, got to see more of the state, and even got to play with a couple well-known Pernambucano musicians, including Nilsinho Amarante, Enok Chagas, and Maestro Spok.
>
> —Derek

Students were witnessing the influence of community on music making and coming to understand that informal learning outside of a university setting can be as powerful as the formal learning taking place in the academy. As future educators, students were learning an important principle, that "the ability to make music is directly linked to the musical and music-educational influences of family, friends, and teachers" (Campbell 2004, 8). This notion that everyone could make music—that music is "alive and more inclusive," was a strong thread running through students' final narratives.

> The thing that really entices me is the energy around the music. Everyone knows the words and dances and sings along enthusiastically; it's a rush just to watch. The focus isn't on musical precision or ability but on the pure excitement and community created by the music.
>
> —John

Changing Perspectives

In the semester following the first groups' return from Brazil, students began to articulate and demonstrate several ways their study abroad in Brazil was leading to new perspectives: (1) musical vocabularies learned in Brazil were stimulating creativity and openness to assuming new roles as a musician, (2) music taking place outside the university played an important role in their experiences inside the university, (3) learning from and with others in a collaborative fashion is what makes music come alive in classroom and rehearsal settings, and (4) music making is an inclusive rather than exclusive experience that often "just happens."

One student remarked that his time in Brazil had led to expanding musical vocabularies that were stimulating his creativity and diversifying his music-making choices (Drummond 2005). As a percussionist and jazz studies major, he was eager to arrange music for the newly formed university Brazilian Ensemble as a way to draw upon the music he had learned in Brazil. He also arranged music for several small jazz groups that performed both on and off campus. His passion for Brazilian music and his desire to educate others to the new sounds and rhythms of northeast Brazil prompted him to host several radio programs on the campus station that were devoted to Brazilian music.

During the second year of the exchange, collaboration between American and Brazilian students increased, and a new Brazilian ensemble was formed. When American students who had studied in Brazil were reunited with Brazilian students in the United States, the idea to play together seemed obvious. Add to this collaborative venture those students recently selected to travel on exchange in the coming year, and a nucleus of students with shared interests and experiences came together to form a new ensemble.

Within the ensemble rehearsal, informal practices were playing out as students relied on learning several tunes orally and aurally that were not available in printed form. Students transcribed music from recordings and YouTube performances as needed in order to reconstruct parts for various members of the group. Several alternately suggested interpretations and offered ideas for new instrumentation. In many ways the rehearsals mirrored the inclusive process students experienced in Brazil where musicians often gathered in homes for impromptu music making or met on weekends to jam. As one student remarked, "In Brazil everyone makes music. . . . Music just happens."

American students are embracing the chance to listen to and participate with their international peers. The interplay of students from Brazil and the United States who are now performing and learning together is leading to new sounds and arrangements. One violin player who joined the Brazilian Ensemble was soon playing solos and covering accordion parts; a trumpet and bass player joined in alongside percussionists to learn Maracatu rhythms on the booming alfaia drums.

Students returning from Brazil eagerly share what they learned and assume new roles as "culture translators" (Irwin, Rogers, and Wan 1999). American students and professors who have traveled to Brazil as part of the Music Alive! exchange are now collaborating in performances and also giving music education workshops. Together they are teaching side by side, introducing and translating the language, rhythms, and dances they learned in Brazil as a result of their common experiences. The notion of students-as-teachers represents a shifting paradigm that is beginning to take hold.

Similarly, Brazilian students studying in the United States find themselves in the role of culture bearer, introducing their music in both ensembles and music education classes. Several examples stand out: Music education students listened intently as Rolsy taught a children's game song in Portuguese to the general music methods class; dancers in the African ensemble mirrored Ju's fluid movements of Maracatu during an evening class that she taught; percussionists relied on Claudio's expertise to learn the art of alfaia drumming and panderio that permeate the northeast traditions of Maracatu and Forro; and Diego's arrangement of a tune for one of the big-band jazz ensembles taught everyone that there is much more to bossa nova than "The Girl from Ipanema."

OPENING DOORS TO FUTURE POSSIBILITIES

As American music students exchange places with Brazilians and cross borders to study for a semester in Brazil, they undoubtedly find themselves standing in the shoes of the Other, initially feeling like strangers in unfamiliar territory. This perspective has the potential to give "rise to glimpses of possibility, to what is not yet, to what ought to be" (Ayers 1995, 321).

At the end of two years, we are on the verge of knowing some of the ways the study-abroad experience is enriching students' lives and positioning them for the future. Although not conclusive, we know that students' who spend a semester in Brazil return with a new awareness of the inseparable nature of music and life. Their ears are opening to new rhythms, melodies, and unique timbres of Brazilian music. We see evidence that American students are now rethinking the role of informal music making as a result of experiencing music that is alive in Brazil's communities. Another important transformative idea is that music is an inclusive rather than exclusive enterprise.

Green argues that "music in the classroom needs to draw upon the world of informal popular [vernacular] learning practices outside the school" (2008, 1), and students who participate in the Music Alive! exchange in Brazil will return open to this idea. Even if these future teachers have yet to design strategies for moving music from outside to inside the music classroom, they will more than likely try as a result of this experience. Another shift involves challenging the status quo: The chance that these future teachers will replace "taken for granted" approaches with innovation is promising (Green 2008, 2). In the end it is the work of mindful teachers who are culturally sensitive and responsive that will make a difference (Campbell 2004).

Before the Music Alive! program began, we could only imagine what a semester-long study-abroad experience might mean for undergraduate music students. Very few music students elect to study abroad. Perhaps the losses outweigh the benefits when thinking about leaving behind ensembles, close ties with studio teachers, social networks, and tradition. Fortunately we have the stories of students who have chosen to participate—stories that point to the immeasurable rewards of their study abroad in Brazil.

This border crossing is far more than a surface encounter. In just one semester, students are exposed to a "lifeworld of culture" (Irwin, Rogers, and Wan 1999, 209) that will potentially make them more empathetic to the diversity of people and musics in their own communities. By taking this one step outside familiar territory, they have opened themselves to becoming more tolerant and curious. They have felt the "familiar heart of the stranger" (Ayers 1995, 322), and this has left a lifelong impression. There were obstacles and uncertainties along the way as students experienced being the Other for the first time, but these are precisely the experiences that lead students to reach beyond their familiar world and come to know themselves anew.

After students return and their memories begin to fade, one hopes that these lived experiences will never be far from the surface. As a professor who has been to Brazil four times with the Music Alive! exchange, I suspect that students' sensations are similar to mine. The sounds of Portuguese remain on the tip of the tongue, the undulating rhythms of forro and samba set hips and feet in motion, and the beauty of Brazil's sparkling seas and Southern Cross continue to offset images of poverty and crime.

Now that we are more than halfway through the four-year project, the community of students and faculty who have been touched by this border crossing is growing. Portuguese classes that were dormant for years are now back on the books, faculty who previously performed internationally in Europe are heading south to Brazil, the Brazilian Student Association on campus is full of energy, and announcements of university-wide efforts to promote global literacy and study abroad appear regularly in e-news. Change is in the air.

Already two of the seven students who have studied in Brazil have returned to visit and pursue further study. Another who studied last semester is planning to return: "There is no doubt in my mind that I will return to Brazil; this experience has opened up a whole world of options for my future." We all need to seize the opportunity to travel and study abroad; only then will we really know what it means to be home.

NOTE

1. Music Alive!—a U.S.-Brazil Higher Education Music Arts Consortium—received a four-year grant (2006–2010) from the Federal Improvement Program for Secondary Education (FIPSE).

REFERENCES

Ayers, W. 1995. Social imagination: A conversation with Maxine Greene. *Qualitative Studies in Education* 8 (4): 319–28.

Campbell, P. S. 2004. *Teaching music globally: Experiencing music, expressing culture.* New York: Oxford.

Drummond. J. 2005. Cultural diversity in music education: Why bother? In *Cultural diversity in music education: Directions and challenges for the 21st century,* ed. P. Campbell et al. Brisbane: Australian Academic Press.

Green, L. 2008. *Music, informal learning and school: A new classroom pedagogy.* Hampshire, UK: Ashgate.

Greene, M. 1995. *Releasing the imagination: Essay on education, the arts, and social change.* San Francisco: Jossey-Bass.

Irwin, R., T. Rogers, and Y. Wan. 1999. Making connections through cultural memory, cultural performance, and cultural translation. *Studies in Art Education* 40 (3): 198–212.

24

The Rock Project:
Informal Learning in
Secondary General Methods

Katherine Strand and Daniel Sumner

ABSTRACT

This curricular innovation focused on informal learning and rock music in order to expand *preservice* music education students' perspectives on school music. Through the creation of rock bands, dialogue, and journaling, the music education students gathered experiences and ideas for how to teach through informal learning. It is hoped that new experiences during teacher training will help future music teachers expand the range of classes and teaching strategies in their practice.

INTRODUCTION

One of the biggest challenges we face in secondary general music education methods courses is teaching our undergraduates to appreciate and consider teaching in ways that are not part of the traditional ensemble canon. Many music education majors seem to view the junior high and high school students who are not in band, choir, or orchestra as nonmusicians. In reality, with less than half of the students in any given school likely to participate in traditional ensembles, nontraditional approaches to music instruction may encourage participation, learning, and enjoyment for many more secondary students than we currently reach.

We hoped to find ways to encourage our music education students to meet the needs of children whom they will teach in secondary general music classes—kids who may or may not be interested in traditional ensembles and formal instruction. We designed an action research study to field-test a project to help our students appreciate and imagine designing instruction to support informal music-making practices. To do this, we asked our students to form rock bands, to learn and perform tunes, and to explore ways of encouraging their future students to engage in informal learning practices.

BACKGROUND

The rift between "high" and "low" music, the music created for formal occasions and the music best suited for everyday use, has existed for millennia. Throughout history, many have made the assumption that only "high" music is singularly worthy of scholarly interest and use in music instruction for young students. Swanwick (1968) examined this idea in a time when popular music had become firmly established as the preferred musical style of school-age students. He suggested that a rich musical understanding of a piece of popular music is more valuable than a shallow understanding of a classical symphony. If teachers can look beyond their personal cultural and social biases, they will find that much popular music has real merit. Music teachers need to focus on the musical attributes of popular music that can be taught to students.

Green (2001) argued that informal methods of music learning have been used throughout history. Informal music learning often combines elements of listening and imitating, formal or informal apprenticeship-type relationships with older, more experienced musicians, peer-directed and group learning, and individual practice. Although the term *informal* implies that the learners may not be systematic in their approach to music learning, Green found that popular musicians who engaged in informal music learning described their approach as disciplined, systematic, and focused on technical proficiency, musicality, and interpersonal musical relationships (Green 2001).

The strength of an informal approach to music learning is that the process of learning is developed and implemented by the music makers rather than by teachers. Green suggested that musicians who learn music in informal ways may be more likely to continue to engage in musical activities throughout life. To the end of developing pedagogy to teach through informal music making, she suggested that music teachers begin to realize the potential of informal music-learning by engaging in informal music-making themselves.

Green undertook a research project from 2002 to 2006 with twenty-one secondary schools, thirty-two classroom teachers, and over 1,500 students. The project began with classroom discussions on the ways in which popular musicians learn. Students then grouped themselves into small "bands" and were instructed to listen to a selection of their own CDs and decide on a song to learn and perform. The students were responsible for organizing their group, selecting a song, arranging the song, developing the necessary technical proficiencies on the instruments, and running rehearsals. The teachers set dates for preliminary and final performances.

Green found that students were enthusiastic at the outset of the project and that they particularly enjoyed the opportunity to select the song for their group. Teachers, some of whom were initially apprehensive about dedicating precious instruction time to the project, found that on-task behavior improved during the project. Some teachers found it difficult to refrain from stepping in to assist when students struggled with musical or technical issues. However, most teachers offered little actual instruction and observed that students were generally able to work through their difficulties either alone or with peer assistance. The vast majority of teachers and students expressed enjoyment and satisfaction with the project, and several teachers were surprised at the amount of music learning that took place. Both teachers and students expressed a nearly unanimous desire to repeat the project.

In order to learn whether we could encourage our music education majors to consider informal music making as a potential teaching approach, we decided to involve them in a curricular innovation to test informal learning in our classroom. The students would learn a piece of music informally and perform the piece for their peers. In class discussions we would explore the possible ways that informal music-making might be applied within a secondary general music class. Our classroom project soon became known by the sobriquet "The Rock Project."

EXAMINING THE ROCK PROJECT

The action research study that accompanied our curricular innovation allowed us to examine the process of developing and implementing instruction and the process of student learning. The study also allowed us to assess the success of students in order to improve future repetitions of the project. Data collection included informal student interviews, guided class discussions, instructional artifacts, performance artifacts, student-rated performance rubrics, and teacher evaluations of student work. Students also kept journals of their learning experiences and reflected on the pedagogical implications for their future teaching careers.

Data were analyzed through emergent category coding. We examined the data to discover themes in the students' spoken and written thoughts. Next, we reorganized the data into categories and reexamined the reorganized text in light of the process of instruction and the success of the innovation. The findings are presented here to provide insights into the students' thinking about the project and their beliefs about the value of informal learning in a general music classroom.

Implementing the Project

Our class was an undergraduate general music methods K–12 course that met two days a week for fifty minutes over fifteen weeks. The twenty-five students in this class were all music education majors within a school of music and had auditioned and been accepted into the school of music based on GPAs, standardized test scores, interviews with music education faculty members, and performance auditions with studio faculty. In short, these students had been fairly successful both in their academic careers and in learning how to perform on their instruments. All of these students had participated in traditional performance ensembles and private instruction on their instruments.

Because students would have limited time to learn both repertoire and how to play the instruments, we chose well-known rock songs by singers and groups like the Beatles, the Bangles, the Beach Boys, Feist, Nirvana, Regina Spektor, and the Rolling Stones. Song choices were based on (1) instrumentation (guitar, keyboard, drums, and bass), (2) form (hook, chorus, and verses), (3) simple and repetitive chord progressions, and (4) vocal harmonies. We then divided our students into groups of five, checking first to see if we could place a student with some experience on guitar and a percussionist into each group. Checking for resources, we asked if anyone had access to a bass guitar and amplifier and found that two students could use their own or borrow these instruments. To ensure instrumentation, we had also secured permission to borrow a base guitar and amplifier in case other groups might need them.

Each group was given two of the chosen songs and allowed to se-lect one of the two. We tasked them to re-create songs on authentic instruments (rather than on their primary instruments), and prepare a performance over the course of three weeks. Each group was given one additional task, to "create something new" with their band. The students decided as a class that the new musical creation should last between two and four minutes and that all group members should be involved. The groups were told that they would perform their learned songs and created music for each other and an invited audience.

The students kept journals of their experiences in musical learning, the rehearsal process, and speculations about pedagogical implications. We asked the students to write in their journals after each group meeting and rehearsal and once again after the final performance. We gave the following questions to the students to guide their writing, asking that they consider each question in each journal entry:

1. What is it like to collaborate informally in preparing a performance piece of music?
   - What was my role in the group?
   - What roles did other group members take?
   - What worked well, and what obstacles did we face?
   - How did we work with/overcome these obstacles?
2. What kinds of musical learning took place?
   - How was the learning experience the same as, and how was it different from, traditional teacher-led music instruction?
3. How can I imagine facilitating and mentoring informal music-making in a classroom setting?
   - What obstacles may need to be overcome?
   - What solutions can I imagine to overcome the obstacles?

Students rehearsed and journaled outside of class. In class we asked them to set project goals and determine assessment criteria. We asked them to imagine how they might integrate informal learning in their own classrooms and what learning goals they would set for their students. The class decided upon the following learning goals:

- technique on instruments
- thinking skills—strategies to recreate a song by listening
- ensemble skills—rehearsal skills, blend, and balance
- confidence as a performer
- self-assessment skills

Next, we asked them to imagine how they would assess the success of student learning and to develop appropriate assessment tools. They decided on the following assessment criteria and tools:

- creativity versus authenticity in reproduction of song, as assessed in a grading rubric
- competence in music making in performing the song, as assessed in a grading rubric
- performance skills on instruments, as assessed in a grading rubric
- the music-learning process indicated in the journals and rated in a grading rubric
- learning related to the collaborative process indicated in journals and rated in self- and peer-assessments

Finally, they designed rubrics to assess each of the criteria above. The discussion on how to weight the different aspects of each criterior took a great deal longer than we anticipated, for the students began arguing over how to assess experienced versus novice guitar players, how to determine if self- and peer-assessments were valid, and whether journaling could, indeed, accurately capture the learning process while they were working on their rock songs.

The two final performance rubrics indicated that students had begun to consider the all of the different aspects of the performances. Among the criteria discussed, the class decided that stage presence should be part of the performance rubric so as to encourage lively and engaging performances. This would also provide groups with less musical skill an opportunity to show other strengths. The performance rubric for the Rock Project is listed in table 24.1.

To assess the musical creation, the students all agreed that the rubric should address three criteria: complexity, length, and originality. The students were particularly concerned to find ways to support novice instrumentalists with opportunities to earn points in case the demonstration of technical skills was not equal among the groups. Table 24.2 is the assessment rubric that the students designed for their compositions.

The journal rubrics were written to assess student efforts to answer each question and reflect after each rehearsal. They decided that thoroughness, evidence of reflection, and the number of entries would make the best assessments on the learning process. Table 24.3 shows the journal rubrics.

The students decided that rubrics for peer- and self-assessments were needed to determine if each group member participated in

Table 24.1 Assessment Rubric for Rock Performance

Performance Rating	0	1	2	3	4
Accuracy	band does not perform	band produces meter, but incorrect form and/or chord progressions	band produces meter, form, and chord progressions accurately	band produces (2) and melodic lines correctly	band produces (2), (3), and harmonies accurately
Creativity	band does not perform	band performs tune in exact replication	band performs tune that replicates with expressive variation	band performs new work with some new elements	performance has new ideas and complexity
Precision	band does not perform	band performs, but performers do not stay together	band performs and band players stay together most of the time	band performs together well with 1 or 2 mistakes	band is "tight" throughout entire song
Stage Presence	band does not perform	band does not relate to audience, no facial expression or movement	band shows some facial expression, some relating to audience	band shows some facial expression, relates to audience, some appropriate movement	band is very entertaining on stage: facial expression, relates to audience, and appropriate movement

Table 24.2. Assessment Rubric for Musical Creation

Performance Rating	0	1	2	3	4
Complexity	band does not perform new work	band performs unison or solo work	band performs work with discernable layers and form	band performs work with layers and melodic or harmonic progression	band creates (3) and has interesting melodic and harmonic lines
Length	band does not perform new work	band performs new work less than 30 seconds long	band performs new work less than 1 minute long	band performs new work about 1 minute long	band performs new work longer than 1 minute
Originality	band does not perform new work	band performs known tune	band performs known tune with ininnovations or performs new tune	band performs new work that does not replicate any known music	band performs new work that is very innovative

Table 24.3. Assessment Rubric for Journal

Process Rating	0	1	2	3	4
Thoroughness	no journal	journal reports events without reflection	journal answers some reflective questions	journal answers most reflective questions	journal answers all questions
Content: evidence of process	no journal	journal reports feelings without evident process	journal reports process, demonstrating little effort	journal reports process, demonstrating thorough learning process	journal reports (3) *and* reflective learning
No. of journal entries	no journal	1 entry	2 entries	3 entries	4 or more entries

rehearsals and the performance. Each student in a group would assess the other group members, and him- or herself, rating attendance and role taking during each rehearsal.

Finally, the students argued over the amount of weight to give each rubric in a final grade for the project. After a prolonged discussion, they decided to weight the journal rubric as 50 percent of the grade, the song performance as 15 percent, the musical creation as 10 percent, and the peer-/self-assessments as 25 percent. Their reasoning was that many students, if told that their performances would be counted heavily in a project grade, would "freeze" and be unwilling to take chances. They decided that it was important for project participants to enjoy the process of learning and ensemble playing and that performance skill development was more of an ancillary benefit to the experience.

On performance day, each group played their rock songs and musical creations for each other. They dressed in clothing they thought suitable for "rock stars." As audience members they cheered and clapped through the songs, encouraging each other into acts of bravado on stage. While one group performed another group used the rubrics to evaluate their peers, so each student in the class had the opportunity to test the rubric as well as to perform. The performances themselves were all rated (both by peers and teachers) as successful, as were the musical creations.

FINDINGS

We found that the students' experience in learning and performing their rock songs were highly successful. The students worked together, rehearsed, learned new instruments, and re-created each song for performance. They graded each other using rubrics that they had designed to experience the assessment procedure, they handed in journals, and they gave self- and peer-assessments. They stated in our debriefing session that they loved the chance to step out of their traditional formal learning experiences and learn music in a new way, to make their own musical decisions. They loved the challenge of learning new instruments. They stated, additionally, that an informal learning experience challenged their former notions of pedagogy.

The journals and informal interviews yielded information on the success of our project. We found five categories of student responses:

1 descriptions of events
2. emotional responses to events

3. descriptions of interpersonal relationships
4. ideas about musical learning
5. questions in the application to pedagogy

By far, the bulk of comments related to descriptions of events and emotional reactions to the project. Descriptions of events recorded an orderly progression of meeting planning and rehearsals. Some groups collaborated more successfully than others, but all recorded progress toward their performance goals. The students expressed global enjoyment in the opportunity to re-create a rock song and invent their own music.

The comments related to interpersonal relationships expressed frustration with, and interest in, the collaborative process. As one student stated: "Everyone was willing to give their own ideas but also to concede if someone else had a better idea. This respect and modesty created a safe and productive environment in which we envisioned our band and the songs that we would play."

Very few students described any changes in musical knowledge that might have been gained through the process of learning their songs and creating a new piece of music. However, they did discuss the processes of learning the music and peer mentoring. As one student explained, "[He] had some issues with picking, and I showed him how I usually anchor the sound, and all that I needed to tell them in order to stop the sound was to just barely release the finger from the fingerboard. The type of learning we did would best be described as experiential. Although it seemed chaotic at times, we somehow managed to accomplish what we set out to accomplish." In our debriefing, the students explained that their focus was not on conceptual learning per se. They focused instead on learning the technical skills needed to re-create the music. Learning about music was a product, not a goal during rehearsals.

The written and spoken comments imagining future pedagogy indicated that the students contemplated both the possibilities that informal learning could include peer mentoring and discovery learning, and the challenges they feared, including student inertia and difficulties collaborating.

Some statements indicated that the students related their informal learning experiences to similar experiences in formal learning. This journal entry expresses surprise that performing groups with no leader could use successful rehearsal strategies: "I was having trouble transitioning from the bridge to the chorus. To overcome this problem, we slowed down the tempo and practiced the transition many times. This obstacle is bound to arise in any teaching situation, and the way we

handled it is exactly how a music teacher would handle the obstacle."
Other comments involved questions about how they might deal with
the sensitive issues that the group faced during their own rehearsals,
as with this student's comments about encouraging a creative process:

> This problem brings up a sensitive subject in teaching creativity and
> improvisation. Without limitations and guidance students are likely
> to create a cacophony. With too much limitation, students do not
> have the adequate freedom to explore and learn musical freedom. In
> this situation I would give models for the band to imitate and address
> potential problems such as . . . leaving the tonal center. This way the
> students are primed for success.

IMPLICATIONS FOR GENERAL MUSIC METHODS COURSES

The students valued the experience in informal learning rather than
simply discussing it as a pedogogical option. We learned, through our
data, that individual reflections tended to focus more on the task at
hand (learning the song and rehearsing together) and the emotional
reactions to the experience rather than on the pedagogical implications. However, the in-class discussions allowed students to imagine
how their experiences might work in a secondary general music class
to encourage their own students to learn, experience music, and enjoy
working together in new ways.

Perhaps most important, their discussions over learning goals and
assessments brought to light many of the issues that we, as teachers,
often lecture about. Through this project, the students discovered the
ways in which teachers can determine how learning occurs and what
to look for when evaluating student growth. Our students expressed
interest in continuing the project when moving on to public-school
teaching. Personal experiences in informal learning allowed them
to imagine teaching strategies that they had never considered viable
before.

Our plans for future implementation include a number of recommendations. First, we decided that the students needed more guidance
in the journaling process to encourage reflection on musical learning,
the value of informal learning processes, and pedagogical implications.
Journal checks and feedback midway through the process may help to
focus student reflections. We considered the value of providing more
group-based guidance to the students in their learning process. One
student suggested that the class could have a strategy-sharing discus-

sion early in the process to allow groups who were collaborating successfully to assist those who were not as successful. We determined that the students would need to continue to develop their own learning outcomes, assessment criteria, and grading rubrics for other projects to help them explore the questions about student learning that emerged during this process.

Finally, we decided that our efforts within the classroom could be best evaluated by re-creating the study with an element of longitudinal exploration. Interviewing students several years after their college experience, in the midst of their own practices, will allow us to learn if they make use of informal learning in their classrooms.

We hope that this innovation will encourage novice teachers to move beyond their formal learning experiences and embrace future students who will respond enthusiastically to informal learning opportunities.

REFERENCES

Green, L. 2001. *How popular musicians learn: A way ahead for music education*. Burlington, Vt: Ashgate.
———. 2008. *Music, informal learning and the school: A new classroom pedagogy*. Burlington, Vt.: Ashgate.
Swanwick, Keith. 1968. *Popular music and the teacher*. Oxford: Pergamon Press.

㉕

Rekindling the Playful Spirit:
Learning to Teach through Play

Sarah H. Watts

ABSTRACT

Play is a natural and normal aspect of the childhood experience. In order to tap into children's playful natures as an avenue to musical proficiency and understanding, it is useful for preservice music educators to rekindle their own playful spirits and channel them into musical encounters for children. Techniques for Teaching Music to Children is a university-level teacher-preparation course for undergraduate and postbaccalaureate students that invites future music educators to build musicianship skills as applied in the elementary-music setting while allowing them the opportunity to playfully engage in various music-learning activities that would be appropriate for the elementary classroom. This course has encouraged students to feel more connected to children, experience more comfort in working with children, bond socially, and participate more fully in playful musical encounters without inhibition.

THE IMPORTANT WORK OF PLAY

According to Goodkin (2004), "Play is nature's schooling, and its curriculum has been developed for thousands of years to fit children just right" (11). He further noted that "if play is the process, children's games are the textbooks of Nature's schooling. These games are bursting with rich language, patterned math, colorful history, scientific observation, physical challenge, visual design, rhythmic dance and exuberant music—a complete curriculum by any school's standards" (11).

Play is an inexorable aspect of the childhood experience. It serves to engage the imagination and inquisitive nature (Sutton-Smith 1997) and provide opportunities to explore social roles, learn how to set rules, and acquire leadership skills (Knapp and Knapp 1976; Harwood 1998). The context of play is a safe place where friendships are built, experimentation occurs, and children are empowered to take control of their environment (Factor 2001).

In acknowledgment of play as the heart of childhood, several central pedagogical approaches to the teaching of music make use of play in order to effectively engage children in musical exploration and skill building. Frazee (2006) noted that "Orff's pedagogical ideas are rooted in the idea of children's play and fantasy" (21). Singing games in Kodály and various types of games in Dalcroze Eurythmics also serve to engage the playful nature of children. Frazee further explained that "playful discovery leads naturally to accomplishment, given time and opportunities for practice" (31), suggesting the effectiveness of incorporating children's natural inclination to play into learning situations. Goodkin (2004) shared that "by honoring the wisdom of playing games, we speak to the child in the child" (12). He further observed that "though most teachers understand the role of games in the preschool music program, by middle school, the spirit of play in the curriculum tends to be severely diminished" (15).

With playful natures declining as we age, it is important for those of us who work with children in elementary-music settings to rekindle the playful spirit, to recall the carefree feeling of uninhibited absorption in pleasurable pursuits. It makes sense, then, to provide opportunities for preservice teachers to recultivate their inner playfulness, to acknowledge play as a conduit between them and their future students, and to channel that playfulness into effective music teaching.

LEARNING TO TEACH THROUGH PLAY:
A PREPARATORY COURSE

Techniques for Teaching Music to Children (TTMC) is a 300-level course designed for undergraduate music education majors and those seeking postbaccalaureate teacher certification at a large university in the Pacific Northwest. Students enrolled in the course have been enrolled in core music courses for two to three years, entering TTMC with foundations in music theory, aural skills, music history, and applied performance in various instruments or voice. The course meets twice weekly for fifty minutes each meeting, and runs for the duration of a ten-week academic quarter.

TTMC exists to serve a variety of purposes: It is a prerequisite course for music education majors that occurs in the sequence prior to the full-scale elementary teaching-methods course. While TTMC does not delve deeply into the particulars of theory and pedagogy, it provides a context in which students may further develop musicianship skills as applicable in an elementary-music classroom setting—that is, building skills in sight-singing, solfège (with Kodály-Curwen hand signals), leading song activities in front of a group, and piano skills that are applicable to the classroom situation. Additionally, TTMC helps familiarize students with and build a repertoire of songs appropriate for use in the K–5 elementary-music setting. TTMC makes use of the folk musics of Anglo and African American traditions, a useful and familiar point of departure. (Subsequent coursework focuses on world musics; students are by no means denied exploration of other musics.)

With regard to study materials for each class, students are assigned anywhere from two to four songs to prepare for each class meeting. Preparation requires students to be able to perform the following tasks: sing each song using the movable do system of solfège, demonstrate appropriate Kodály-Curwen hand signals for each song, sing each song on text, and accompany each song appropriately on the piano, either using a prewritten accompaniment or one of their own design, as applicable to each piece of music. All of these items are to be fully prepared and performance-ready for each class period and are followed by some type of playful engagement with prepared repertoires.

APPLICATION OF THE ALTERNATIVE

It might be easy for a skill-building and repertoire-building course to take on a drill-like nature, rehearsing fundamental skills in a dry and unstimulating manner. The alternative to traditional skill/drill sessions employed by TTMC is, quite simply, to play. The singing and instrumental skills, while of utmost importance, are not the end objective of the course; rather the skills are a means to a playful end, ways in which to imaginatively engage children in making music. Musical encounters for children are not merely discussed or observed—they happen right in the classroom during each class meeting. Through activities ranging from kneeling on the floor in front of barred percussion instruments improvising over a bordun, to festive folk dances, to singing along with storybooks, to engaging with various fun and colorful manipulatives, these preservice teachers are invited to immerse themselves in playful musical experiences that demonstrate the child's point of view. As one TTMC student explained, "Music isn't something you can learn by reading about it; you have to *do* it!" Others reflected that "I enjoy play and found it, in context, to be an effective way of teaching [the] subject matter" and that "I loved learning through play. At first it was rather intimidating, but I feel much more comfortable now with engaging with young children."

A TYPICAL CLASS

A typical class begins with a vocal warm-up in the form of a round, lovingly known as Round of the Week. Round of the Week may involve a two- to four-part round, frequently featuring movement of some type, concentric circles, motions that demonstrate the text, or "beats in the feet." Following this warm-up, the class attends to the business of the repertoire assigned for that particular class period. As a group, the students sing through the assigned piece unaccompanied on solfège syllables. (At the beginning of the term as students are gaining facility with the hand signals, I invite them to sing with solfège syllables with no hand signals the first time through and then add the hand signals on subsequent performances. As students become more familiar with the hand signals, I eliminate the first step and move immediately into singing solfège with hand signals.) I occasionally ask students to sing in small groups so that I can assess progress and preparation. Following the singing of the prepared pieces, students come to the front of the classroom, three at a time, and accompany the class on the piano. These several repetitions of the song in addition to outside preparation sufficiently familiarize students with the songs to participate fully in the next phase of the class.

Following the skill check-in and assessment, the songs are spun out into some type of playful activity, which may include a singing game, a play party, a folk dance, a story, or the like. The song "Noble Duke of York" (Langstaff and Langstaff 1970) may serve as an illustration of this two-part sequence. As part of the skill-building segment, students sing "Noble Duke of York" on solfège syllables with hand signals and then take turns coming to the front of the class to accompany at one of the three pianos that are set up ahead of time. The remaining students sing along on solfège or song text. Once everyone has had the opportunity to accompany at the piano, the second part of the sequence begins, where the class moves "Noble Duke of York" from a skill-building exercise into a three-dimensional activity—in this instance, a contradance involving two parallel lines. Following the physical engagement with the piece of repertoire, we deconstruct the activity through a teacher's lens: What must be considered as a teacher implements this activity? What are the space requirements? How would a teacher break down the movements into easily understandable segments? How would she move children from their seats into the dance formation? The answers to these questions emerge more easily after having the activity embedded within the body.

ASSESSMENT

The two-pronged approach to this course manifests itself in the assessment strategies, as well. The skill-building aspect of the course is assessed through two proficiency examinations where students are asked to sight-sing a children's folk song, play common chord sequences that would be useful in accompanying children's music, sight-read a piano accompaniment intended for children, and prepare a children's folk song to perform, both singing and accompanying, with an appropriate introduction. In these examinations, singing and piano progress as applicable to the elementary music setting is evident. Skills are further assessed through short teaching episodes where students lead a song using solfège, then text, then accompany the class while providing an appropriate introduction and some sort of conducting gesture from the piano.

Regarding the repertoire-focused aspect of the class, students are asked to design short activities for use with children, such as a brief ostinato for unpitched percussion instruments, a body-percussion piece, and an orchestration of a one-chord song using instruments of the Orff Instrumentarium. An integrative final project concludes the course where students are asked to compile a collection of thirty folk songs. Students integrate their singing and piano skills with their repertoire and idea-building skills by creating a recording of themselves singing and playing each folk song while completing a template that requires them to analyze important features of each song (form, important rhythmic and melodic figures) and provide suggestions for using each piece of music in the classroom.

It may seem redundant to reinforce sight-singing and piano skills cultivated in classes outside of TTMC. However, this approach allows students to contextualize and integrate these skills in a way that will be practical in the elementary-music classroom. Students who have completed the course have shared that "I really needed help with sight-singing, and I found this class to be very beneficial with practicing that" and that their "piano skills definitely improved." One student even shared, "We had so much fun, but the class was challenging at the same time, because it forces you to prepare."

CONSTRAINTS AND CHALLENGES

While learning to play through play may sound like nothing but fun, there are certainly obstacles to overcome in successfully carrying out this type of coursework encounter. Largely, the constraints in successful participation in this course are imposed on the students by the students themselves. Many step into TTMC certain that they will pursue teaching careers in secondary school ensemble performance settings. While gearing one's self toward secondary teaching is entirely normal, natural, and necessary, some students struggle with actually envisioning themselves in an elementary setting, thereby cutting themselves off from grasping the importance of interaction with elementary-focused teaching techniques. This situation may translate into lack of commitment in classroom activities and the inability to let go of inhibitions and just *be* in the playful musical moments. However, it is of utmost importance for those future secondary teachers to recultivate their inner playful natures in order to process what the elementary-music experience is like and to realize that young people walk into high school performing ensembles not as blank slates but as blossoming musicians who have come from very real and rich musical places. To combat this "too cool" syndrome, I simply try to provide a consistent and enthusiastic model of elementary teaching, encourage students daily, and cite examples of why we do what we do the way we do it, relating our class mission to real world teaching situations. To this end, one student reflected that "as someone who thought they would only teach high school, it really opened up my view on childhood education and has henceforth moved me in that direction. I am so grateful to have that experience now."

Students frequently encounter the challenge of overcoming personal inhibitions with regard to the movement component of the course. Many may be accustomed to engaging with an instrument as their primary means of musical communication and may encounter difficulty in experiencing music within and without the body. Connecting physically with music in TTMC is intended to build preservice teachers' comfort level with movement as applied in the elementary-music teaching setting with the goal of providing a quality movement model for future students. Composed and improvised movements, movements with partners, folk dances, movement as demonstration of other musical concepts, and other ways of channeling music through the body are brought into the mix throughout the course. One TTMC student reflected that "we all got a new perspective with what we could do with our bodies and music." Another shared, "Yes, I had to get outside myself, but as the quarter went on, I became much more comfortable. I'm definitely taking that with me from this class (comfort in getting up in front of people/being silly)." Others indicated that the movement in class "engaged me kinesthetically and emotionally—I had to get beyond my shyness or embarrassment, but once I did, it was pure joy!" Not only did the movement aspect of the class serve to heighten students' awareness of their bodies as vessels of music, but it served to reinforce important concepts related to the act of teaching in the elementary setting. One student commented that "all the movement and interaction really helped me grasp the concepts. I always looked forward to this class." Another explained that "I think it will be easy for me to remember the games better that way," which is consistent with Goodkin's (2004) assertion that "because of the repetition within games and the delight of playing them over and over, the children will get the practice they need without ever knowing they're 'practicing'" (13).

BENEFITS TO THE MUSIC EDUCATION COMMUNITY

Providing preservice music educators with the opportunity to both learn through play for themselves and to facilitate learning through play for children has brought about a variety of positive outcomes in this university's music education community. Professors who have worked with these preservice teachers in coursework following TTMC have noted that these preservice teachers have had the benefit of working through activities using the child's eye as a lens. This revisiting of the childlike point of view has allowed these preservice teachers to become more conscious of children and to cultivate comfort in working with children. As one TTMC student noted, "It was hard but valuable to think from a child's perspective. Thinking about the limitations of children's abilities was new to me." Another shared that "you had to approach activities with a realistic idea of if children could do it too and if they would enjoy it. It was a new way of thinking." These new ways of thinking and playful hands-on approaches helped students to emerge from the course with a more realistic picture of the musical life that is possible in an elementary classroom.

An additional benefit of inviting preservice teachers to learn in and through play was the extent to which engaging in play brought about a sense of social cohesion among class members of TTMC that extended beyond their work in this particular course into subsequent coursework. A sense of interconnectedness with one another as a result of communal music making characterized these collegial bonds in addition to providing a model for bonding in the elementary classroom situation. A TTMC reflected that "[play] was a good way to let the class bond with each other; being open and uncaring about self-image allows other students to open up as well," suggesting that stepping outside one's own comfort zone in the play arena may have provided motivation and support for other students who may have been struggling with participating actively. Another TTMC student shared that "I loved the interaction between students. We all had fun in these activities!" indicating that it was not simply the games or the repertoire that were appealing but also the communal doing of music, becoming part of a musically engaged whole.

A further benefit that has permeated this university's music education community has been the building of musical repertoires for teaching music to children. Preservice teachers were invited to build this child-friendly repertoire in active, participatory, and child-centered ways so that rather than simply collecting songs, they were amassing approaches for spinning these songs out into music-learning encounters for children. A TTMC student noted that it was "fun to build a rep[ertoire] of what to teach kids. Definitely have a new respect [for] folk music now." This accumulation of repertoires, ideas, and approaches has translated into increased comfort in planning and executing preservice music-teaching encounters that are built into subsequent coursework.

CONCLUSION

Techniques for Teaching Music to Children has become an invaluable asset to students within this university's teacher-training program.

Emerging with enhanced musicianship skills as well as a wealth of child-friendly repertoire and ideas for musical encounters, these pre-service teachers are well prepared to move into the next phase of their study of music for children. TTMC serves as a reminder for those who work with children in musical settings that the playful spirit must never be allowed to fade away. Play comes naturally to children but not always for adults. Embracing the opportunity to revisit a child-like place and, in turn, making use of that information to engage young people in making music is vital to those who will step into the music classroom to work effectively with children. A TTMC student summed up her experience thusly: "Even now I am approaching educational philosophies with a desire for more musical-play engagement. Musical play is the heart of musical pleasure—I hope to use all that I've learned in this class in the future."

REFERENCES

Factor, J. 2001. Three myths about children's folklore. In *Play today in the primary school playground*, ed. J. C. Bishop and M. Curtis, 24–36. Buckingham, UK: Open University Press.

Frazee, J. 2006. *Orff Schulwerk today: Nurturing musical expression and understanding*. New York: Schott.

Goodkin, D. 2004. *Play, sing, & dance: An introduction to Orff Schulwerk*. Miami: Schott.

Harwood, E. 1998. Music learning in context: A playground tale. *Research Studies in Music Education* 11:52–60.

Knapp, M., and H. Knapp. 1976. *One potato, two potato: The secret education of American children*. New York: W. W. Norton.

Langstaff, N., and J. Langstaff. 1970. *Sally go round the moon*. Watertown, Mass.: Revels Publications.

Sutton-Smith, B. 1997. *The ambiguity of play*. Cambridge, Mass.: Harvard University Press.

About the Contributors

Volume editor **Ann C. Clements**, Ph.D. (The Pennsylvania State University), is associate professor of music education at the Pennsylvania State University where she teaches undergraduate courses in secondary general music methods, world and popular musics, materials and repertoire, and guitar techniques. At the graduate-level she teaches courses in philosophy and sociology of music education. Her research interests include music participation, secondary general music, choral music, and ethnomusicology. Currently she serves as the upper-school general music teacher and choir director at the State College Friends School and is the choir director of the Foxdale Village Retirement Community Chorus.

CONTRIBUTORS

Frank Abrahams, Ed.D. (Westminster Choir College of Rider University), is professor and chair of the Music Education Department at Westminster Choir College of Rider University in Princeton, New Jersey. He is author of several texts and articles on the subject of critical pedagogy for Music Education and is a frequent clinician, speaker, and workshop facilitator.

Joseph Abramo, Ed.D. (Teachers College of Columbia University), is assistant professor of music education at Hartwick College in Oneonta, New York. He has previously taught guitar classes and music theory in Middletown, New York, and has taught courses at Kean University in New Jersey and the State University of New York at Orange.

Carlos Abril, Ph.D. (Northwestern University), is associate professor of music at the Northwestern University Bienen School of Music, where he teaches courses in general music, multicultural music education, and philosophy. His research focuses on cultural diversity in music education, music perception, and music education philosophy.

Sarah J. Bartolome, Ph.D. (Louisiana State University, Baton Rouge), is assistant professor of music education at the Louisiana State University in Baton Rouge. She completed a Ph.D. program in music education in 2009 from the University of Washington. Sarah teaches general music methods and is a frequent clinician and presenter of workshops at local and regional conferences across the United States.

Nancy Beitler (Lehigh Valley Area School District) presently teaches instrumental music at Southern Lehigh Middle School in Center Valley, Pennsylvania. She is a Ph.D. candidate at the Pennsylvania State University with a focus on her creative activities for middle school instrumental music students and the reflective practices of students and educators.

Ruth O. Boshkoff (Director Emerita of the Indiana University Children's Choir) is a nationally known teacher and composer who specializes in elementary general and children's choral music. She is director emerita of the Indiana University Children's Choir.

Brenda Brenner, D.M. (Indiana University Jacobs School of Music), is associate professor of music education (strings) at the Indiana University Jacobs School of Music. She is also codirector of the Indiana University String Academy, where she has taught since 1993.

Lily Chen-Hafteck, Ph.D. (Kean University), is associate professor of music education and assistant chair of the music department at Kean University in New Jersey. Her research interests include multicultural music education, cultural issues in early childhood musical development, and the relationship between tonal languages and children's singing.

Don D. Coffman, Ph.D. (University of Iowa), is professor of music education at the University of Iowa. He also directs the Iowa City/Johnson County Senior Center New Horizons Band, which provides an opportunity for "chronologically gifted" adults to learn or reacquaint themselves with wind and percussion instrumental music.

Mary L. Cohen, Ph.D. (University of Iowa), is assistant professor of music education at the University of Iowa, where she teaches undergraduate choral methods, elementary methods, and graduate courses and also supervises general music-methods courses. Her research interests include choral singing and well-being—particularly in the context of prison choirs—the history and philosophy of music education, and the relationship of movement theories to learning.

Megan Clay Constantine (Case Western Reserve University) is pursuing her Ph.D. in music education at Case Western Reserve University and is currently a lecturer at Cleveland State University in musicianship and education. She was a music educator for eight years and continues to perform on string bass and piano throughout the Cleveland area.

Robert Gardner, Ph.D. (The Pennsylvania State University), is assistant professor of music education at the Pennsylvania State University, specializing in stringed-instrument playing and teaching, alternative styles for string ensembles, and orchestral conducting. A double bassist and conductor with experience in a variety of musical genres, he has written articles for the *American String Teacher* and GIA Publications and has given presentations at conferences and workshops throughout the country.

Brent M. Gault, Ph.D. (Indiana University Jacobs School of Music), is associate professor of music education in the Indiana University Jacobs School of Music and also serves as the program director for the Indiana University Children's Choir.

Beth Gibbs, Ph.D. (Grand Valley State University), is assistant professor of music education at Grand Valley State University in Allendale, Michigan. In 2009 she earned her Ph.D. in music education from the Pennsylvania State University. Beth teaches undergraduate elementary methods and supervises student teachers. Previously she taught as an elementary and middle school general music specialist.

Elizabeth M. Guerriero (The Pennsylvania State University) is a Ph.D. candidate at the Pennsylvanian State University and adjunct assistant professor at Westminster Choir College of Rider University. She holds a master of music degree from the University of Denver and specializes in string music education.

Jonathan D. Harnum (Northwestern University) is a doctoral candidate in music education at Northwestern University and is author of three commercial textbooks on music education topics. His research interests include high school general music, community music, and informal music teaching and learning.

Matthew Hoy (North Penn School District) holds a bachelor of music degree in music education from Bucknell University in Lewisburg, Pennsylvania, and a master of music degree from Temple University in Philadelphia. He has worked in the Pennsylvania public schools for five years.

Sheri Jaffurs (University of Michigan–Flint and the Farmington Public School District) is lecturer at the University of Michigan–Flint and a music teacher in the Farmington Public School District with research interests in teaching and learning in informal and formal music education and in democracy in education. She has taught for over twenty years in many venues to all ages in "real life," face to face and virtually, in synchronous and asynchronous contexts.

Victor Lin (Teachers College of Columbia University) is a doctoral student in music education at Columbia University, Teachers College in New York. He is an active freelance jazz pianist and violinist and teaches jazz at Columbia University.

Lisa M. Meyer (Dearborn Public Schools, Dearborn, Michigan) has been an educator for twenty-two years. She has taught a wide range of ages, from kindergarten- through college-age students. For the past fourteen years she has served as the music resource teacher for the Dearborn Public Schools.

Douglas C. Orzolek, Ph.D. (University of St. Thomas, St. Paul, Minnesota), is associate professor of music education and associate director of bands at the University of St. Thomas in St. Paul, Minnesota. He teaches undergraduate and graduate courses in music education, directs the Symphonic Band, and holds a keen interest in secondary general music education and assessment.

Catherine Odom Prowse (Dearborn Public Schools, Dearborn, Michigan) graduated from Wayne State University and Marygrove College in Detroit, Michigan, receiving her bachelor of music education degree and master in the art of teaching degree. She teaches vocal music for Dearborn Public Schools, is the choir director and church organist at St. Thomas Aquinas, and is married to Dr. Ron Prowse, also a musician and director of music at Sacred Heart Seminary in Detroit.

Joshua S. Renick (Teachers College of Columbia University) is a doctoral student and director of student teaching in the Department of Music and Music Education at Teachers College, Columbia University. Before pursuing his doctorate, he taught elementary and middle school instrumental music in the San Francisco Bay Area.

Barbara J. Resch, D.M.E. (Indiana University–Purdue University Fort Wayne), is associate professor and director of music education at Indiana University–Purdue University Fort Wayne, where she teaches courses in foundations of music education and in psychology of music. In 2009 she begins her term as president of the Indiana Music Educators Association.

Alison M. Reynolds, Ph.D. (Temple University), is associate professor of music education at Temple University in Philadelphia, where she teaches music learning and development, general music for inclusive populations, and graduate research courses; she also guides undergraduate and graduate research. She is published in the *Bulletin of the Council for Research in Music Education, Research Studies in Music Education, Perspectives*, and *Journal of Music Teacher Education* and is coauthor of *Jump Right In: The Music Curriculum* (revised edition) and *Music Play: Guide for Parents, Teachers, and Caregivers*.

Janet Robbins, Ph.D. (West Virginia University), is professor of music education at West Virginia University, where she teaches undergraduate and graduate courses and also coordinates the music student teaching program. Her recent involvement with *Music Alive*, a federally funded student-faculty exchange project with two Brazillian universities, has led her to travel and to the study of traditional music and dance in northeast Brazil.

Christopher Roberts (University of Washington) has taught elementary music in Seattle, Washington, for over ten years and is pursuing a Ph.D. in music education at the University of Washington. An active workshop clinician, he was awarded the 2009 Outstanding Research Award by the Organization of American Kodaly Educators.

Mark Ross (The Penn State Child Development Lab), a blues professional guitarist, toured the United States, Canada, and Europe as part of the critically acclaimed and Grammy-nominated *Queen Bee and the Blue Hornet Band*. Previously he has taught special-needs preschool children at the Rainbow School, in State College, Pennsylvania, and currently he is the children's music specialist at the Penn State Child Development Lab on the University Park campus.

Cecilia Roudabush (Iowa City Community School District) received a bachelor of fine arts degree in music education and music therapy in 1989 and a master in music education degree, specializing in music therapy, in 1998, both from the University of Iowa. She has taught general/adaptive music at the elementary level for thirteen years and is currently in her seventh year as a general/adaptive music teacher at North Central Junior High in North Liberty, Iowa, where she also teaches personal development.

Katherine Strand, Ph.D. (Indiana University Jacobs School of Music), associate professor of music in the Jacobs School of Music, Indiana University, where she teaches courses in general music methods and education philosophy at the undergraduate and graduate levels. She has published articles in the *Journal of Research in Music Education, Music Education Review, Bulletin of the Council for Research in Music Education, Journal of Music Teacher Education, Arts Education Policy Review, Music Educators Journal, Teaching Music, General Music Today,* and the Indiana *Musicator* and has presented research and workshops in international, national, regional, and state music-education conferences.

Daniel Sumner (University of Louisiana at Monroe) is a music educator, jazz guitarist, and composer. Currently he is assistant professor of music education at the University of Louisiana at Monroe. Previously he taught in Indiana University's Jacobs School of Music and in the New Orleans public school system.

Linda Thornton, Ph.D. (The Pennsylvania State University), is associate professor of music education at the Pennsylvania State University.

Her research and teaching interests include the development of young instrumentalists and teacher development and assessment.

Terese Volk Tuohey, Ph.D. (Wayne State University), is associate professor of music education at Wayne State University in Detroit, Michigan, where she teaches instrumental music education courses. Her primary research interest is multicultural music education; she is author of *Music, Education, and Multiculturalism*.

Sarah H. Watts, Ph.D. (University of Washington), completed a Ph.D. in music education in 2009 from the University of Washington in Seattle. Her research interests include children's musical cultures and transgenerational musical play. She is currently a designer for the company Musically Minded in Seattle, Washington, where she creates lesson plans and curriculum for preschool music classes.

Betty Anne Younker, Ph.D. (University of Michigan), is associate professor of music education and associate dean for academic affairs in the School of Music, Theater, and Dance at the University of Michigan. Her teaching experience spans twenty-six years in public school, private studio, and university settings, while her research is focused on creative and critical thinking and issues related to philosophy and curriculum in music education.

Breinigsville, PA USA
29 September 2010
246375BV00001B/2/P